The Green Office Manual

The Green Office Manual

A Guide to Responsible Practice

WASTEBUSTERS LTD

Earthscan Publications Ltd, London

First published in the UK in 1997 by
Earthscan Publications Limited

Reprinted 1998

Copyright © Wastebusters Ltd, 1997

A catalogue record for this book is available from the British Library

ISBN: 1 85383 447 5

Page design by Paul Sands, S&W Design
Typesetting by PCS Mapping & DTP, Newcastle upon Tyne

Printed and bound in Great Britain by
Biddles Ltd, Guildford and King's Lynn

Cover design by Simon Rosenheim

Printed on Evergreen Offset paper which has been manufactured from recycled pulp (100% de-inked post-consumer waste) and is totally chlorine-free.

For a full list of publications please contact:
Earthscan Publications Limited
120 Pentonville Road
London N1 9JN
Tel. (0171) 278 0433
Fax: (0171) 278 1142
Email: earthinfo@earthscan.co.uk
WWW: http://www.earthscan.co.uk

Earthscan is an editorially independent subsidiary of Kogan Page Limited and publishes in association with WWF-UK and the International Institute for Environment and Development.

Contents

List of Figures

List of Tables

Foreword

The Department of the Environment, Transport and the Regions welcomes this guide which has been designed by Wastebusters to help managers green their offices and save money at the same time.

Business in the Environment recently surveyed Britain's top 100 companies. The results showed that it can be tempting for office based companies not to give a great deal of priority to assessing their environmental performance. Offices do not, after all, have such an obvious potential impact on the environment as the mining, manufacturing or petrochemical industries, for example. Yet ordinary office activities use energy and other resources, produce waste and add to carbon dioxide emissions. There is a great deal of scope for steps to improve the quality of the environment through better management practices and looking carefully at the efficient use of resources.

But the lessons of this manual have a much wider application. It would be odd to regard what we do in the office as somehow isolated from our other everyday activities. If saving energy and reducing waste make sense at work they make sense at home too. And if they make sense for one company then they also make sense for its customers and suppliers. A company that manages its environmental impact properly is likely to manage its other affairs properly. It is the kind of company that people will be keen to do business with. And it is in a position to influence the behaviour of a wide range of people and other organisations. I hope that the need for everyone to adopt a greener lifestyle will be kept in mind in developing green office policies, and that every opportunity will be taken to spread the message beyond the office door.

Alex Galloway
Head of Environmental and Energy Awareness
Department of the Environment, Transport and the Regions
January 1997

About Wastebusters

Wastebusters Ltd is an independent environmental consultancy specialising in the office sector. The consultancy was established by Lesley Millett in 1991 in response to a market need for a practical approach to green office auditing and environmental programmes, in particular:

☐ balancing environmental concerns with practicalities and financial considerations;

☐ producing concise, jargon-free communication to make environmental practice accessible to all organisations;

☐ the development of office guidelines and corporate environmental policies and programmes;

☐ encouraging staff participation through creative environmental awareness training; and

☐ helping organisations develop environmental programmes which result in action.

Wastebusters have worked with a wide range of organisations: small companies, multinational organisations, local and central government and schools. Wastebusters felt that this information could be made available on a nationwide basis in a form that would be relevant to all offices and so published the *The Green Office Handbook* in October 1994. This was the first guide of its kind to offer practical advice for organisations intending to manage the environmental effects of their buildings and office activities.

The Green Office Manual – A Guide to Responsible Practice is a revised edition which is substantially updated to promote best practice within offices.

LESLEY MILLETT – AUTHOR

Lesley is a sales and marketing professional with 15 years experience of the corporate sector. Her particular strengths are balancing environmental concerns with the practicalities and financial considerations of introducing sound environmental practice into offices. Lesley is Director of Wastebusters.

Lesley is a recognised speaker at industry seminars and participated at the Department of the Environment Regional Road Shows 'Making Waste Work: A competitive opportunity' in June 1996.

Project management experience includes Waste Minimisation Programme for Dorset County Council and Lehman Brothers, and Environmental Audit for Union Bank of Switzerland. She wrote *Wastebusting for Schools* for Dorset County Council.

Lesley aims to make environmental improvement accessible to all by presenting environmental issues in a practical and highly accessible way.

She has developed environmental awareness training programmes for a number of organisations and leads workshops and training sessions.

Wastebusters Ltd
3rd Floor
Brighton House
Brighton Terrace
London SW9 8DS
Tel: 0171 207 3434
Fax: 0171 207 2051
Email: manual@wastebusters.co.uk

Acknowledge-
ments

The author would like to acknowledge the help of the following people and organisations in the preparation of this manual.

Joss Tantram and Merlin Hyman at Wastebusters for their hard work, additional writing and research and commitment to this project; Joss particularly for his work on purchasing and environmental awareness, including the production of graphics; Merlin for his extensive research on transport and environmental management.

Chas Ball and Rob King at SWAP (Save Waste and Prosper) for their help with the section on batteries; Mark Stevenson at the Northmoor Trust for his contribution to the grounds maintenance section.

Jan McHarry at the Buy Recycled Programme (BRP) for her support and contribution to additional information on the BRP; Michael Jones at the UK Ecolabelling Board for contributing information on Ecolabelling.

Elise Smithson at BICC Cables for her help with environmental management and transport; Simon Forsyth at Computer Peripherals in Bristol for his help with transport; the Environment Council, particularly Edwin Datschefski for his contribution to benchmarking.

All Wastebusters clients who provided case study material (all case studies are based on Wastebusters clients unless otherwise credited).

Alex Galloway and Roger Hinds at the Department of the Environment, Transport and the Regions; Steve Waring and Martin Gibson at the Environmental Technology Best Practice Programme (ETBPP); Steve Norgrove, Terry Martin and Jim Bellingham at the DTI, for their support and encouragement with the project.

Kogan Page/Earthscan for supporting our second publication.

Glossary of Terms and Acronyms

AMA	Association of Metropolitan Authorities
BEMS	Building Energy Management Systems
BiE	Business in the Environment
BOD	biochemical oxygen demand
BRE	Building Research Establishment
BRESCU	Building Research Energy Conservation Support Unit
BREEAM	Building Research Establishment Environmental Assessment Method
BSI	British Standards Institute
BSRIA	Building Services Research And Information Association
BTCV	British Trust for Conservation Voluntccrs
CBI	Confederation of British Industry
CCT	compulsory competitive tendering
CFC	chlorofluorocarbon
CFL	compact fluorescent lamp
CHP	combined heat and power
CMHR	combustion modified high resilient
COD	chemical oxygen demand
COSHH	Control of Substances Hazardous to Health
CRN	Community Recycling Network
EA	Environment Agency
ECF	elemental chlorine free
EDTA	ethylene diamine tetra-acetate
EEO	Energy Efficiency Office
EMAS	Eco-Management and Audit Scheme
EMERG	Electronic Equipment Manufacturers Recycling Group
EMF	electromagnetic field
EMS	environmental management system

EPA	Environmental Protection Act
EPA	Environmental Protection Agency (USA)
ETBPP	Environmental Technology Best Practice Programme
ETSU	Environmental Technology Support Unit
FECRS	Federation of European Cartridge Recyclers and Suppliers
FSC	Forest Stewardship Council
GAP	Global Action Plan
GWP	global warming potential
HCFC	hydrochlorofluorocarbon
HDRA	Henry Doubleday Research Association
HFC	hydrofluorocarbon
HMIP	Her Majesty's Inspectorate of Pollution
Hoshin	breakthrough objective
HSE	Health and Safety Executive
HUNC	Halon Users National Consortium
ICC	International Chamber of Commerce
ICER	Industry Council for Electronic Equipment Recycling
ICO	International Coffee Organisation
IEEP	Institute for European Environmental Policy
IEM	Institute of Environmental Management
IPCC	International Panel of Climate Change
ISO	International Standards Organisation
IUCN	World Conservation Union
LA-EMAS	Local Authority Eco-Management and Audit Scheme
LARAC	Local Authority Recycling Advisory Committee
LGMB	Local Government Management Board
LPG	liquefied petroleum gas
MDF	medium density fibreboard
MEL	Maximum Exposure Limit
MRF	material recovery facility
NAPM	National Association of Paper Merchants
NFFO	Non-fossil fuel obligation
NRA	National Rivers Authority
NRF	National Recycling Forum
NTA	nitrolotriacetate
OBA	optical brightening agent
ODP	ozone depleting potential
PET	polyethylene terephthalate
PFC	perfluorocarbon
RCEP	Royal Commission on Environmental Pollution
RMA	Retread Manufacturers Association

RSPB	Royal Society for the Protection of Birds
SAD	seasonal affective disorder
SCEEMAS	Small Company Environmental and Energy Management Assistance Scheme
SEPA	Scottish Environmental Protection Agency
TCF	totally chlorine free
UKAS	UK Accreditation Services
UKCRA	United Kingdom Cartridge Recycling Association
UNCED	UN Conference on Environment and Development
VOCs	volatile organic compunds
WBCSD	World Business Council for Sustainable Development
WES	Watch Education Service
WWF	World Wide Fund for Nature

1: Pressures for Change

There is increasing pressure on organisations to develop responsible environmental practice. Organisations are often keen to respond but the pressures of their core business mean that they are short of the time and resources necessary to research and implement sound environmental practice. There is plenty of information available telling organisations what they should be doing, but a lack of practical information on how to do it.

The Green Office Manual aims to solve these problems by giving you clear, concise information about environmental issues and the practical steps you need to take to create a greener office environment and cut costs at the same time.

The *Manual* is aimed at the person with responsibility for running the office, generally the office or facilities manager. It will assist all types of organisations, from a large manufacturing company who wishes to ensure the office is not ignored in their environmental programme, to a small organisation where there is no one specifically appointed to take care of environmental issues. It is equally applicable to local authorities, central government and schools. The *Manual* is therefore designed for people who are extremely busy, have very little time to spare and are probably already struggling to try and work their way through all their existing reading material!

The *Manual* tells you how to structure your own simple environmental programme. This covers: a review to assess your current environmental performance, an environmental policy and a simple action plan. The environmental programme will:

❑ identify what to do, how it can be done and who can help;
❑ help you plan a successful and cost effective approach to environmental issues; and

❑ provide a framework to develop and implement a formal environmental management system.

Wastebusters' experience of implementing successful environmental programmes has enabled us to highlight common problems and make sure you avoid them!

WHY GO GREEN?

Improving environmental performance is no longer optional. The minimum standards demanded by legislation alone require an awareness of the impacts of an organisation on its wider environment that was unlikely to exist in the past. However, the range of pressures are wider than purely legislative. All the stakeholders in organisations are beginning to demand improvements and potentially substantial cost savings from cutting energy use and waste should not be ignored. These pressures and opportunities can combine together to exert a powerful influence on organisations.

The Government is encouraging companies to respond to these pressures and has set a target that '50 per cent of companies with more than 200 employees to have management systems in place to give effect to their environmental policies by the end of 1999.'

The Business Case

LEGISLATIVE PRESSURE

The last 20 years have seen environmental legislation grow from a few specific measures to a comprehensive programme of regulation. The European Union has enacted over 200 pieces of legislation covering pollution of the atmosphere, water and soil, waste management, chemicals and biotechnology safeguards, product standards, environmental impact assessments and nature conservation. In the UK a new Environment Agency has been created whose mission is to protect and enhance the environment. The Agency provides a 'one-stop shop' for environmental regulation.

This new environmental legislation has considerable power. Failing to comply is costly and does major damage to an organisation's reputation. There is also the prospect of directors being held responsible for their company's action and receiving jail sentences.

Recently legislation has broadened its approach. The principle of making the polluter pay is being implemented through taxes and duties on pollution. In October 1996 a tax on landfilling waste was introduced which has substantially increased the waste disposal costs of all organisations. This tax is likely to increase in the future. The Government has also pledged to raise duty on road fuel by 5 per cent a year above the rate of inflation as part of its strategy to curb carbon dioxide emissions. Such legislation does not actually prohibit pollution but those organisations that do not respond to these trends will find their waste and energy costs rising swiftly.

A further development is the implementation of the principle of producer responsibility through the Producer Responsibility Obligations. Organisations producing over 50 tonnes of packaging are required to recover and recycle a percentage of their packaging. The obligation to recover waste is therefore being placed firmly on the producer. There are already discussions of how to broaden these responsibilities to small companies and other waste streams.

COST

Many organisations perceive environmental initiatives as costing money but they can, if efficiently managed, be very cost effective. Many companies have achieved large savings through cutting waste and energy use, money which directly affects the bottom line. The National Westminster Bank Plc set out its energy policy in 1991, and annual savings from implementing 350 initiatives in the first year were estimated at £630,000.

WASTE DISPOSAL COSTS

Savings in waste disposal costs can be particularly significant and are often underestimated despite recent substantial increases with the introduction of the Landfill Tax. They are likely to continue to rise as governments discourage landfilling of waste. Efficient recycling and waste minimisation programmes can reduce your waste disposal costs by retrieving materials for recycling and improving resource usage. On average 70 per cent of office waste is recyclable, so there is significant potential for savings.

The Environmental Protection Act Duty of Care Regulations for waste already impose stringent controls on disposal, placing an additional burden on a busy facilities management team. The initiatives described in this manual can help to reduce your liabilities under the Duty of Care and Special Waste Regulations and reduce your Landfill Tax liability.

SUMMARY OF POTENTIAL COST SAVINGS

❑ An average 50 per cent reduction in waste disposal costs and Landfill Tax liabilities.
❑ Revenue from the sale of recyclables.
❑ Waste minimisation and improved resource usage.
❑ Energy savings.
❑ More efficient use of transport.

COMPETITIVE ADVANTAGE

Supply Chain Pressure

Companies who are already committed to sound environmental practice want to deal with like-minded companies. For example, British Telecom, one of the largest purchasers in the country, has a generic environmental standard that all companies tendering are expected to meet. Many other large companies are going down the same route. This trend is putting increasing pressure on smaller companies who will soon find themselves excluded from many opportunities if they do not manage their environmental effects.

Management Standards

Supply chain pressure is being encouraged by the growth of environmental management standards. These are voluntary schemes that aim to improve environmental management practice by ensuring that it is addressed as an integral part of the management process. The British Standard BS 7750 was the first such standard which has been followed by the European Eco-Management and Auditing Scheme (EMAS) and the International Standard ISO 14001 (described in Chapter 9). Certification provides an internationally recognised and externally verified testament to your commitment to continuous improvement of environmental performance. Organisations registering to these standards have found them an effective way of gaining a competitive advantage.

Consumer Pressure

Pressure from customers is a key consideration for companies selling direct to the consumer. Consumer pressure is particularly powerful when focused by pressure groups like Greenpeace and Friends of the Earth. This was graphically demonstrated by the impact on Shell of plans to dispose of the Brent Spar oil rig at sea. The resulting international boycott cost Shell millions of pounds and its carefully nurtured green image. Other recent boycotts have included those of margarines using fish oil from industrial fishing. The European Union Ecolabelling scheme aims to give consumers objective information on which to base environmental purchasing decisions. This could substantially increase pressure on companies that have not as yet been exposed to environmental campaigning.

There is also a commercial opportunity in satisfying the desire of consumers for greener products. This has been successfully exploited by a number of companies including the Body Shop, Ecover and the Cooperative Bank.

STAKEHOLDER CONCERNS

Potential investors are increasingly interested in an organisation's environmental performance. For instance the Cooperative Bank ethical investment policy includes the pledge not to invest in companies that needlessly pollute the environment, a trend that is being reinforced by the growth of ethical funds. Pressure groups and commercial companies have pledged to produce green ratings of companies as information for investors; this is likely to increase ethical investments among smaller lenders.

Insurers

Insurance companies have been quick to realise the potential impact of large scale future claims due to environmental problems and are increasingly including environmental criteria in their calculation of premiums. Organisations who have not fully assessed their risks and taken steps to manage them will find that insurance companies will demand higher premiums and may even refuse insurance altogether.

Banks

Minimising environmental risk is critical to commercial lenders whose loans are secured on the basis of the physical assets of a company. If the assets of a company default to a bank, that bank will be responsible for the company's environmental liabilities. The cost of cleaning up contaminated land could end up far outweighing the value of the original loan. This is a risk few banks would be willing to take. Major banks such as NatWest are already including environmental risk assessments in their lending policies.

Staff Morale

Employee awareness of environmental issues is on the increase; pressure to implement sound environmental practice, particularly recycling, often comes from staff rather than management. This enthusiasm needs to be tapped; it is a useful resource, providing motivation and creating awareness. The successful introduction of recycling schemes can have a very positive effect on staff morale and can improve communication, since it cuts across all business functions.

SUMMARY: BENEFITS TO SMALL BUSINESSES

Developing environmental initiatives will help small organisations to:

❑ save money – waste reduction measures are easier to control in small organisations;
❑ respond positively to supply chain pressure;
❑ make sure that you comply with legislation;
❑ provide opportunities for good publicity; and
❑ encourage staff involvement in your business.

Graduate Recruitment

Environmental issues are now included in the school syllabus. Graduates are increasingly aware of and concerned about the environmental credentials of any company they might wish to work for. A company which is seen to be responding positively to environmental issues is perceived as acting responsibly.

Corporate Responsibility

In all the talk of legislation, cost savings and management control the basic motivation of protecting the Earth for ourselves and for future generations is sometimes sidelined. It is the reason why this manual has been written and may well be the reason you purchased this copy. Many companies' environmental policies enshrine this principle with a commitment to 'sustainable development'. This has been defined as 'development which meets the needs of the present without compromising the ability of future generations to meet their own needs' (World Commission on Environment and Development, 1987).

Small Businesses, Local Authorities and Schools

The pressures identified above apply to all organisations, whether public or private sector, large or small. However, there are specific pressures for certain sectors.

SMALLER ORGANISATIONS

Very few small companies have seen environmental issues as an immediate pressure but they can gain considerable benefits from environmental awareness. Energy efficiency and waste minimisation measures can be implemented with no capital investment and can produce surprising savings. A simple environmental policy and action programme can have marketing benefits and may well become essential for selling to some companies and local authorities. For example, the printing company Beacon Press has just 75 staff but has gained a great deal of publicity due to its extensive award winning environmental programme. (See Beacon Press Case Study in Chapter 9).

LOCAL AUTHORITIES

Local authorities have different pressures to businesses, but are also working to tight budgetary constraints. Directorates increasingly operate as individual business units and compete for work against commercial organisations. Examples are direct services organisations and print departments. Cost savings from waste reduction and energy efficiency will help competitiveness in tendering for work.

Agenda 21

Some 90 per cent of UK local authorities are now committed to Local Agenda 21. This agenda for action provides a strong motivating pressure for local authorities for action within the authority and in the wider community. An increasing number of local authorities are using the European Eco-Management and Audit Scheme for local government (LA-EMAS) to structure their Local Agenda 21 programmes.

The success of Agenda 21's global action plan for achieving sustainable development ultimately depends on practical projects and local action. It has been estimated that over two-thirds of the statements in Agenda 21 – the most significant outcome of the 1992 UN Conference on Environment and Development (UNCED) – cannot be delivered without the cooperation and commitment of local government.

All local authorities should be developing a local strategy for achieving sustainability, a Local Agenda 21, and involving the whole community in doing so. Achieving a sustainable community will mean each local authority taking a lead in education and the provision of information promoting individual lifestyle changes, as well as reviewing its own planning and policy functions.

As part of this commitment to Agenda 21, it is important that local authorities demonstrate good practice within their own operations. For example, all local authorities are working towards achieving the target of recycling 25 per cent of household waste by the year 2000. It is therefore important to introduce waste minimisation and recycling measures in-house.

SCHOOLS

Schools are under increasing financial pressures and simple cost-effective initiatives which save money and generate income are highly valued. Environmental education is now part of the curriculum, and there is tremendous potential to link

---

SUMMARY: BENEFITS TO LOCAL AUTHORITIES

Developing a planned approach to the environment will help local authorities to:

❑ achieve cost savings;
❑ act consistently with the messages they promote to the public;
❑ demonstrate good house-keeping practices and sound management control;
❑ make sure that they comply with environmental legislation;
❑ build a positive environmental profile; and
❑ contribute to Local Agenda 21 and provide opportunities to involve staff.

SUMMARY BENEFITS

❑ Legislative compliance.
❑ Cost savings.
❑ Competitive advantage.
❑ Increased investment.
❑ Improved staff moral.
❑ Better graduate
   recruitment.
❑ Improved management
   control.

sound environmental practice within the running of schools with curriculum activities. For example, the introduction of recycling and waste reduction measures helps to raise awareness of the value of resources, and setting up initiatives such as a wormery in the school grounds is both fun and educational! Encouraging participation from children helps to produce environmentally responsible adults.

Summary

Developing environmental initiatives will help schools to:

❑ save money;
❑ promote environmental awareness and support curriculum activities;
❑ contribute to waste minimisation at a local level;
❑ enhance the school's image within the local community and encourage involvement; and
❑ produce environmentally responsible adults!

2: Getting Started

HOW TO USE THIS MANUAL

This manual will help you to reduce the environmental impacts of your office. Every office has activities which impact upon the environment, regardless of its size or function. You can help to minimise these impacts by recognising where they occur, planning ways to avoid them and implementing your plans. This book is designed to do this in two ways according to the progress you have already made:

1. If you are just getting started on environmental improvements the *Manual* sets out a structured approach to identifying and tackling the key environmental issues within a planned programme. The next section shows you how to build a planned approach.

2. If you have an established environmental programme but you need help with specific issues in the office you can use this manual as a reference book. Where you need questions answered or need further information about legislation, alternative products or contacts just turn to the relevant section in each chapter.

Each of the main chapters covers a specific functional area, highlighting the key environmental issues, relevant legislation and the practical action you can take to reduce the environmental impact of your office. Chapters are further divided into subsections, each describing a specific issue. Each subsection ends with a summary of the points you should cover in your environmental programme. You can use these Summary Guidelines as a checklist to make sure you have covered all the important points.

FINDING THE INFORMATION YOU NEED

To find information on a particular subject:

- ❑ look at the contents list at the beginning of the Manual;
- ❑ search for the subject in the index;
- ❑ look at the overview at the beginning of each chapter; or
- ❑ look at the summary at the end of each chapter for a list of its essential conclusions.

The Glossary lists definitions of the common environmental terms and acronyms used in the Manual.

To find information about a supplier or service provider, refer to the contacts at the end of each chapter.

In addition the *Manual* contains:

- ❑ Common pitfalls and how to avoid them.
- ❑ Case Studies, covering a broad cross-section of industry sectors and company sizes, used to illustrate particular issues. (The Case Studies are based on Wastebusters' auditing work and on the experience of other organisations.)
- ❑ Contacts for each key subject area and industry organisations. All organisations mentioned in the text are listed at the end of each chapter.

A PLANNED APPROACH

If you are just starting, or have established a few *ad hoc* environmental initiatives you need to take a planned approach to make sure of long term success. In our experience organisations that rely on informal initiatives or depend on volunteers find it difficult to maintain momentum. Volunteers have other calls upon their time and schemes that use the enthusiasm of a single individual can collapse if that person leaves.

Making sure that the environment remains part of your common practice after initial enthusiasm wears off often presents a major stumbling block for organisations. The challenge is to make environmental issues part of your company culture.

This section outlines a simple process that you can follow to establish and maintain an environmental programme. References are made in the text to chapters in the *Manual* that provide information and support at each stage. Following this structure will help you demonstrate that you are taking a responsible approach to your environmental issues.

If you are looking to implement a formal environmental management system or considering accreditation to any of the independent environmental management standards, guidance is given in Chapter 9. You can also refer to this chapter for more detail on the steps outlined below.

KEY STEPS

Initial Commitment

If you want to develop a meaningful environmental programme you need to accept that you will have to change the way you do things.

The first step is to get senior management commitment. Without this commitment you will be unable to overcome the barriers to change or tackle difficult issues such as transport and purchasing.

To convince top management to commit themselves to an environmental programme you will need to spell out the business benefits. Chapter 1 sets out the business case for sound environmental practice.

Setting up a Project Team

The next stage is to agree who is going to do the work. A successful approach is to give responsibility to a manager and for them to establish a project team to coordinate the environmental programme. Each key functional area should be represented on the team (in small organisations, a team member may be responsible for multiple areas). These key areas are set out in Chapters 3 to 7.

REVIEWING YOUR POSITION

In starting any new initiative you need to establish where you are at present. A review of current practice and how this affects the environment will provide a baseline from which you can improve.

Gaining Commitment

The key to the success of an environmental programme is to involve people in the process. This enables them to contribute their ideas and helps to gain their commitment to the introduction of the programme. It is important to include staff who are keen to go green, whether or not they have any specific responsibility for any of the areas covered by the review.

Many organisations involve staff in the design of initiatives at an early stage and in our experience this is often a successful way of sustaining initiatives (Chapter 8 gives you information on involving staff to generate ideas and action).

Methodology

The structured review can be used as a starting point and adapted to your own circumstances. For example, in a small organisation, each member of the audit team might have responsibility for several areas; the 'team' may even consist of one person – the office or facilities manager. In a large organisation, each team member will have responsibility for a particular functional area; the structured nature of the methodology means that it can be extended to cover multiple-site organisations.

KEY FUNCTIONAL AREAS

- ❑ waste management;
- ❑ IT services;
- ❑ purchasing, including catering and cleaning services;
- ❑ building and energy management;
- ❑ transport;
- ❑ sales and marketing; and
- ❑ personnel, human resources and training.

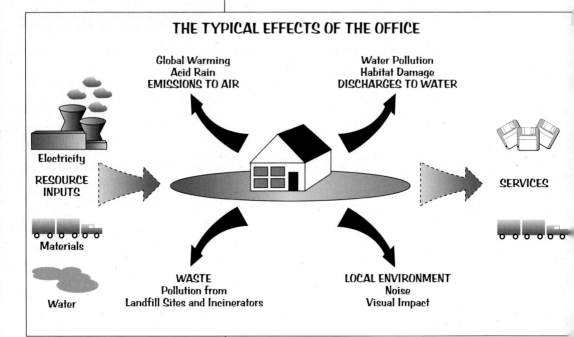

THE TYPICAL EFFECTS OF THE OFFICE

Global Warming
Acid Rain
EMISSIONS TO AIR

Water Pollution
Habitat Damage
DISCHARGES TO WATER

Electricity

RESOURCE INPUTS

SERVICES

Materials

Water

WASTE
Pollution from
Landfill Sites and Incinerators

LOCAL ENVIRONMENT
Noise
Visual Impact

FIGURE 2.1

Typical environmental effects of the office

AIMS OF THE REVIEW

❑ establish your current status in terms of environmental performance;
❑ identify potential for improvement;
❑ identify areas of weakness, particularly concerning legislative compliance;
❑ gauge staff awareness levels of environmental issues: an important consideration in planning an environmental launch programme; and
❑ identify potential cost savings.

Review Process

Hold meetings with staff and management. In large organisations, each team member would discuss issues with their department. Some organisations, such as local authorities will have regular team meetings at which the review can be held. In small organisations, the project team are likely to provide all the necessary information themselves. To make sure that you are identifying all the relevant information you can use the Summary Guidelines at the end of each chapter of the *Manual* as a checklist.

Identifying Your Effects

In order to help you to recognise the general effects that you have on the environment use Table 2.1 below. This identifies the typical environmental effects of an office. The table links the activity and effect to the chapter heading. Use the table to identify the issues relevant to your organisation.

DRAWING UP A POLICY

The review will identify your current position. The next stage is to decide what you can do to improve and how you can do it. A policy setting out your commitment to environmental improvements provides the framework for this process.

If the environment is to be integrated into normal business practice a commitment from senior management is essential. A formal policy signed by senior management adds this essential credibility. (Chapter 9 gives further information on designing policy statements.)

DEVELOPING ENVIRONMENTAL ACTION PLANS

There is often a large gap between policy and action. Environmental policies need to be backed up with a realistic and achievable action plan. An action plan is simply an organised way of making sure that staff know what they can do, when and how (Table 2.2 gives an example of a simple action plan that can be used to structure your environmental initiatives).

Use the information contained in Chapters 3 to 8 to develop your action plan. Identify the practical action you can take, set improvement targets and allocate responsibilities.

TABLE 2.1

Typical environmental effects of the office

ACTIVITY	OUTPUTS	ENVIRONMENTAL EFFECT	CHAPTER
EMISSIONS TO ATMOSPHERE			
Energy use (heating, lighting, PCs etc.)	CO_2	Global warming	6
Refrigeration, fire fighting, air conditioning	CFCs, HCFCs & Halons	Depletion of the ozone layer	6
Transport	CO_2, NO_x, SO_2, particulates	Global warming Ill health	7
DISCHARGES OF WATER			
Cleaning and grounds maintenance	Various chemicals	Pollution of water courses	5
NATURAL RESOURCE USE			
Water Use	Water	Energy required to deliver to your office	6
Paper Purchasing	Paper	Reduction in diverse wildlife habitats	4
Furniture	Wood	Destruction of old growth forests	4
WASTE			
All areas of the office	General waste	Wastes natural resources and causes air and water pollution	3
Use of IT equipment	IT Waste	Wastes natural resources and contains toxic materials	3

MONITORING AND REVIEW

Your action plan may look impressive but it is only effective if you monitor improvement over time. Reviews help you to find out what you have achieved, where your problems lie and what you can do about them. An annual review will help to define new objectives and targets to ensure continuous improvement.

THE FORMAL APPROACH: ONE STEP BEYOND?

If, having developed a planned approach, you wish to go one step further into a formal environmental management system, Chapter 9 gives you a full description of the necessary steps and certification schemes. The formal route has a number of advantages, in particular it can be externally verified to give your environmental programme public credibility.

TABLE 2.2
A model action plan

OBJECTIVE AND TARGET	TARGET DATE	PROJECT MANAGER	COSTS	INDICATOR	KEY ACTIONS
WASTE					
Recycle 90% of waste paper	January 1999	A. Manager	Reduction in waste disposal cost	Amount of paper being recycled	Set up office paper recycling scheme. Encourage staff to use scheme. Donate savings on disposal costs to charity.
Reduce total yearly waste production per person by 5%	January 1999	R. Waste	Reduction in waste disposal cost	Total yearly waste per person.	Use Email for all internal memos. Print & photo-copy double sided where possible. Ask suppliers to take back waste packaging.

3: Office Waste

INTRODUCTION

Efficient recycling and waste reduction measures significantly reduce waste disposal costs by retrieving materials for recycling and reducing the use of raw materials. The practical actions described in this chapter reduce the environmental impact of an office by reducing the volume of waste going to landfill. You should also consider the recyclability and ultimate disposal of a product when making purchasing decisions (see Chapter 4).

This chapter:

❏ identifies a number of key areas for waste reduction – which is environmentally and commercially the best option;

❏ explains how to identify recycling opportunities within the office and ensure their efficient introduction;

❏ highlights common obstacles to recycling and describes how to overcome them;

❏ explains how to quantify the volume of waste you produce and the costs of waste disposal and potential cost savings; and

❏ describes the new legislation affecting waste, particularly the Landfill Tax and the Producer Responsibility Obligations.

The introduction of the Landfill Tax in October 1996 has significantly increased the cost of waste disposal. It is widely speculated that this tax will be increased in successive budgets. The impact on the office will be to further increase the cost of using landfill which will encourage waste minimisation and recycling. The Producer Responsibility Obligations (Packaging Waste) Regulations place a producer responsibility obligation on certain businesses to recover and recycle specific tonnages of packaging waste. Although this does not directly affect the office, it is likely to have a wide ranging effect on how waste is handled. Offices with effective recycling schemes in place will benefit from increased demand for the material.

There are important legislative requirements for the correct disposal of waste. Failure under the Environmental Protection Act (EPA) Duty of Care can result in prosecution and embarrassing publicity. Finding suitable waste disposal contractors involves making sure that they meet the legislative requirements of the duty of care on your behalf. This chapter summarises the implications of the duty of care for the office and gives guidelines on how to verify contractors' legislative compliance.

In small offices, the volume of waste produced is usually quite low. In this case, it may be difficult to find a contractor willing to collect material for recycling, and storing the material for later collection can be a problem due to limited storage space. The answer is to reduce the waste at source, as described under Waste Reduction, later in this chapter. Offices in multi-tenanted buildings should approach other tenants, and landlords, to create joint recycling schemes.

Schools are under increasing financial pressures. The introduction of mixed paper recycling schemes in schools will reduce disposal costs and can also raise additional revenue for the school from recycling credits. Waste reduction measures improve use of resources and are also cost effective.

Local authorities are responsible for encouraging waste minimisation and recycling by the general public. It is therefore important that their in-house practices are consistent with these messages. Many local authorities are conducting office waste minimisation audits and implementing improvement plans in order to demonstrate good practice.

Waste Regulation

THE ENVIRONMENT AGENCY

The Environment Agency was set up on 8 August 1995, and took over responsibility for waste regulation on 1 April 1996.

The creation of the Environment Agency has brought together responsibilities for waste regulation, water pollution (formerly discharged by the National Rivers Authority (NRA) and for controlling industrial pollution (formerly Her Majesty's Inspectorate of Pollution (HMIP)). The aim of bringing all these functions together into a single national agency is to provide a more coherent and integrated approach to environmental protection and enhancement.

It is one of the most powerful regulators in the world. It provides a more comprehensive approach to the protection and management of the environment by combining the regulation of land, air and water. Its creation is a major positive step merging the expertise of the National Rivers Authority, Her Majesty's Inspectorate of Pollution, the Waste Regulation Authorities and several smaller units from the Department of the Environment, Transport and the Regions.

The Agency exists to provide high quality environmental protection and improvement. This is achieved with an emphasis on prevention, education and vigorous enforcement wherever necessary.

'MAKING WASTE WORK' – THE WASTE HIERARCHY

The Government White Paper on Sustainable Waste Management *Making Waste Work* (DoE, 1995) sets out the Government's strategy for achieving more sustainable waste management. This document highlights the importance of the waste hierarchy of reduction, re-use, recovery and disposal. Waste reduction at source is always the best commercial and environmental option.

The primary targets are:

❏ to reduce the proportion of controlled waste going to landfill to 60 per cent by 2005; and

❏ to recover 40 per cent of municipal waste by 2015.

Office waste is classified as controlled waste.

Secondary targets are set for specific waste streams. The most important is the existing household waste recycling and composting target:

❏ To recycle or compost 25 per cent of household waste by the year 2000.

Composting receives a high profile within the Strategy, and local authorities are encouraged to establish central composting schemes for garden and organic waste (see section on organic waste).

The White Paper states:

Many companies that have introduced waste reduction strategies have found that there can be significant savings to be gained both in terms of the costs of the raw materials and energy needed to produce the waste, as well as the costs of disposal or recovery itself. Companies which do

FIGURE 3.1
The waste hierarchy

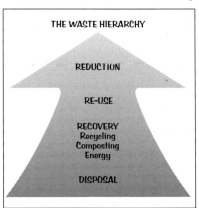

THE WASTE HIERARCHY

REDUCTION

RE-USE

RECOVERY
Recycling
Composting
Energy

DISPOSAL

not take steps to reduce the amount of waste they produce, thus miss out on a potentially significant opportunity to increase their competitiveness.

The White Paper highlights the lack of awareness of many organisations of the costs of waste disposal, and suggests that companies need to give greater recognition to waste disposal costs.

The Government is also committed to the reduction of its own waste, and the Department of the Environment, Transport and the Regions has set targets for minimising the solid waste it produces and will advise other government departments to achieve these standards. The aim was for two-thirds of government departments are to have office waste minimisation targets in place by the end of 1996.

Copies of *Making Waste Work* are available from HMSO and there is a useful summary of this document available from the Department of the Environment, Transport and the Regions.

LEGISLATION

What is Waste?

The legal definition of waste is 'any substance or object which the producer or the person in possession of it discards or intends or is required to discard'.

'Controlled waste' is any household, commercial or industrial waste such as waste from a house, shop, office, factory building site or any other business premises.

Duty of Care

The management of waste is tightly controlled by legislation Section 34 of the Environmental Protection Act introduced the duty of care which places everyone involved in the waste chain from producer, to transporter, to disposer, under a duty to ensure that waste is handled responsibly and that each participant in the waste management chain is carrying out their obligations under the legislation.

In *Waste Management: the Duty of Care – a Code of Practice* (DoE, 1996) the duty is imposed on the producer of the waste

---

MAIN IMPLICATIONS OF THE EPA

- ❏ A business must know how much waste it generates and what it consists of.
- ❏ A business must ensure that its waste is collected by a Registered Waste Carrier or Exempt Carrier.
- ❏ A waste transfer note containing a description of the waste for disposal or recycling must be raised. This is normally issued annually and must be kept on file for two years
- ❏ A business must satisfy itself that its waste is dealt with properly and legally through the disposal chain, to the extent that it can reasonably be expected to control events.
- ❏ Material collected for recycling is still classed as a waste and its disposal or recycling is governed by waste regulations.

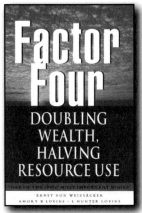

CORPORATE ENVIRONMENTAL MANAGEMENT

SYSTEMS AND STRATEGIES

Richard Welford

Presents a comprehensive analysis of the role of business in safeguarding the environment. It introduces the general issues and context, and then gives a detailed, critical examination of all the key tools of corporate environmental management, including environmental management systems and standards; environmental policies, guidelines and charters; environmental auditing; life-cycle assessment; the measurement of environmental performance; and environmental reporting.

Written in a clear and informative style, with checklists, explanatory notes and references for further reading, the book draws on the existing environmental strategies of a number of leading firms.

This is the most authoritative guide to contemporary environmental management. Its 'how to' focus makes it essential reading – not only for students and researchers but for managers faced with the challenge of introducing environmental strategies into their own organisations.

£15.95 Paperback ISBN 1 85383 308 8 1996 288 pages

CORPORATE ENVIRONMENTAL MANAGEMENT 2:

CULTURE AND ORGANISATIONS

Edited by Richard Welford

It is important to recognise that no technique or technology can be successful without the human element; the cooperation of everyone involved in the organisation. In this sequel to *Corporate Environmental Management: Systems and Strategies,* Richard Welford and the contributing authors, including Tony Emerson, Ralf Meima, David Jones, John Dodge and Romney Tansley, explore the various organisational and cultural concepts which firmly place the corporate environmental management agenda within the human dimension. The issues this book addresses will be of interest to human resource managers; students in business schools; and managers within both large firms and SMEs.

£15.95 Paperback ISBN 1 85383 412 2
£40.00 Hardback ISBN 1 85383 417 3 June 1997 240 pages

FACTOR FOUR

DOUBLING WEALTH, HALVING RESOURCE USE

Ernst von Weizsäcker, Amory B. Lovins, L. Hunter Lovins

"One of the 1990's most important books, Factor Four opens up a new way of thinking about efficiency." GEOFF MULGAN, DEMOS

The book contains a wealth of examples of revolutionising productivity, in the use of energy, from hypercars to low-energy beef; materials, from sub-surface drip irrigation to electronic books; and transport, from video conferencing to CyberTran, demonstrating how much more could be generated from much less, today. It explains how markets can be organised and taxes re-based to eliminate perverse incentives and reward efficiency, so wealth can grow while resource use does not.

£15.99 Hardback ISBN 1 85383 407 6 352 pages May 1997

EARTHSCAN

Earthscan, 120 Pentonville Road, London N1 9JN
Telephone 0171 278 0433 • Fax 0171 278 1142 • email earthsales@earthscan.co.uk
http://www.earthscan.co.uk

and all other parties who handle the waste until the material is finally disposed of or reclaimed. It was updated in March 1996 to take into account the application of the duty of care to the scrap metal industry from 1 October 1995 who were previously exempt.

WASTE STORAGE

Proper storage of waste is required under the Duty of Care Regulations. Waste producers must ensure that waste is secure to prevent leakage and spillage. The nature of office waste is relatively innocuous, however, storage of wastes should at least comprise the following:

❏ Secure area for storage of skips holding general wastes. Access to skips by third parties could result in the illegal deposit of hazardous or Special Wastes with general wastes. In the case of multi-tenanted premises where the company has little control over wastes from other tenants being mixed with their general wastes for disposal, you are responsible for checking that the storage facilities are satisfactory.

❏ Hazardous and Special Wastes should be stored in a secure and preferably contained area to control spills or leaks. Flammable wastes in sufficient quantity require specifically designed storage. Incompatible wastes must be segregated (see Chapter 6).

LEGISLATIVE COMPLIANCE: CONTRACTORS

Under the Environmental Protection Act – Duty of Care, you must follow the correct procedures regarding the disposal of your general waste. This duty lies with the original waste producer: you cannot delegate this legal responsibility to your contractors. However, failure to comply with the Duty is not an offence of strict liability once the waste has been transferred to a carrier or disposal contractor – if, and only if, the waste producer can prove that all reasonable measures have been taken to ensure that the waste has been dealt with properly and legally. Since no precise definition of 'reasonable measures' is given in the Regulations or the Approved Code of Practice, it is essential to use reputable contractors who will comply with the Duty of Care on your behalf. Non-compliance can result in costly prosecution.

To verify a contractor's compliance, you should:

❏ Make sure that the contractor provides the necessary

documentation: each waste stream has a transfer note which covers the specific waste stream description and the waste contractor and carrier used.
❏ Check that the waste carrier has a certificate of registration or exemption and make sure you see a copy of it.
❏ Check that the disposal sites used are licensed to accept the wastes being taken to them: either check the waste disposal site licence or contact the Environment Agency. Check the exemptions of sites receiving waste for recycling.
❏ Find out what happens to the material when it leaves your premises. Visit the contractor's premises and disposal sites to make sure that what the contractor tells you happens actually does happen. The waste producer must show that he has 'taken all such measures applicable to him in that capacity as are reasonable in the circumstances'.
❏ Ensure that you are happy with the security of the contractor's operations.

Waste Management Licensing Regulations

The disposal or keeping of waste in or on land requires a waste management licence. There are a number of waste management activities which do not require a licence, including sorting, shredding and baling wastes for recycling and storing waste ready for these operations. From 1 January 1995 it is an offence for an establishment to carry on an exempt activity if the exemption has not been registered.

Waste Management Licensing Regulations (DoE, 1995), were introduced on 1 May 1994 and updated in April 1995 to include the recovery of scrap metal and waste motor vehicle dismantling. The primary aim is to comprehensively license waste management activities, including the competence of operators. The likely effect on the office is to further increase the cost of waste disposal; waste brokers must now be registered.

The term 'broker' is defined as follows:

An establishment or undertaking which acts as a broker has control of waste in a sense that it arranges for the disposal or recovery on behalf of another and is outside the chain of people who handle waste (the producer, holder, carrier, recovery operator, or disposal operator).

The objective of the waste management licensing system is to ensure that waste management facilities:

❑ do not cause pollution of the environment;
❑ do not cause harm to human health; and
❑ do not become seriously detrimental to the amenities of the locality.

The Landfill Tax

In October 1996 the government introduced the Landfill Tax. The tax is levied according to the weight of waste disposed and is charged through the waste disposal contractor, back to the waste producer. The Landfill Tax is currently rated at £10 per tonne of waste. Producers of waste are charged higher rates for disposal as an incentive to reduce the quantities of waste produced. An organisation taking steps to reduce waste will see immediate financial benefits.

The Landfill Tax is intended to reflect the indirect costs of disposing of waste to landfill which are not represented through the disposal charge. The tax intends to raise revenue through waste disposal which can be used by newly established environmental trusts to minimise the effects of landfill.

Producer Responsibility Obligations (Packaging Waste) Regulations

These regulations, which were finally published on 29 January 1997, aim to raise the level of recovery and recycling of packaging waste. The regulations stem from the requirements of the EC Packaging and Packaging Waste Directive and from the Government's producer responsibility challenge to producers and users of packaging to recover 50–75 per cent of packaging waste by the year 2000.

Businesses with, initially, a turnover of £5m or more (later £1m) and which handle more than 50 tonnes of packaging or packaging materials in any one year will have to meet specified legal obligations.

These obligations are to:

❏ register with an appropriate agency (the environment agency (EA) or the scottish environmental protection agency (SEPA)) or join a registered collective collection scheme;
❏ recover and recycle a percentage of their packaging waste (specific percentages will depend on where the business is the packaging chain); and
❏ provide data on the amount of packaging handled, recycled or recovered.

Business in the following sectors will have to recycle the following percentages of packaging:

Packaging raw materials production – 6 per cent of total to be recovered/recycled.

Packaging manufacture (converting) – 11 per cent of total to be recovered/recycled.

Product packing and filling – 36 per cent of total to be recovered/recycled.

Selling to consumers or final users – 47 per cent of total to be recovered/recycled.

In practice each obligated business will have to recover and recycle the percentage of that waste relevant to their activities They can do this by:

1) Recycling that amount themselves or purchasing certificates from a reprocessor showing that the appropriate tonnages have been recycled on their behalf. In this case a yearly certificate should be issued to the EA or SEPA by a director or company secretary which states that the obligation has been met.
2) Becoming a member of a collective scheme which will take on legal responsibility in exchange for meeting its conditions. VALPAK, established during 1996, is a cross sectoral collective scheme which will undertake this responsibility on behalf of its members.

Companies need to have registered with the Environment Agency and have produced Packaging Flow Data by the end of August 1997. The Department of the Environment, Transport and the Regions has produced a PC operable disk to help businesses calculate their individual obligation. Contact Sall Campbell at the DETR.

The Government has set targets that 52 per cent of packaging waste should be recovered and 15 per cent recycled by the end of 2001 with a minimum of 15 per cent for each packaging material, however recovery and recycling obligations do not apply until the end of 1998 when interim targets of 38 per cent recovery and 7 per cent per material recycling will take effect.

Failure to comply with the regulations is a criminal offence.

WASTE DISPOSAL

The majority of office waste is disposed of to landfill (85 per cent), 7.5 per cent to incineration and 7.5 per cent recycled or re-used. It is estimated that in the UK approximately 120 million tonnes of controlled waste per year goes to landfill. There is some energy recovery from landfill from the methane gas produced.

There is also an increase in the incineration of waste for energy recovery. There are concerns regarding the local impacts of incineration, particularly the emissions of hazardous gases.

The disposal of general waste has a significant environmental impact:

❑ Landfill sites can emit landfill gases (primarily methane and carbon dioxide). Methane is a significant greenhouse gas.
❑ Landfill sites can cause groundwater contamination.
❑ Landfill is unsightly and inefficient in land use.
❑ There is a shortage of landfill sites: some of London's waste is transported to Oxfordshire for disposal.
❑ There is concern over the control of emissions from incinerators.

Waste disposal is expensive, costs have increased with the Landfill Tax and are likely to continue to escalate.

Assessing Current Arrangements

As part of the review process, you need to investigate your current waste disposal arrangements in order to assess the potential reduction in waste disposal costs to be gained from recycling. In a multi-tenanted building, it is difficult for individual tenants to calculate waste disposal costs, since these costs are usually included in a service charge. To achieve real improvement, all the tenants must develop a programme for the whole building to reduce total waste disposal costs.

Investigate the following:

WASTE DISPOSAL COSTS

Establish the current costs of waste disposal. Charges are usually based on the size and number of containers and the frequency of collection. Retrieving materials for recycling will enable you to reduce the size and frequency of collection and therefore reduce costs. Although for small organisations the costs of waste disposal are minimal (and the benefits of waste disposal reduction therefore less), the costs can still be calculated. For example, if your waste is collected by your local authority, find out how charges are worked out (charges are often per sack).

TYPE OF CONTAINERS

Identify the size and type of containers and the volume of material they will take. You may be able to reduce the size of a compactor or even replace it with a smaller container. Ernst & Young reduced its collections from daily to weekly which resulted in savings in excess of £15,000 per annum.

COST OF SECURITY SHREDDING

TABLE 3.1

Typical waste stream analysis for a school and office (President's Commission on Environmental Quality; Solid Waste Task Force, January 1993)

This cost should be included in the assessment of waste disposal costs. Identify how charges are assessed, e.g. minimum volume or number of sacks. If you have an in-house shredding machine, identify the cost in man-hours. It may be more cost effective to have a specialist company handle this or, better still, reduce the volume of confidential shredding.

WASTE TYPE AS A PERCENTAGE OF TOTAL WASTE	SCHOOL	OFFICE
Cardboard	11	6
White paper	19	57
Other mixed paper	16	6
Newspaper	4	9
Glass	1	2
Plastic	8	5
Drinks cans	1	1
Wood	7	
Remainder	33	14

CONTAINER SIZE (LITRES)	APPROXIMATE WEIGHT OF GENERAL WASTE CONTAINED (KG)
A black sack	10–15
1,100 (Euro bin)	220
950 (paladin)	190
660	132
360	72
240	48
120	24

TABLE 3.2

Standard capacities of waste bins based on landfill tax calculations (HM Customs & Excise)

WASTE TYPE AND QUANTITY	WEIGHT
4000 glass wine bottles	1 tonne (0.25 kg each)
50,000 drinks cans	1 tonne (0.02 kg each)
250,000 plastic vending cups	1 tonne
200,000 sheets A4 paper (80 g/m)	1 tonne

TABLE 3.3

Weight of common waste products

STORAGE AREAS

Identify storage restraints and potential areas for additional short-term storage.

ASSESSING MATERIALS

To assess the potential for recycling in your waste stream, you need to conduct a waste stream analysis. This will identify the estimated volume of recyclable products entering the waste stream. In the absence of definitive figures, the average figures quoted in Tables 3.1–3.6 can be used as a guide.

Use the ready-reckoner in Table 3.4 to calculate your total waste produced.

An example of how to use this ready-reckoner is given in Table 3.5.

TABLE 3.4

Ready-reckoner – total waste produced

NUMBER OF WASTE BINS USED AND THEIR CAPACITY	APPROXIMATE WEIGHT OF GENERAL WASTE CONTAINED	FREQUENCY OF COLLECTION PA	TOTAL WASTE PRODUCED PA
4 x 660 litre bins	4 x 132 kg = 528 kg	50 collections pa	50 x 528 kg = 26,400 kg

WASTE TYPE	PERCENTAGE OF TOTAL WASTE PRODUCED PA	TOTAL WEIGHT OF WASTE PRODUCED PA	ESTIMATED WEIGHT OF WASTE TYPE
Cardboard	11%	12,000 kg	1320 kg

TABLE 3.5

Ready-reckoner – waste composition by weight

Selecting Waste Management/Recycling Contractors

RECENT DEVELOPMENTS

The major waste management companies are starting to respond positively to the pressures on industry to implement waste reduction and recycling measures, and many are expanding their services to include recycling. As landfill site operators they are also investing in improved technology to meet higher standards of environmental protection.

Therefore when assessing waste disposal contracts consider waste management companies as well as specialist recycling companies. Equally, several recycling companies are developing their services to include waste management. There are benefits of using one contractor for both services. However ensure that they are equipped to deal with both services and that you are not losing out on revenue for recycling or paying too much for waste disposal.

For example, Biffa Waste Services have a high profile in terms of commitment to environmental protection and investment in improving standards of landfill sites. They now see their activities as resource management and have developed an alliance with SCA Recycling to provide a national collection capacity for all types of waste paper. This also maximises the efficiency of the use of their existing fleet of vehicles.

UK Waste now provide recycling services which include electronic equipment, and Hannay Recycling now provide a service for waste disposal. Several toner cartridge remanufacturing companies are expanding their collection systems to include other materials used in offices such as fluorescent tubes.

There is also a growth in materials recovery facilities (MRFs). One of the most established is at Milton Keynes. Grundons have recently developed a Waste Management Park at Colnbrook, which includes an MRF. The benefit of using

WASTE	WASTE CLASSIFICATION	METHOD OF DISPOSAL
Confidential paper	General, commercial	In-house shredding and recycling or secure disposal by contractor
Non confidential white paper	General, commercial	Recycling
Cardboard	General, commercial	Flattened and tied for recycling
Glass bottles: wine, mineral water and mixers	General, commercial	Colour separated for recycling
Aluminium and steel cans	General, commercial	Recycling
Plastic vending cups	General, commercial	Recycling via Save-a-Cup scheme
Disposable items: hand towels, napkins, paper plates, plastic dishes and bottles, sandwich wrappings	General, commercial	General waste disposal
Toner cartridges	General, commercial	Returned to supplier for recycling
Building waste from reorganisations and refurbishment	Difficult	Re-use within building, donation to local group for recycling
Electrical waste e.g. obsolete computers, printers and associated parts	Difficult	Re-sale via specialist brokers, return to supplier for recycling
Used cooking oil	Difficult	Recycling
Food	Organic	Composting
Feminine hygiene products	Clinical	Disposal by specialist contractor
Fluorescent light tubes	Difficult	Disposal by hazardous waste contractor
Chemical wastes from cleaning and building and grounds maintenance	Hazardous	Responsibility of contractor undertaking work, disposal as special waste

MRF is that no pre-sorting of materials is necessary prior to collection, the material is sorted on site and sent to reprocessors for recycling.

However, the revenue received on high quality sorted material will be much higher. There are often collection charges for the use of MRFs. It is also more difficult to promote a strong message in-house since you are not asking people to separate at source.

However, many local authorities are considering plans for MRFs in response to the Landfill Tax and the need to respond

TABLE 3.6

Main office waste arisings and recommended disposal routes

COMMON PROBLEMS

Drop in Revenue/Increase in Costs

❑ Less reputable companies will initially offer a high level of revenue, particularly on white office paper, in order to secure your business, only to drop the price or increase the charges once the scheme is in operation. Ensure you agree terms in writing preferably with a formal contract.

Fluctuations in the Paper Market

❑ There are genuine fluctuations in the paper market and therefore it is difficult to guarantee revenue. Use the prices quoted in *Materials Recycling Week* as a guide.

Contamination

❑ Promote the scheme effectively to avoid contamination. Agree an acceptable level of contamination with the contractor, otherwise you may find that your expected revenue has been substantially reduced.

Beware of Cowboy Operators

❑ Make sure your waste/recyclables are sent to landfill/recycling. Check the final destination.

Paying Too Much for Waste Disposal

If you use one contractor for recycling and waste, check how the charges are calculated and monitor closely.

PRACTICAL ACTION

Choose the Right Contractor

Consider both specialist recycling companies and waste management companies. Smaller specialist recycling companies often provide additional flexibility and are generally well placed to handle smaller organisations. There are often specialist local companies providing a good service. For example in the Bristol area, Resourcesaver is a well established independent company who collect a wide range of recycled materials from households and offices.

Clarify Costs

Clarify exactly how costs are calculated. If the contractor is handling waste and recycling, is the revenue on paper off-set against the collection charges for waste? Make sure you receive a breakdown of costs/revenue.

Carry Out an Audit Trail

Find out what happens to the material once it leaves your site. Is all material collected for recycling actually recycled. What happens to contaminated material?

Go Out to Tender

If you are a large organisation, go out to tender, preferably to a minimum of three companies. Use the information collected in the waste stream analysis to give an indication of the potential volume of material. The market is highly competitive, ensure you are offered a competitive deal. Using the total potential volume of recyclables from a large organisation can help to include smaller offices in collection arrangements.

HM Customs & Excise has recently used the information gathered on the total waste from all 320 offices to negotiate a national contract for paper recycling. This has provided a consistent approach to recycling throughout the organisation and enabled small sites to participate.

Contract Terms

For larger organisations, make sure the terms agreed are written into a contract, with clarification costs and time period for which they apply. Make sure you take into account price fluctuations within the paper market.

Environmental Standards

Check the environmental policy and standards of the contractor. Is there a commitment to maximise recycling and reduce the volume of material sent to landfill? If they are a landfill operator, are they investing in environmental technology?

to the government target of recycling 25 per cent of household waste by the year 2000. The use of MRFs enables authorities to provide mixed collection of recyclables from households.

There are considerable regional variations in the recycling facilities provided. It is more difficult to find recycling contractors in rural areas.

WASTE REDUCTION

Waste reduction is always preferable to recycling and is the most environmentally and commercially beneficial option. You should promote waste reduction measures as well as recycling. Remember that all waste is originally brought in as an asset.

PRACTICAL ACTION

There are a number of areas of potential waste reduction, the most obvious being paper and better use of technology.

Promote Re-use

Smaller offices can re-use paper very effectively, since it is easier to control. For example, paper that has only been used on one side can be fed back through the fax machine. Obsolete letterhead paper can be turned into scrap pads.

Promote Double-Sided Copying

Most photocopiers have a double-sided copying facility, but staff are often unsure which button to press. A poster above the copier can help.

SUMMARY GUIDELINES

- ❑ Assess the volume and type of waste materials.
- ❑ Identify storage restraints.
- ❑ Clarify how waste disposal costs are calculated.
- ❑ Ensure specific details are written in to contract documentation, particularly confirmation of costs and how long prices are held.
- ❑ Check environmental credentials of contractors.

Case Study

Subject –	**WASTE REDUCTION – OHPS**
Organisation –	**TETRA PAK UK**
Organisation type –	**PACKAGING MANUFACTURING**
Location –	**STOCKLEY PARK, HEATHROW**
No. of staff –	**250**

BACKGROUND

A high number of OHPs are produced for internal meetings. OHPs are produced by the IT department. The production of one OHP currently costs £2.20. Approximately 25 packs of film are used per month: a total cost of £33,000 per year.

ACTION

The reduction of high volume use of OHPs can be achieved by introducing a Macintosh computer to the meeting rooms and using a software package, such as Persuasion. Pictures and text are stored on floppy disk; the disks are used in conjunction with the Macintosh, which links directly to projection equipment to display the 'OHPs' on the screen.

The reduction in the use of OHPs will result in a cost saving of approximately £15,000 per annum. This figure takes into account that not all meeting rooms have this facility and that OHPs will also be used for external meetings and presentations.

The reduction in OHP usage also reduces the security problem of disposing of polythene colour transparency rolls which frequently contain confidential information.

RESULTS

❑ Cost savings of £15,000 pa.
❑ Reduction in costs of security shredding.
❑ Reduction in consumption of polythene film.
❑ Improved environmental profile.

Case Study

Subject –	**WASTE REDUCTION – ZERO WASTE INITIATIVE**
Organisation –	**B&Q**
Industry sector –	**RETAILING**
Location –	**SCARBOROUGH AND WEYMOUTH**

BACKGROUND

Since 1990 it has been B&Q's policy to reduce the environmental impact of its business. B&Q's 280 stores and 18,000 staff impact on the environment both locally and globally, and waste minimisation plays an important part in reducing our impacts at store level.

ACTION

The Zero Waste project was launched as a small scale pilot in August 1994; the aim being to encourage pilot stores to recycle or reuse their waste and then roll out the pilot scheme to other stores. In 1995, the project was extended to ten B&Q Supercentres and a B&Q Warehouse. The work done in these stores showed that the majority of our waste was in fact a resource; either we could recycle it or donate it to local schools and charities where it could be re-used.

BENEFITS

❏ Waste disposal costs reduced by diverting waste from the skip.
❏ Cardboard and plastic film generate revenue through recycling.
❏ Reduced environmental impact by reducing waste to landfill.
❏ Good community links by donating materials for re-use to schools and local charities.
❏ Several Zero Waste stores reduced their general waste by

RESULTS

Scarborough

❏ Damaged carpet tiles, broken ceramic tiles and netting donated to a local wildlife charity to build a pond.
❏ Scout groups use B&Q's heavy duty polythene as ground sheets.
❏ Unsaleable wallpaper and paint have been donated to the community service and used by young offenders to redecorate disabled and elderly people's homes.
❏ The store recycles all its cardboard and donates broken pallets to local schools for use in woodwork classes.

RESULTS

Weymouth

❑ Plastic film and cardboard are recycled via B&Q's Central Warehouse.

❑ Scrap office paper is made into jotter pads.

❑ Excellent community links by donating heavy duty chainreels to a local school for children with learning difficulties. The children find the feel of them interesting.

❑ Unsaleable wallpaper and paint are also donated to local schools.

The waste management programmes undertaken by these stores will provide the blueprint for other stores to develop a waste minimisation culture.

between 40 per cent and 75 per cent in 1996. It gave additional motivation to other stores which already had well developed waste minimisation programmes who reduced their store waste to only one small skip per month.

❑ The most successful stores are those with a voluntary Environmental Officer to coordinate waste management projects.

(Contributed by B&Q.)

Control Office Copying

Increase the use of print room facilities for volume copying. This helps minimise wastage and ensures greater use of double-sided printing and copying. The print room's policy should be to print double-sided unless otherwise specified. Double-sided copying and printing also saves money on paper, postage and storage requirements.

Better Use of Technology

Train staff and include E-mail in your induction programme. Discourage the printing of hard copies, unless absolutely necessary. Electronic diaries and voice mail are becoming increasingly common and considerably reduce paper consumption and improve efficiency.

Gouldens, solicitors in the City of London has introduced a number of measures which have improved efficiency, and reduced costs and paper consumption. Research materials are increasingly purchased on CD-ROM. Staff increasingly work from home using laptop computers with direct links to the network. The litigation department scan in documents for court cases which allows targeted production of paper for participants. The dramatic increase in the use of the internet and CD-ROMs is significantly reducing paper consumption and improving efficiency in communication technology.

Use PC-Based Faxes

Using a PC-based fax helps reduce the production of hard copies and systems are becoming increasingly sophisticated. However, faxes are often backed up by a posted hard copy: encourage staff to ask themselves whether this is really necessary. Make sure machines are set not to print out a transmission report for every fax.

Case Study

Subject –	**WASTE REDUCTION**
Organisation –	**CAMBIO**
Sector –	**BIOTECHNOLOGY**
Location –	**CAMBRIDGE**
No. of staff –	**5**

BACKGROUND

Cambio is a small team of biotechnologists who sell over 5000 products in over 35 countries. It has been trading for eight years and has always taken a keen interest in protecting the environment within a business framework. The company spends a large part of its effort in transferring technology from University laboratories (mainly Cambridge University) to the market place of molecular biology.

Cambio ships products world-wide. Many of these products are intrinsically unstable which means that most parcels require polystyrene boxes and frozen inserts to preserve their biological activity.

ACTION

Cambio has devised a re-use policy for polystyrene boxes. This has decreased the stockpile of used polystyrene boxes at laboratory sites and reduced the cost of replacement packaging for Cambio by £600 per month. The policy was introduced in 1987 and has a large pool of dedicated users who return polystyrene on a regular basis. Cambio pays the user a 50p credit for returned boxes, and provides regular pick-ups from customers who are largely local organisations including the university and the hospital. More recently it has started to encourage the re-use of cold packs, cardboard boxes and chips (either polystyrene or corn starch).

In addition all paper and stationery products are made from 100 per cent recycled material and are totally chlorine free. Paper is re-used where possible and collected for recycling.

RESULTS

- ❑ Cost savings of £7200 from the re-use of product packaging.
- ❑ Involvement of customers in the re-use of packaging with a financial incentive.
- ❑ Successful use of recycled paper and stationery products with no loss in quality.
- ❑ Positive environmental profile with customers who are environmentally conscious.

Office photocopiers have energy saving buttons, staff cycle to work including the Managing Director. Cycle couriers are used for local deliveries.

Savings made from recycling are given to charity. In 1995 £250 was donated to Castle Projects Print Finishers, a local organisation dedicated to the rehabilitation of the mentally ill.

(Contributed by Cambio.)

SUMMARY GUIDELINES

- ❑ Do you need it!
- ❑ Investigate opportunities to use less.
- ❑ Investigate re-usable, recyclable alternatives.
- ❑ Increase use of technology to reduce paper usage.
- ❑ Encourage staff to come up with ideas on waste reduction.
- ❑ Promote waste reduction initiatives (see Chapter 7).

Avoid Using Header Sheets

Adjust printers to avoid wasteful header sheets; use fax tabs where possible.

Design Publications to Avoid Waste

Choice of design and font size can significantly reduce paper usage. Consider the size of the print used, page layout and the weight of paper. This is particularly important in the case of documents with a large circulation. Reducing the size of an annual report by one page results in substantial savings in paper.

Reduce OHP Use

Information can be projected directly from a PC screen, avoiding the need for acetate OHPs.

Additional Areas

For waste reduction initiatives in catering see Chapter 5.

Energy Use

Simple in-house initiatives such as a 'switch off' campaign can result in significant energy savings: see Chapter 6.

Exchange/Repair Furniture and Equipment

See Chapter 4 and Chapter 6.

Control Stationery Use

Hold a stationery amnesty to retrieve all those stray pens, pencils, etc. Office moves can be an opportunity to order new stationery. Make sure departments take their stationery with them.

Encourage Staff Suggestions

Use your Environment Committee to encourage suggestions from staff on waste reduction. See Chapter 8.

Local Authorities

A specific area for potential waste reduction in local
authorities is in the reduction in circulation of Committee
Papers. Discuss circulation with members and offices to
identify areas of reduction. Members are often grateful
to have more targeted information to read!

Kings Lynn and West Norfolk Borough Council
reduced paper consumption by 4 tonnes per year and
saved £3750.

Schools

Schools often have a strong culture in re-use due to very
tight budgets. For example at Prince of Wales First School
in Dorchester, parents have been very responsive to
requests to donate materials for use in art and technology classes. Materials such as toilet rolls, corks, drinks
cans and yoghurt pots are collected and sorted for ease
of access and use. They are displayed in an efficient and
attractive way, and clearly labelled to encourage use.
They are treated and handled as resources, not waste.

The message is: encourage recycling, but not by producing
more waste! Follow the waste hierarchy; reduce, re-use,
recycle.

RECYCLING

Recycling does have an environmental impact. However,
generally, the recycling process provides clear environmental
benefits over virgin materials. The more recyclate used, the
less virgin raw materials need to be extracted and the greater
the environmental benefits seen in production.

PRACTICAL ACTION

When investigating the feasibility of recycling schemes
establish:

Potential Volume of Material

The contractor needs to know the anticipated volume in order to assess viability of collection.

Contractor to be Used

You must have a market for the material. Recycling facilities vary considerably depending on the area of the country. It is pointless collecting recyclable materials if no one will come and collect them, so find a contractor prior to setting up your scheme. Look in the Directory or contact your local authority Recycling Officer, who should know what is available in your area. Local Friends of the Earth groups are often a good source of information, or the Community Recycling Network (CRN).

Collection Arrangements

Collection charges and/or potential revenue are linked to volume. For example, a contractor may charge to collect a small quantity of paper (especially if it is mixed and of poor quality). However, you may be able to negotiate payment for high quality white paper if the volume is sufficient. Note that the price is affected by fluctuations in the paper market.

Storage Restraints

If the volume of material produced is small, and storage is limited, it is rarely practical to store the material for several weeks to reach the minimum volume required by the contractor. The fire risk needs to be considered when assessing suitable storage areas.

Volume of General Waste

Establish the approximate tonnage of your waste to clarify the environmental impact of the waste going to landfill/incineration. This will help you identify recycling potential: on average, 60–70 per cent of office waste is recyclable. Small offices may have difficulty finding contractors to collect small volumes of material for recycling; lack of storage space may also be a problem. The answer is to reduce the volume of general waste at source: see Waste Reduction, in this chapter, for details.

The Type of Material

Assess what the contractor will collect prior to setting up a scheme. For example: some toner cartridges are recyclable, but not all; high quality white paper has a value, but mixed paper may not.

Communication and Retrieval System

It has to be easy for staff to recycle, otherwise it will not happen! Staff need to know what the bins/containers are for, so make sure you tell them.

PAPER

Environmental Issues

Paper, which accounts for over a third of our waste, is currently disposed of in landfill sites or by incineration (although the use of incineration for energy recovery is increasing, it is still in its infancy in the UK). Recycling paper has many environmental benefits and has a high profile:

❏ High quality recycled paper can be made without re-bleaching, if it is correctly sorted.

❏ Recycling paper helps to reduce the pressure on natural habitats resulting from intensive forestry. The paper industry plants more trees than it chops down, but natural habitats are being destroyed to make way for intensive tree farming. It takes 17 trees to make one tonne of high quality white office paper.

❏ Recycling paper is more energy-efficient than making virgin paper from wood.

❏ Paper goes to a recycling mill rather than to landfill sites or for incineration.

For more detail on the environmental issues associated with paper see Chapter 4.

Changes in the Paper Market

Increases in paper prices during 1995 gave additional incentive to collect paper for recycling (however, this market is renowned for fluctuations). The exceptionally strong demand in 1995 was caused by world-wide economic growth which led to an increase in demand for pulp and paper, particularly in SE Asia, at the same time as large areas of N American forestry were taken out of production, a position which has since stabilised.

The construction of two new de-inking plants in the UK at Aylesford (SCA) and Kemsley (UK Paper) has increased the demand for paper collected for recycling. UK Paper are now producing a high quality white copier paper 'Evolve' from the Kemsley plant which provides an excellent opportunity to close the recycling loop.

In spite of the fluctuations in the paper market, paper recycling schemes are still cost effective because they reduce waste to landfill and therefore waste disposal costs.

The increase in the purchase price of paper has helped to increase awareness of paper consumption and the benefits of tighter control over usage.

COMMON PROBLEMS

Non-Recyclables

❑ Some paper products can be difficult to recycle, particularly glues and heavily laminated finishes. Check with your contractor to find out what they will not take. Tell staff what can and cannot be recycled. Reduce the use of laminates in your publicity material.

Storage Restraints

❑ Your storage restraints will determine the frequency of collection required. For example, in Central London, storage is generally very tight, since space costs money. The fire risk also needs to be considered when assessing suitable storage areas. If you have storage space, you may be able to store half a tonne of paper and therefore receive revenue.

PRACTICAL ACTION

High quality office paper and computer paper can be recycled very efficiently to make more office papers and tissue paper. Mixed waste paper and the lower grades are generally used for low-grade paper products and packaging material.

There is an expansion of recycling schemes for mixed paper, which helps reduce some of the traditional problems of contamination. Mixed paper schemes minimise the volume of material sent to landfill. However, separation of white paper where volume is sufficient will give a higher revenue.

When considering the viability of paper recycling schemes, identify all the paper products going into the waste stream.

Assessment

Potential Volume of Material

The contractor will need to know the anticipated volume of paper in order to assess the viability of collection. Collection charges and/or potential revenue are linked to volume. Paper must be of reasonable quality. Mixing white paper with cardboard and newspapers will probably ensure that the paper merchant leaves your load behind!

Type of Material

Assess what the contractor will collect prior to setting up a scheme. Some merchants will collect mixed coloured and white paper, so that you don't have to separate it. However, it's better to separate white office paper, since it can be used to make high quality office paper. Mixed paper can usually only be used to make low grades of paper.

Recycling Low-Grade Waste

Cardboard, newspapers, brochures and magazines are potentially recyclable, but are all low-grade waste. These have a low market value, so paper merchants will often make a charge to collect them. Charges vary considerably and it is often easier to find a willing contractor if they are also collecting your higher grade waste. A more practical alternative for cardboard is to ensure that suppliers retrieve packaging materials from deliveries: see section on the Producer Responsibility Obligations.

Negotiations with Paper Merchants

Negotiations with the paper merchant should include the collection of all paper products. It may be more cost effective to combine security waste with non-confidential paper and therefore find a contractor to handle both.

Revenue and Collection Charges

The paper market is fairly volatile: prices paid for recycled paper do fluctuate. High quality white office paper has a market value and some paper merchants will pay a small amount per tonne. However, this is generally based on large quantities of half a tonne upwards. For smaller quantities, you are very unlikely to receive revenue, but should have your paper collected free of charge. Small organisations may be able to find other outlets for paper: for example, Ernst & Young's Southampton office (180 staff) dispose of some of its shredded paper to be used as guinea pig bedding! Cheshire County Council's is being used as duck bedding.

Confidential Waste

If the contractor chosen for non-confidential paper operates to good levels of security, it should be possible to reduce the volume of material sent for confidential shredding. Obviously some material is highly sensitive, but there is often room for more discrimination. Staff must realise that there is a cost to the company. Are internal memos really confidential? If the remaining material is highly sensitive, be extremely vigilant regarding the

Contamination

❑ Many companies introduce a dual-bin system, whereby a bin for paper recycling is placed under each desk alongside the general waste bin. This system obviously encourages staff to recycle, but it also encourages contamination. A frequent problem is that everything goes into the paper recycling bin including plastic cups, sandwich wrappers, etc. If paper recycling schemes are heavily contaminated, paper merchants will not collect or will charge for collection. This is where most schemes fail.

Communication

❑ The key to the successful introduction of recycling programmes is effective communication. Without the commitment of individuals, the programme will never be successful and achieve the potential cost savings identified. See Chapter 8 for effective launch programmes.

SUMMARY GUIDELINES

❏ Assess the potential volume and type of material.
❏ Find a market for the material.
❏ Investigate collection arrangements.
❏ Consider storage restraints.
❏ Decide on the method of retrieval.
❏ Launch the scheme: refer to Chapter 8 for details.

level of security provided by the contractor. Follow these guidelines:

❏ Ensure confidential waste bins are clearly labelled and locked. Security risks can be of concern in-house as well as externally.
❏ Ensure the contractor provides tagged security sacks and certificates of destruction.
❏ Verify the level of security provided by the contractor. They must have a system of security clearance for waste handlers and their security procedure must extend to the transit of the materials. Vehicles should be kept locked and transit time minimised.
❏ Give clear instructions to the contractor regarding subcontractors: sub-contracting should not be allowed without clearance from yourselves. Regular monitoring of the contractor's performance is important.
❏ Clarify: the cost per tonne of security shredding, minimum quantities for collection and the amount of material to be shredded.
❏ Visit the contractor's site to check the security of their premises and operations.

Retrieval Systems

It has to be easy for staff to recycle paper, otherwise it will not happen. However, you must create a balance between having enough containers (so that staff do not have to go far to use them) and making it too easy (so that everything is thrown into the bin, causing contamination problems). Many recycling companies can provide you with suitable containers.

Use medium-sized bins (holding, for example, about 10 kg of paper) distributed evenly around the office, allowing one container per 7–10 staff. This means that staff need to think before they throw paper away, but don't have to do a route march to reach the bins! In addition, place extra bins in key areas such as copier and print rooms.

Individual desktop trays can be added to supplement the scheme recommended above. If this system is adopted, enlist the support of your staff and make them responsible for emptying the desktop trays into the larger bins. These can be over-printed with your company logo. An alternative is to use the lids from photocopier boxes and ask your print department to produce labels.

Case Study

Subject –	**WASTE MINIMISATION**
Organisation –	**WEST MOORS MIDDLE SCHOOL**
Organisation type –	**SCHOOL**
Location –	**WEST MOORS – DORSET**
No. of students–	**450**

BACKGROUND

As part of Dorset County Council's commitment to good house-keeping practice, four schools in Dorset including West Moors Middle School took part in a pilot project to reduce waste and save money. The school has 450 pupils aged 9–12 years. There is a strong recycling culture within the school from both staff and pupils. Awareness of waste reduction and recycling was high, and a number of initiatives were already in place.

ACTION

Recycling

Staff retrieve plastics, glass and cans for recycling and take them to the local recycling banks. Some cardboard is re-used in the art department prior to recycling. A mixed paper recycling scheme has been introduced. Paper banks have been sited in the playground since 1 December 1995 for the collection of mixed paper waste and cardboard from the school and waste paper bought in from home. By mid-September 1996 they had collected 3.7 tonnes – this equates to 37 trees! (It takes 0 trees to produce 1 tonne of newsprint, and 17 trees to produce 1 tonne of high quality office paper.)

Children are responsible for leaving and collecting recycling bags from each classroom. Recycling bins are placed in each year group. The scheme is run by the Humanities Department and any income generated is used for history and geography books. Paper which is partially used or damaged is placed in a scrap paper tray to be used for rough work. Spare cut-off card from a local business is used as scrap for teaching and office staff.

The scheme has been promoted to parents through the local newsletter, and the response has been excellent. Newspapers are even used by the art department prior to recycling in the paper banks! Text books are repaired where possible to extend their life. When obsolete they are offered free to the local community or sent to the developing world. Parents donate materials for use in the art department eg toilet rolls, drinks cans and yoghurt pots.

The paper recycling initiative has saved the school an estimated £200 pa in waste disposal costs.

Building and Grounds

The re-use of materials from building waste was impressive. Metal was sold to a local scrap metal merchant which has raised £100–200. Waste wood was used in the school woodwork shop or given away as firewood. Bricks were kept for re-use in new building work. Any top soil removed in building work was used in the garden areas. Obsolete doors and other sheet material were offered to the local community/parents at no cost. Replaced glazing and brackets were kept for re-use.

Environmental awareness is very strong in the maintenance of the grounds. There is no burning on site. Grass cuttings are left. Wildlife areas are left round the edge of the playing field. This encourages the growth of seedling trees which are re-planted. Waste from pruning etc. is cut up into mulch, or removed by grounds maintenance staff for firewood.

Environmental Education

The introduction of the re-use and recycling measures within the school helps to promote a strong message of the value of materials. This supports curricular activities; the school grounds are used for ecology and local field trips are organised regularly particularly by Years five and seven. There is potential to introduce a wormery for the composting of kitchen waste. The science staff felt this could be linked to the curriculum.

RESULTS

- ❏ Low disposal costs and volume of waste produced due to effective waste reduction measures.
- ❏ Introduction of the mixed paper recycling scheme has reduced volume to landfill by 3.6 tonnes and disposal costs by £200 pa (by reducing frequency of the paladin collection).
- ❏ Toner and deskjet cartridges: collection for recycling ensures safe disposal. Use of remanu-factured cartridges reduces costs by 20–50 per cent.
- ❏ Increase in environmental awareness from students, particularly the value of paper.

UK Paper has been creative in its packaging of its new copier paper 'Evolve'. The lids of the boxes are designed for use as paper trays.

Cleaning Contractors

Cleaning contractors play an important role in the success of recycling schemes. It is very frustrating, if you have religiously collected paper for recycling, to find that your cleaning staff have thrown it out! Involve cleaning staff in the planning stage. For example, a change of cleaning contractor at Lehmans to Lancaster Cleaning, has had a significant impact on the success of the paper recycling scheme. Lancasters was enthusiastic and also recognised the opportunity to improve waste handling arrangements by the introduction of a more efficient recycling scheme. It monitored the scheme daily and allocated a specific member of staff to managing the recycling.

Conversely, one of our clients thought they had been recycling for three years, when in fact the cleaning staff had been putting the green bags in the skip! Cleaning staff need to know what the arrangements are and what is expected from them. Follow these guidelines:

❑ Collection of recyclables needs to be coordinated with the cleaning schedule. The cleaners will need to retrieve the recycling sacks to meet collection times.
❑ Establish contact points for cleaners and recycling contractors to handle any problems on a day-to-day basis.
❑ Find out if there is an additional charge for handling recycling schemes. Most cleaning companies appreciate that they need to be receptive to recycling. After all, they are not handling any extra waste.
❑ Find a short-term storage area for recyclables prior to collection.
❑ Make sure that the cleaners retrieve and replace recycling sacks when the bins are full. It is demotivat-

ORGANIC WASTE

Environmental Issues

Every year, landfill sites receive three to four million tonnes of putrescible household waste, and two million tonnes of garden waste collected at civic amenity sites. The environmental and economic impact of using landfill sites is discussed under Waste Disposal in this chapter.

The importance of composting has been recognised in *Making Waste Work* with specific targets set for composting and local authorities being encouraged to introduce central composting facilities. Three secondary targets have been set to encourage recycling and composting, which have strong implications for local authorities.

1) '40% of domestic properties with a garden to carry out composting by the year 2000.
2) All waste disposal authorities to cost and consider the potential for establishing central composting schemes by the end of 1997.
3) One million tonnes of organic household waste per annum to be composted by the year 2000.'

For further details on grounds maintenance and green waste see Chapter 5.

COMMON PROBLEMS

❑ Do not include meat and fish in compost material: they attract vermin.
❑ Keep wormeries out of direct sunlight to prevent destruction of the worms.
❑ Do not put grass in any quantity into wormeries: it heats up and gives off ammonia, which will kill worms.
❑ Do not put weeds with seeds into a wormery: the wormery does not produce enough heat to break down the seeds, which will germinate when the compost is used.
❑ Wormeries tend to need more looking after than traditional heaps. Ensure sufficient man power is available.

PRACTICAL ACTION

Donate Waste Food

In the past, it has been possible to dispose of food waste (from company restaurants, for example) as pig swill. However, food hygiene regulations have been tightened up and it now has to be sterilised first, which is generally prohibitively expensive.

However, Crisis, the national charity for single homeless people, has set up Crisis Fairshare. It will collect quality surplus fresh food and redistribute to hostels and day centres providing meals to homeless people in London. It has strict controls over food handling and ensures that all sites are adhering to the food hygiene regulations and ensures correct food storage and preparation at all times.

It asks that donated food is of good quality and within its use by date. It needs to be stored and prepared according to current legislation. If it is pre-prepared it needs to be kept chilled and covered.

Introduce Composting

If your food waste is unsuitable, or this facility is not available in your area, consider introducing a composting system, to cope with both food and, if your company has its own grounds, garden waste. Composting is the biological decomposition of organic waste under controlled conditions. The traditional compost heap, where oxygen is supplied or restricted, can aid decomposition as can the introduction of a wormery. There are three main methods of composting: wormeries, traditional composting and large-scale composting.

Wormeries

❑ A wormery uses tiger worms to digest waste and can reduce its contents by as much as 80 per cent. A wormery needs more attention than the aerobic system (compost heap). It can be kept indoors or outdoors and is suited to small volumes of material. A 50:50 split between garden and food waste is preferable. Wormeries produce good quality compost and liquid fertiliser. The compost produced is richer than that produced by traditional methods and can be used to refine compost from traditional heaps. Wormeries are ideal for use by smaller offices in rural locations.

Traditional Composting

Traditional composting is suited to a large volume of material and can cope with a higher garden waste content than a wormery can, since compost heaps generate enough heat to kill weed seeds. They must be outdoors with good drainage to cope with run-off. Traditional compost heaps do not break waste down as finely as wormeries. An additional outlet may be needed for excess compost: local schools, nurseries, allotment growers and your own staff may be grateful recipients! Your local council may be a good source of information.

Large-Scale Composting

Where the volume of compost is sufficient, it may be more practical to take organic waste to a composting plant. Some local authorities have developed composting facilities for household waste. However, there is normally a charge for this, so it is only viable if there is a substantial volume of material.

Carlisle City Council set up their own composting plant for green waste collected at the civic amenity site. They sell the compost to local allotment associations and community groups. Make sure you establish a market for your compost.

SUMMARY GUIDELINES

- ❏ Donate quality excess food to Crisis Fairshare (if in the London area).
- ❏ Install a wormery if the volume of material is small with a high proportion of kitchen waste (particularly useful for small companies with their own kitchen facilities).
- ❏ If the majority of the material is garden waste, use a traditional compost heap.
- ❏ Take material to a municipal site where volume ensures it is cost effective.
- ❏ Find additional outlets for the compost, if necessary, for example, schools and nurseries.
- ❏ Monitor the quality of material going into the composting system.
- ❏ Buy back compost.

Assessment

Potential Volume and Type of Material

This will determine the most suitable composting option. Wormeries are not capable of handling large volumes of waste, unlike traditional compost heaps. Wormeries cope better with a 50:50 split between garden and kitchen waste. If the volume of garden waste is greater than kitchen waste, then a traditional compost heap is more suitable.

Retrieval Systems

If you introduce an in-house system, you can easily retrieve materials from your restaurant and grounds. However, if the volume is substantial, you will need to arrange transportation of the material to the nearest site. The assessment of volume will determine financial viability.

Schools

Schools have good potential to introduce traditional composting and wormeries as part of the curriculum as well as encouraging waste reduction. Composting schemes, particularly wormeries are popular with children, and can be linked to environmental education through the science curriculum.

Henry Doubleday Research Association (HDRA) is a national organic gardening organisation and aims to encourage composting in households, schools and local authorities. It is an excellent source of advice and provides leaflets on composting as well as information on the wide range of composters on the market – there are at least 30. It works with a number of local authorities to help them develop composting programmes.

HDRA is also very active with schools and runs a number of activities including the Schools Recycling Week. According to its Education Officer, recycling and composting can be linked to six curriculum subjects: science; mathematics; English; art; design and technology; geography; and history.

In addition to composting it is important to buy compost made from organic waste. Dorset County Council has a policy to compost all green waste. It uses the the local composting plant, Eco-Composting at Christchurch and buys back compost for use in its grounds maintenance (see grounds maintenance in Chapter 5).

GLASS

Environmental Issues

The raw materials used to make glass are not expensive or rare, but silica (sand) is extensively quarried and causes unsightly damage to the landscape. Glass is also relatively heavy and bulky, constituting a large percentage of waste by weight. Glass can be recycled very efficiently, with an energy saving of 25 per cent. One tonne of recycled glass saves 30 gallons of oil.

The glass industry is committed to achieving a 58 per cent recycling rate by 2000.

The companies that are most likely to have glass for recycling are those with staff restaurants and client function rooms.

PRACTICAL ACTION

Assess the Current Usage

Assess current usage to find out the potential volume for recycling. Note that contractors often need glass to be separated by colour.

Establish a Retrieval System

Glass can often be retrieved directly by the catering contractors when trays are cleared from the staff restaurant and hospitality suites cleared after functions. Glass is often already separated from general waste for health and safety reasons.

Find a Contractor

Some local authorities offer glass collections and there are a number of organisations throughout the country offering this service. For smaller organisations, and where volume is low, it will be difficult to find a contractor to collect the glass: you can take small amounts to the local bottle bank. An alternative to using bottled water is to introduce an in-house water purification system, which means that bottles can be re-used (see Chapter 5).

VENDING CUPS

Environmental Issues

Plastics rely on oil for their production, which is a finite raw material and in most cases does not biodegrade.

PRACTICAL ACTION

Single-walled polystyrene (that is, plastic) cups can easily be recycled. Following collection, the polystyrene is formed into pellets. The material is used for a variety of non-food applications, including video cassettes, office equipment and industrial reels.

Assessment

There are at least three different types of vending cup on the market, but there are only established collection systems for one, so you must identify the recyclability of the type you are using:

Waxed Paper Cups

Facilities for recycling waxed paper cups are not currently available. The wax coating requires chemicals to break it down for recycling, which rather defeats the object.

Expanded Polystyrene Cups

Expanded polystyrene cups are theoretically recyclable, but collection facilities are not widely available. Collection facilities are available for quantities in excess of one tonne. These can be compacted on site to minimise space problems.

Polystyrene (Plastic) Cups

Facilities to recycle single-walled polystyrene (plastic) cups are widely available.

Using Mugs

Using mugs is environmentally preferable. However, this can be difficult for hygiene reasons. The replacement of vending cups with mugs is usually reliant on staff having (and using) washing-up facilities. This is generally more practical in smaller offices.

You could issue staff with their own mugs overprinted with your company logo and a message – this provides a good opportunity to promote an environmental message. Some vending machines have sensors that enable them to detect that there is a mug in the dispenser: in this case the machine does not issue a cup. Statistics about the percentage vend of cups and mugs can usually be provided by the vending company. These statistics can be used to monitor relative usage and to feed back results to staff.

Retrieval Systems

Save-A-Cup provides a collection service for single-walled polystyrene (plastic) cups. It is continually expanding its collection services and collects in the main regional centres. It provides Beca bins and labelled sacks. Beca bins are specifically designed to stack cups, which substantially reduces the space they occupy. Cleaning staff must put the cups into the labelled sacks for weekly collection. Save-A-Cup provides back-up publicity to encourage staff to recycle.

It also provides flaking machines which reduce on-site storage requirements and improve the efficiency of its operations. In the collection of unflaked cups, 30 per cent of the gross weight is liquid. Flaked cups can be collected by your normal supplier of cups.

Save-A-Cup has also developed a range of office stationery products made from recycled vending cups. These are useful and functional promotional tools. For example rulers – it takes seven vending cups to make one ruler.

CANS

Environmental Issues

The raw materials used to manufacture cans are iron ore, tin and bauxite. This involves mining operations in developing countries which are very destructive to the environment. Following extraction, the raw material is transported to smelting plants: the smelting of all metals is very energy intensive. Once filled and transported, cans have a relatively short shelf-life before they are disposed of in the waste stream. In the UK, cans are made from tinplate and/or aluminium and can be recycled.

SUMMARY GUIDELINES

- ❏ Use vending machines with sensors that allow mugs to be used. Using mugs is preferable to increasing the number of plastic cups being recycled.
- ❏ Where vending machines are used, ensure that single-walled polystyrene (plastic) cups are used, rather than expanded polystyrene or waxed paper.
- ❏ Check that Save-A-Cup provides collection facilities in your area.
- ❏ Eliminate vending machines in smaller offices where storage of used cups is impractical. Use mugs instead.
- ❏ Feedback the results of recycling, to maintain motivation. Use Save-A-Cup publicity material and stationery products made from vending cups.
- ❏ Place Beca bins by each vending machine.

SUMMARY GUIDELINES

- ❏ Obtain containers and publicity material from ACRA and British Alcan.
- ❏ Find a local contractor and establish what they will collect prior to setting up the scheme.
- ❏ Find out whether you will receive revenue on aluminium cans.
- ❏ Install can crushers if the volume of cans used is high.
- ❏ If the volume of cans is too small to make collection by a contractor viable, take the cans to your nearest recycling facility.

PRACTICAL ACTION

Assessment

SEPARATING MATERIALS

Aluminium has a higher value than steel and some contractors will pay for aluminium cans. Some contractors will collect aluminium only, so that you have to separate it in-house. Although it is generally more practical to collect mixed cans, the advantage of splitting the cans is that you will receive revenue on the aluminium.

USING CAN CRUSHERS

Can crushers will reduce the space the cans occupy. Wall-mounted can crushers are available that have magnets for testing cans to see whether they are aluminium or steel (aluminium does not stick to the magnet). Alternatively, bins with can crushing devices that sort steel and aluminium are available.

CHOOSING A RETRIEVAL SYSTEM

The restaurant is generally a good location for a can bank, relying on staff retrieving cans from their trays. This scheme can easily be extended if successful. Assessment of current usage will help identify potential volumes.

SOURCING COLLECTION CONTAINERS

Halcyon Plastics provide collection boxes made from white cardboard and clearly labelled in blue. They are 2.5 feet high and 18 inches across. Clear plastic sacks to go in the boxes are provided. The Aluminium Can Recycling Association provides back-up publicity material.

Sell-A-Can provide 'banks' – similar sized containers in the shape of a can that may be over-printed with your logo and message.

FIND CONTRACTORS

British Alcan or ACRA will provide details of regional collection arrangements. Some paper recycling companies will also collect cans.

PROMOTE THE SCHEME

Large electronic can crushers are available which automatically separate steel and aluminium. They also give out a token for every can and are a very useful promotional tool.

OFFICE EQUIPMENT

Some 100,000 tonnes of electronic equipment reaches the end of its life each year. This will increase further when products bought during the consumer electronics boom of the 1980s enter the waste stream. The scrap value of this waste could be as much as £50 million annually. There is increasing pressure for manufacturers to respond to this issue. Technological changes are speeding up obsolescence, landfill costs are rising and pressure for legislation throughout Europe is mounting.

There is an increasing number of companies who specialise in electronics recycling. Some computer manufacturers are beginning to develop equipment which is designed for ease of disassembly and recycling but this is still a new development. The majority of computers disposed of currently are not designed to be easily recyclable. See Chapter 5.

PRACTICAL ACTION

Upgrade Existing Equipment

Avoid purchasing new equipment by upgrading existing equipment where possible. Don't over-specify. Not all staff need high specification machines.

Encourage Exchange of Equipment

Encourage exchange of equipment within your organisation. Another department may have a use for what you are throwing out.

Return to Manufacturer

Return to the manufacturer for refurbishment. Computers can be broken down into component parts for re-use and recycling. Copper and silver from cables can be recycled, as can plastic and metal casings.

Find Specialist Recycling Company

There are a number of specialist recycling companies. For example, Mann Recycling is a specialist company which dismantles computers for re-assembly. If the volume is sufficient it offers a free collection service. UK Waste also provides a specialist collection service. If the material is of a high enough value, you may receive revenue.

Case Study

Subject –	**RECYCLING PROGRAMME**
Organisation –	**LEHMAN BROTHERS**
Industry sector –	**BANKING**
Location –	**CITY OF LONDON (BROADGATE)**
No. of staff –	**1000**

BACKGROUND

US investment bank Lehman Brothers commissioned Wastebusters to conduct a waste management audit as part of its drive for business efficiency. The audit examined existing waste recycling and disposal arrangements and a recommended improvement programme was given. The aim of the project was to reduce the costs of waste disposal and increase the revenue received for recycling.

ACTION

Waste Minimisation

A number of initiatives were being undertaken by the company or were being planned. Additional recommendations included training staff to make use of an existing facility to send PC generated faxes and to review both archiving arrangements and controls on the quantities of PR and research material produced.

Collecting Recyclables

A number of improvements were suggested to the existing paper recycling scheme, to reduce contamination of the collected paper with non-recyclables and to increase participation in the scheme. It was also recommended that cardboard, plastic cups, drinks cans, glass and waste catering oil were collected for recycling.

Recycling Schemes Launch

Board level support was obtained for the initiatives, with the Chairman signing the memo giving notice of the launch. Displays were held in the building reception on the day of the recycling schemes launch, providing facts about recycling and environmental protection and the role to be played by the company. A variety of personalised cartoon posters drawing attention to the various recycling initiatives are displayed prominently around the building.

Monitoring and Review

The staff committee is being used to explore any staff concerns about the waste minimisation programme and to give feedback on its success.

Duty of Care

Visits have been made to the sites of recycling and waste management contractors to ensure that appropriate arrangements are made for the handling and disposal of the company's waste.

RESULTS

- ❑ Cost savings of £18,000 pa estimated through waste disposal costs avoided and revenue on recycling and reduction in Landfill Tax liability of £7,000 pa.
- ❑ Board level support gained for all initiatives.
- ❑ Improvements to existing paper recycling schemes achieved much higher retrieval rates and an improved quality of paper collected.
- ❑ Establishment of high profile launch programme designed to give maximum publicity to schemes and encourage staff participation.
- ❑ Use of creative publicity material and feedback to ensure continued staff motivation.

Sell or Offer to Staff

Staff will often be pleased to purchase equipment. Offer to staff at reduced rates.

Give to Charity or Schools

Charities will often be glad of your obsolete equipment. In the case of local authorities, equipment can often be passed on to schools.

SUMMARY GUIDELINES

- ❑ Do not put computers in the skip.
- ❑ Upgrade equipment where possible.
- ❑ Work with manufacturers to set up return schemes.
- ❑ Use specialist recycling companies to handle obsolete equipment.
- ❑ Donate to schools or local charities.

SUPPORT AVAILABLE

Environmental Technology Best Practice Programme (ETBPP)

The ETBPP is a joint Department of Trade and Industry and Department of the Environment, Transport and the Regions Initiative. It is managed by AEA Technology plc through ETSU and the National Environmental Technology Centre. The programme offers free advice and information for UK businesses and promotes environmental practices that increase profits for industry and commerce and reduce waste and pollution at source.

The ETBPP provides an Environmental Helpline giving free up to date information on a wide range of environmental issues, legislation and technology. They have a strong focus on encouraging waste minimisation and provide a number of free publications showing how to save money through waste minimisation which includes Best Practice Case Studies. They have also produced a useful booklet of 200 tips for reducing waste

REGIONAL WASTE MINIMISATION CLUBS

Regional waste minimisation clubs offer companies the opportunity to share experiences and spread the cost of consultancy. Demonstration projects including the Aire and Calder regional club and North West based 'Project Catalyst' have shown major cost savings and waste reductions for their member companies

Stimulating the formation of waste minimisation clubs throughout the UK is one of the jobs of the ETBPP. As part of this remit the ETBPP also independently monitors the financial savings and environmental benefits generated by a number of clubs. The benefits of the regional clubs to individual companies can be great and intermediaries can also help their local businesses by forming a club. The ETBPP is assisting partnerships of business support organisations by providing training guidance and leaflets to help in minimising waste. Contact the Environmental Helpline.

Environment Agency

The Environment Agency also has a strong remit to promote waste minimisation to businesses and is also encouraging the development of partnerships by providing support in terms of funding and advice. A recent initiative in Surrey between the Environment Agency and Surrey County Council has resulted in the production of the Waste Wise Business Manual to help local businesses implement waste minimisation measures. This was launched in spring 1997 with a series of seminars at a number of locations throughout Surrey – No Time to Waste.

CHAPTER SUMMARY

- ❏ Identify and publicise waste reduction initiatives.
- ❏ Assess the potential reduction in waste disposal costs.
- ❏ Ensure contractors are licensed and comply with the Duty of Care on your behalf.
- ❏ Introduce recycling schemes where practical and monitor them.
- ❏ Launch recycling and waste reduction programmes to staff.
- ❏ Renegotiate waste disposal arrangements when recycling is established.

Sources of Information

Electronics Recycling

INTEX COMPUTERS LTD
Unit M4
Hazleton Interchange
Lakesmere Road
Horndean
Hampshire PO8 9JU
Tel: 01705 594 999
Fax: 01705 594 888

MANN RECYCLING ORGANISATION
Ashburton Industrial Estate
Ross on Wye
Herefordshire HR9 7BW
Tel: 01989 768 899
Fax: 01989 561 021

RECYCLE-IT
c/o SFK (UK) Ltd
Sundon Park Road
Luton
Bedfordshire, LU3 3BL
Tel/fax: 01582 492 436

Recycling

Paper Recycling Companies

A W LAWSONS & CO
55 Lant Street
London SE1 1QP
Tel: 0171 407 5296
Fax: 0171 403 7741

GREENER WORLD LTD
Airport Business Centre
427 Great West Road
Hounslow
Middlesex TW5 0BY
Tel: 0181 571 0100
Fax: 0181 843 0500
Also collects glass and cans

BPB RECYCLING UK
(previously Davidsons)
Folds Road
Bolton BL1 2SW
Tel: 01204 364141
Fax: 01204 372727

JOHN HANNAY & CO. LTD
Linwood Avenue
College Milton
East Kilbride G74 5NE
Tel: 013552 25455
Fax: 013552 31463

PAPER ROUND LTD
3rd Floor
42 Kingsway
London WC2B 6EX
Tel: 0171 404 4848
Fax: 0171 831 6244

PEARCE RECYCLING GROUP
Pearce House
Acrewood Way
St Albans
Herts AL4 0JY
Tel: 01727 861522
Fax: 01727 846428

RESOURCE SAVER
New Stadium Road
Eastville
Bristol BS5 6NL
Tel: 0117 9525100
Fax: 0117 9518197

SCA RECYCLING
543 New Hythe Lane
Aylesford
Kent ME20 7PE
Tel: 01622 883000
Fax: 01622 719841

SEVERNSIDE WASTE PAPER LTD
The Pines
Heol-y-Forlan
Whitchurch
Cardiff CF4 1AX
Tel: 01222 615871
Fax: 01222 692120

Vending cups

SAVE-A-CUP
Suite 2
Bridge House
Bridge Street
High Wycombe
Bucks HP11 2EL
Tel: 01494 510167
Fax: 01491 510168

Cans

ALUMINIUM CAN RECYCLING ASSOCIATION (ACRA)
5 Gatsby Court
176 Holliday Street
Birmingham B1 1TJ
Tel; 0121 633 4656
Fax: 0121 633 4698

HALCYON PLASTICS
St Michaels House
Norton Way South
Letchworth
Hertfordshire SG6 1PA
Tel: 01462 682271
Fax: 01462 480056

STEEL CAN RECYCLING INFORMATION BUREAU
69 Monmouth Street
London WC2H 9DG
Tel: 0171 379 1306
Fax: 0171 379 1307

Glass

Greener World (see paper recycling)

BRITISH GLASS RECYCLING COMPANY LTD
Northumberland Road
Sheffield S10 2UA
Tel: 0114 268 4067
Fax: 0114 268 7914

Organic Waste

CRISIS FAIRSHARE
296/302 Borough High Street
London SE1 1JG
Tel: 0171 403 8588

Distributes excess quality food from restaurants and hotels to single homeless people in London.

TRELAWNEY DAMPNEY
ECO Composting Ltd
Chapel Lane
Parley
Christchurch
Dorset BH23 6BG
Tel: 01202 593601
Fax: 01202 581119

HENRY DOUBLEDAY RESEARCH ASSOCIATION
National Centre for Organic Gardening (see Chapter 5)
Ryton-on-Dunsmore
Coventry CU8 3LG
Tel: 01203 303 517
Fax: 01203 639229

Waste Management Companies

BFI
The Pickeridge
Stoke Common Road
Fulmer
Bucks SL3 6HA
Tel: 01753 662700
Fax: 01753 662464

BIFFA WASTE SERVICES
Coronation Road
Cressex
High Wycombe
Bucks HP12 3TZ
Tel: 01494 521221
Fax: 0171 248 1404

GRUNDONS
Lakeside Road
Colnbrook
Bucks SL3 OEG
Tel: 01753 683277
Fax: 01753 686002

UK WASTE MANAGEMENT LTD
Gate House
Castle Estate
Turnpike Road
High Wycombe
Bucks HP12 3NR
Tel: 01494 449944
Fax: 01494 537779

Associations

COMMUNITY RECYCLING NETWORK (CRN)
10–12 Picton Street
Montpelier
Bristol BS6 5QA
Tel: 0117 9420142
Fax: 0117 9420164

ENVIRONMENTAL SERVICES ASSOCIATION
Mountbarrow House
20 Elizabeth Street
London SW1W 9RB
Tel: 0171 824 8882
Fax: 0171 824 8753

INSTITUTE OF WASTE MANAGEMENT (IWM)
9 Saxon Court
St Peter's Gardens
Northampton NN1 1SX
Tel: 01604 20426
Fax: 01604 21339

INDEPENDENT WASTE PAPER PROCESSORS ASSOCIATION
25 High Street
Daventry
Northants NN11 4BG
Tel: 01327 703223
Fax: 01327 300612

LOCAL AUTHORITY RECYCLING ADVISORY COUNCIL (LARAC)
C/o Arun District Council
Civic Centre
Littlehampton
West Sussex BN17 5LF
Tel: 01903 716133
Fax: 01903 733059

SWAP (SAVE WASTE AND PROSPER)
74 Kirkgate
Leeds LS2 7DJ
Tel: 0113 243 8777
Fax: 0113 234 4222

VALPAK
Macmillan House
Business Centre
96 Kensington High Street
London W8 4SG
Tel: 0171 937 1440
Fax: 0171 937 1577

WASTE WATCH
Gresham House
24 Holborn Viaduct
London EC1A 2BN
Tel: 0171-248-1818
Fax: 0171-248-1404

LONDON PRIDE WASTE ACTION PROGRAMME
157–166 Millbank
10th Floor
Riverwalk House
London SW1
Tel: 0171 217 3055
Fax: 0171 217 3145

Environment Agency Regional Offices

ENVIRONMENT AGENCY EMERGENCY HOTLINE
0800 80 70 60
Head Office
Rivers House
Waterside Drive
Aztec West
Almondsbury
Bristol BS12 4UD
Tel: 01454 624400
Fax: 01454 624409

ANGLIAN
Kingfisher House
Goldhay Way
Orton Goldhay
Peterborough PE2 5ZR
Tel: 01733 371811
Fax: 01733 231840

NORTH EAST
Rivers House
21 Park Square South
Leeds LS1 2QG
Tel: 0113 2440191
Fax: 0113 2461889

NORTH WEST
Richard Fairclough House
Knutsford Road
Warrington WA4 1HG
Tel: 01925 653999
Fax: 01925 01925 415961

MIDLANDS
Sapphire East
550 Streetsbrook Road
Solihull B91 1QT
Tel: 0121 7112324
Fax: 0121 7115824

SOUTHERN
Guildbourne House
Chatsworth Road
Worthing
West Sussex BN11 1LD
Tel: 01903 820692
Fax: 01903 821832

SOUTH WEST
Manley House
Kestrel Way
Exeter EX2 7LQ
Tel: 01392 444000
Fax: 01392 444238

THAMES
Kings Meadow House
Kings Meadow Road
Reading RG1 8DQ
Tel: 01734 535000
Fax: 01734 500388

WELSH
Rivers House/Plas-yr-Afon
St Mellons Business Park
St Mellons
Cardiff CF3 0LT
Tel: 01222 770088
Fax: 01222 798555

Government Bodies

**ENVIRONMENTAL
TECHNOLOGY BEST
PRACTICE PROGRAMME**
ETSU
Harwell
Oxon OX11 0RA
Tel: 0800 585794
Fax: 01235 436461

Trade Press

**MATERIALS RECYCLING
WEEK**
19 Scarbrook Road
Croydon
Surrey CR9 1QH
Tel: 0181 277 5000
Fax: 0181 277 5530

Corporate
Environmental Management 1
Systems and Strategies
Second Edition
edited by **Richard Welford**
University of Huddersfield

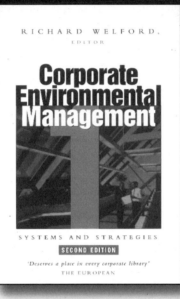

'A readable work which deserves a place in every corporate library'
THE EUROPEAN

'covers everything you could possibly want to know about corporate environmental management ... if you can only afford one book, this is worth serious consideration' SUPPLY MANAGEMENT

This second edition focuses upon EMAS and ISO 14001, while the auditing approach within the ISO 14000 series is also examined. The examination of strategy now places more emphasis on cost reduction and differentiation as a means to achieving a competitive advantage through environmental management, while many areas, such as that on life cycle assessment, have been updated.

Corporate Environmental Management 1 is the first in a series of three books providing basic tools needed by business people and management courses. Other volumes are Corporate Environmental Management 2: Culture and Organisations (1997) and Corporate Environmental Management 3: Towards Sustainable Development (1999)

CONTENTS

Part 1 The Context of Corporate Environmental Management

Part 2 The Tools of Corporate Environmental Management

Part 3 Wider Applications of the Systems Based Approach

Paperback • £15.95 • 1 85383 559 5 September 1998

EARTHSCAN

Earthscan Publications Ltd, 120 Pentonville Road, London N1 9JN Tel: 0171 278 0433
Fax: 0171 278 1142 e-mail: earthsales@earthscan.co.uk Visit the Earthscan Web Site at http://earthscan.co.uk

An A-Z of Health and Safety Law

A Complete Reference Source for Managers
Second Edition
by Peter Chandler

This brand new edition unravels the legal complexities of relevant UK health and safety legislation in a readable and accessible style. *An A-Z of Health and Safety Law* is a fully cross-referenced guide book including all the latest EC directives as well as the rights of employees and duties of employers.

Answering all your questions on health and safety law, this essential second edition simplifies the legal labyrinth and provides valuable advice on such matters as:
- medical examinations
- employee training
- personal protective equipment
- manual handling
- health surveillance
- the maintenance of tools and appliances
- the fencing and guarding of machinery

Complete with a list of relevant HSE publications and useful addresses, this handbook is an invaluable reference source for all employers, personnel managers safety officers, office managers, consultants, solicitors and students of law.

An A-Z of Employment Law
£45.00 Hardback 600 pages
ISBN 0 7494 2444 3
Published 1997
Order No: KT444

Available from all good bookshops or direct from the publisher:
Kogan Page
120 Pentonville Road
London N1 9JN
Customer Services Tel: 0171 278 0545 Fax: 0171 278 8198
e-mail: kpinfo@kogan-page.co.uk

4: Purchasing Products

INTRODUCTION

It is important to recognise that you buy in environmental impacts through your supply chain. Therefore, the performance of the products you buy directly affects your own environmental position. In the service sector, the most significant environmental effects of an organisation may be those that are bought in.

Many organisations see green purchasing as having an inevitable cost premium attached, but this does not have to be the case. Considering environmental criteria in purchasing decisions provides a change in focus away from purely cost based decisions. More fundamental questions need to be asked, such as whether you need a particular item in the first place: a cost-effective and environmentally sound option is to use less and therefore order less. Do all of your staff really need company cars?

This chapter helps you identify environmentally preferable alternatives to common office products. It gives a brief overview of the EU Ecolabel together with information about the Buy Recycled Programme which works to promote recycled products. We also give a number of standard principles to consider before you purchase any product.

This chapter will help you improve the environmental performance of your product purchasing by telling you what you can do now. The following chapter, Purchasing Services, contains information on how to integrate a planned approach to purchasing into your organisation's current practice and covers the most common contracted services.

Closing the Recycling Loop

To maximise the benefits of recycling, the materials that you collect need to be turned into a new product. By buying recycled you are increasing the demand for these products, encouraging the recycling industry and reducing the amount of waste going to landfill. Collecting materials for recycling is only the beginning of the chain. If you're not buying recycled, you're not recycling.

Many organisations operate recycling schemes, particularly in their offices. If successful, they will have a high profile and will have helped to raise awareness of environmental issues in-house. The development of the use of recycled products is a logical step towards closing the recycling loop.

THE BUY RECYCLED PROGRAMME

The Buy Recycled Programme, a National Recycling Forum Initiative, has been set up to support the development of markets for a wide range of collected recyclable materials. It is particularly targeted at the huge purchasing power wielded by private companies and public sector bodies; as major users of goods and services they have a strong influence on current and future markets.

The programme aims to make recycled goods commercially attractive by supporting the growth of markets and providing information to break down myths about product availability, quantity and cost. The programme's long term ideal is to incorporate the buy recycled message into the mainstream business agenda, not as an added extra but at the start of the purchasing decision making process.

The Buy Recycled Programme can undertake to give presentations to significant personnel within public or private sector organisations to raise awareness and promote the scheme. The Programme also produces a newsletter, *Closing the Loop* and can provide information materials and guidance on buying recycled and related market development initiatives (Wastebusters gratefully acknowledge the help of the Buy Recycled Programme in contributing information for this section).

The Recycled Products Guide

The Recycled Products Guide is produced by Waste Watch as part of the Buy Recycled Programme. Costing £30 for a single edition and £50 for a year's subscription, the *Guide* is updated quarterly and includes information on over 800 products in

---

THE BUY RECYCLED PROGRAMME HAS BEEN ESTABLISHED TO

❑ raise awareness and commitment to buying recycled content products and materials;

❑ encourage industry and the public sector to buy more products made with recycled materials;

❑ provide information about product availability across all sectors; and

❑ support the needs of those developing buy recycled purchasing policies and programmes.

wide variety of categories including general stationery, furniture and plastics (see Directory for further information).

PURCHASING TOOLS

European Union Ecolabelling Scheme

The Ecolabel is designed to reduce confusion by providing an authoritative and independent label to identify those goods with the lowest environmental impact in specific categories. Established in 1992, the scheme is intended to:

❑ promote the design, production, marketing and use of products which have a reduced environmental impact during their entire life cycle; and
❑ provide consumers and other buyers with a simple and credible way of identifying products which overall cause less harm to the environment than others.

The scheme is administered in each country by a Competent Body, in the UK by the UK Ecolabelling Board. Conditions for awarding an Ecolabel are defined by product groups. Such groups, the specific ecological criteria for each group, and their respective periods of validity, are established through the involvement of the European Commission, Member States and principal interest groups. Criteria are designed to be precise, clear and objective. They must ensure a high level of environmental protection, be based as far as possible on the use of clean technology, and, where appropriate, reflect the desirability of maximising product life. General environmental impacts considered include: global warming, ozone depletion, human toxicity and acid rain.

Companies whose brands qualify for the label can apply for permission to display it on their products. The scheme has had a slow start due to wrangles over criteria and lack of take-up by companies, however it is steadily expanding and the following relevant product groups are covered:

❑ copying paper;
❑ indoor paints and varnishes;
❑ laundry detergents;
❑ refrigerators;

❏ single and double ended light bulbs;
❏ soil improvers; and
❏ toilet paper/kitchen towels;

Criteria are also under consideration for the following relevant product groups:

❏ batteries;
❏ converted paper products;
❏ dishwashers and dishwasher detergents;
❏ floor cleaning products;
❏ furniture care products;
❏ growing media;
❏ insulation material;
❏ passenger vehicles;
❏ personal computers;
❏ rubbish bags; and
❏ textiles.

To date in the UK, labels have been awarded to seven model: of the Hoover New Wave range of washing machines; Co-op Nouvelle and Waitrose kitchen and toilet rolls and Crown and Dulux water based gloss paint.

In August 1996 the Association of Metropolitan Authoritie (AMA) made a policy decision to encourage its members to purchase Ecolabelled products. To implement this decision the AMA plans to draw up guidelines showing how its 86 member can support the scheme (ENDS, 1996.)

The label can be used as part of a purchasing policy by usin; the label itself and also by using the criteria established for th label as part of your purchasing specification (Wastebuster gratefully acknowledges the help of the UK Ecolabelling Boar in contributing information for this section).

Life-Cycle Analysis

The technique of life-cycle analysis is a useful tool for integra ing environmental criteria into purchasing decisions; provides a structured approach and creates a greater aware ness of the full environmental impacts of a product. It take into account all stages of a product life-cycle from the sourcin of the raw material to end-of-life disposal. This concept is als referred to as cradle to grave.

Purchasers are becoming more aware of this techniqu

particularly with the development of the EU Ecolabelling scheme and increased awareness of products with a high profile environmental impact, such as paper. Understanding of this technique increases awareness of environmental impact and helps to reduce overall environmental effects.

It is unrealistic to expect to be able to conduct detailed life-cycle assessments on all your products. To produce meaningful results requires technical expertise and resources. However, the principles do provide a useful approach to integrating environmental criteria into purchasing decisions and help to identify the products with high environmental impact and at what stage of the product life-cycle this occurs.

METHODOLOGY

A useful starting point is to identify the major products/services which you buy and list the key impacts of those products during their life-cycle. The area of highest impact varies considerably from product to product, some, such as furniture, can have a high environmental impact in several stages of the life-cycle. Having considered these impacts, you need to consider what you can do to minimise them. Resource usage is something you can influence directly, but other impacts may be directly affected by your supplier's environmental stance.

The Total Cost Approach

The total cost approach is a methodology, like life-cycle analysis, which helps you to look beyond the purchase price of a product. There is a strong link between purchasing and waste management, but this is often not recognised, there being little communication between those responsible for each function. It often costs more to dispose of a product than it does to buy it in the first place, but you should not wait until you have to dispose of a product before you find this out. The true costs of waste disposal are often underestimated (see Chapter 3 for further information).

Substantial reductions in waste disposal costs and therefore Landfill Tax liability can be achieved by the consideration of recyclability and disposal in purchasing decisions:

❑ Effective communication between purchasing and waste management teams will reduce disposal costs and promote a better understanding between departments.

> ### LIFE-CYCLE ANALYSIS KEY ISSUES
>
> ❑ sourcing of raw materials;
> ❑ manufacturing processes;
> ❑ packaging;
> ❑ distribution;
> ❑ usage; and
> ❑ re-use, recyclability and disposal.

Increased awareness of the environmental impact of a company's activities will highlight the link between purchasing and waste management, and help to reduce environmental effects.

❑ Considering recyclability and ultimate disposal of a product in purchasing decisions can significantly reduce costs. Reusing or recycling a product at the end of its life diverts it away from disposal to landfill and reduces waste disposal costs.

❑ Replacing a hazardous material with a more benign substance reduces administration since COSHH (Control of Substances Hazardous to Health) Safety Data Sheets are no longer required. General waste disposal can be used and the increased cost of a hazardous waste contractor is avoided. This reduces your liability under the Duty of Care Regulations (1994) by minimising the risks associated with the disposal of hazardous materials.

Using the total cost approach will highlight the cost effectiveness of investing in an initially more expensive product to reduce costs in the long run. For example, efficient light bulbs are more expensive to buy than regular bulbs but use approximately one fifth of the power and last up to eight times longer.

Standard Principles

Before you buy any product ask the following questions:

1. *Do you need to buy it?* The best environmental option is to purchase less. Before purchasing a product or service consider whether you could mend or repair existing equipment or use products more efficiently. Do you need the product in the first place? Office examples include bought-in mineral water and vending cups.

2. *Can you use a lower specification brand?* Some products can be made from a lower specification material which uses less resources without compromising quality. For instance, low grade paper can be sufficient for use in internal note pads.

3. *Does it contain re-used or recycled materials?* Purchasing a product which is manufactured using re-used or recycled raw materials encourages the re-use or recycling of waste. Many office products, such as paper and toner cartridges, are now available with a recycled content.

4. *Which product is cheapest over its whole life?* Look for the lowest whole life cost not just the lowest capital cost. Relatively expensive products, such as energy efficient light bulbs, may last longer and create less waste leading to overall savings.

5. *Does it contain chemicals requiring Safety Data Sheets?* If the product, such as a cleaning chemical, is potentially harmful it will be supplied with a COSHH Safety Data Sheet detailing how to handle it. Try to replace these products with alternatives that do not require such precautions.

6. *Can it be re-used or recycled once obsolete?* Try to purchase products that can be re-used or recycled at the end of their useful life. For instance, thermal roll fax paper cannot be recycled and so purchasing this type of fax rather than plain paper models will mean all faxes received must be thrown away.

7. *Will it require special disposal arrangements?* Some potentially hazardous products such as paints, solvents and oils can cause particular damage when disposed of. Try to find an alternative that is safer and cheaper to dispose of, for instance water based rather than solvent based products.

SUMMARY GUIDELINES

- ❏ Do you need it?
- ❏ Can you use a lower specification brand?
- ❏ Does it contain re-used or recycled materials?
- ❏ Which product is cheapest over its whole life?
- ❏ Does it contain chemicals requiring Safety Data Sheets?
- ❏ Can it be re-used or recycled once obsolete?
- ❏ Will it require special disposal arrangements?

GENERAL OFFICE STATIONERY

General office stationery can be one of the most overlooked areas of office purchasing. Items such as filing products, pads, sticky notes and binders are often seen as cheap, disposable items but can represent a significant purchasing spend. One large organisation in London found out after an audit that it spent over £200,000 per year on these cheap items.

Environmental Issues

General stationery offers the opportunity to use recycled products. Most general stationery items are used in-house and there is little justification to use products made from virgin materials where recycled alternatives exist. Filing products can be made from low-grade paper waste which helps to create a demand for the raw material. There are environmental issues associated with writing products; for example, highlighter and marker pens can contain solvents (see Writing Materials in this chapter).

COMMON PROBLEMS

Cost

Some environmentally preferable office supplies are more expensive. However, cost is generally linked to volume. If your supplier is aware that you are serious about using these products and you guarantee the volume, you should be able to negotiate improved rates on this range. Some recycled products · are cheaper than virgin equivalents. Increased market demand will also help to reduce costs.

Labelling

The labelling of environmentally preferable products varies considerably between different stationery catalogues. Some are confusing and you have to search pretty hard to find them. Names of products can be very misleading.

Quality

As with any purchase it is possible to find some green products that do not work. It is therefore important to test them before distributing them throughout your offices (as you should do with any product). For example, while some correction fluids work well, others do not. Some recycled Post-Its stick, whereas others don't. Product performance varies from brand to brand. Be selective about the products you introduce to ensure they are fit for the purpose.

PRACTICAL ACTION

Demand Accurate, Detailed Information

Most stationery catalogues include a range of products labelled 'environmentally friendly'. However, it is important to establish the criteria for this label. Some suppliers' labelling systems can be misleading.

Work with Suppliers

Work with your stationery company to increase the take-up of environmentally sound products in the catalogue. Bars can be put on the purchase of certain products, to ensure that the environmentally sound options are the only ones used. Most stationery companies will source specific products on your behalf if they do not feature in the catalogue.

Use Specialist Suppliers Where Possible

There are a number of specialist suppliers dealing only with recycled products; Paperback is one of the most established (see Contacts). Specialist suppliers can be especially useful for small organisations which can have problems sourcing small quantities of recycled products.

Use an IT-Based Requisition Procedure

Links with stationery suppliers are becoming increasingly sophisticated with technological developments and there are a number of systems used, eg Electronic Data Interchange (EDI). Direct computer links with suppliers, possibly controlled through the office supplies department can save time and money and give you improved management control, eg suppliers can provide you with detailed printouts for improved control.

Investigate Waste Reduction

There is often potential to reduce the cost of office supplies by improving control and making more efficient use of your resources. For example, box files can be relabelled and re-used and a number of products are not strictly necessary. Office moves can often be used as an opportunity to order new stationery!

Case Study

Subject –	**WASTE REDUCTION IMPROVED RESOURCES USAGE**
Organisation –	**STEPHENSON HARWOOD**
Organisation type –	**SOLICITORS**
Location –	**CITY OF LONDON**
No. of staff –	**350**

BACKGROUND

Lawyers are traditionally very heavy users of stationery items, particularly case files. Stephenson Harwood recognised that there was significant potential for improvement in its control and usage of stationery items. Large numbers of ready-numbered file dividers were bought in packets. Each packet was shrink wrapped. A detailed breakdown of usage was conducted: in many cases, a limited number of dividers from a set were used and the remainder were wasted. Six thousand yellow PVC folders are used to distribute faxes around the firm. Twelve thousand plastic folders are used in-house per annum.

ACTION

Dividers are now bought in single-number packs – ordering is consistent with demand. Stephenson Harwood has set up its own core stock of numbered dividers and makes up multi-numbered packs itself.

RESULTS

- ❑ An estimated cost saving on dividers of £7000–8000 per annum.
- ❑ Reduced wastage of dividers.
- ❑ Reduction in packaging material (shrink wrap).
- ❑ Dividers are manufactured from card without any laminates.
- ❑ Stephenson Harwood is renegotiating with the supplier to source dividers manufactured from recycled card.
- ❑ Use of yellow PVC folders has been eliminated; instead, faxes will be printed on coloured paper for ease of identification.
- ❑ Plastic folders are being replaced with folders made from recycled card.
- ❑ Improved, cost-effective use of resources.

Perception

Perception of recycled products can be poor. However, in recent years quality has substantially improved. Good quality recycled alternatives are available to most products.

SUMMARY GUIDELINES

❑ Use recycled products where they are fit for the purpose.
❑ Encourage re-use and waste reduction (see Chapter 3).
❑ Improve control of purchasing of office supplies.
❑ Work with your supplier – demand detailed information.
❑ Reduce usage of disposables.

Buy Recycled

Filing products made from recycled paper and board include:

❑ ring binders;
❑ dividers;
❑ lever arch files;
❑ suspension files;
❑ box files;
❑ record cards;
❑ folders;
❑ memo pads;
❑ post-its; and
❑ shorthand pads.

Hints for Small Organisations

Small organisations obviously do not have the buying power of larger ones but environmentally preferable products are widely available, so shop around. If your office is small, but is part of a larger organisation, make use of national agreements. Improvements to the way resources are used, for instance if paper is re-used internally, can substantially reduce total usage.

BATTERIES

Environmental Issues

The UK uses 600 million batteries per year and consumption is rapidly increasing with the growth of affordable technology such as mobile phones. Batteries are inefficient in their use of energy when compared to mains power. Traditional batteries contain low levels of toxic heavy metals, particularly cadmium and mercury, which contribute to air pollution if burned in a refuse incinerator and present a potential threat of water pollution if landfilled. Environmentally preferable alternatives to batteries are available.

The Batteries and Accumulators Containing Dangerous Substances Regulations 1994

These Regulations stem from the requirements of EC Directive 91/157/EEC which aimed to reduce the quantities of heavy metals (mercury, cadmium and lead) entering the environment from spent batteries. The regulations:

▪ 'Prohibit the sale of alkaline manganese batteries with more than 0.025 per cent mercury by weight; button cells and batteries composed of button cells and alkaline manganese batteries containing 0.05 per cent mercury by weight and intended for prolonged use under extreme conditions are exempted.

▪ Require that appliances using batteries covered by the Directive must be designed to ensure that the batteries can be easily removed.

▪ Introduce a marking system for batteries covered by the Directive to indicate heavy metal content and stress that batteries should be collected separately; this will not apply to those manufactured or imported into the EC before 1 August 1994; nor will it apply to those marketed in Britain on or before 31 December 1995' (NSCA, 1996).

Under the EC Directive, batteries which can be recycled will have to carry a recycling emblem (being designed in the UK).

All member states will be obliged to set up relevant programmes for safe disposal and recycling and inform the EC of progress. However, of the 600 million batteries sold each year in the UK, only 10 per cent would be covered by this Directive.

The battery industry has set a target to recycle a minimum of 90 per cent of lead acid batteries, a commitment which has been welcomed by the Government in its White Paper, *Making Waste Work* (HMSO, 1995). The Government is concerned that lead acid battery recycling should take place under tightly controlled conditions as battery acid and soluble lead salts can present a considerable hazard to humans and the environment (for further information see Chapter 6).

At the time of writing there is no domestic battery recycling facility in the UK. Of the main battery types commonly used in the office (primary – non rechargeable and secondary – rechargeable NiCd (nickel–cadmium)) only NiCd batteries can be recycled (*Making Waste Work* assumes that collected NiCd batteries can be sent to France for recovery).

Implications

Most battery manufacturers have lowered the levels of mercury, cadmium and lead contained in their products. The Directive and Regulations have led directly to the development of nickel hydride rechargeable batteries which in some products are taking the place of nickel–cadmium batteries (which contain the highest levels of cadmium). Manufacturers claim they contain far less toxic material and give out twice the power but NiCds continue to be the predominant portable rechargeable battery used.

PRACTICAL ACTION

Avoid Using Batteries

Use mains electricity wherever possible or, better still, go for solar powered options, for instance, calculators.

Use Rechargeable Batteries

The energy needed to make batteries is 50 times greater than the energy they give out. Rechargeable batteries are more efficient in resource use and give savings in energy and cost. In smaller offices, using rechargeable batteries is often very practical, since it is easier to control.

Use Return Schemes

As there is currently no national collection programme for nickel–cadmium batteries the best options are to establish whether you can send batteries back to manufacturers or to set up a scheme with your supplier.

Some waste management and specialised office service companies are starting to offer a collection service for battery recycling.

WRITING MATERIALS

Environmental Issues

Writing materials can be divided into wet and dry writing instruments. Wet writing instruments include permanent markers and ball point pens. Dry writing instruments cover wooden pencils.

The main issues involved in the use of writing instruments in the office concern:

- the raw materials used;
- the use of chemicals during manufacture: solvents, heavy metals, formaldehyde and benzene;
- the finishes used on dry writing instruments; and
- the environmental and waste problems, including packaging, refillability and disposability.

Solvents and Lacquers

Solvents are major ozone depleters. They are used to dissolve colour pigments. Traditional correction fluids have contained 1,1-trichloroethane, a chemical which is estimated to account for 15 per cent of all ozone depletion and is also a factor in making solvent abuse potentially lethal. Some solvents also give rise to volatile organic compounds (see Chapter 5, Catering and Cleaning Environmental Issues section). Solvents such as toluene and xylene are mild carcinogens and are commonly found in markers specially formulated for writing on problem

SUMMARY GUIDELINES

- ❏ Avoid using batteries where you can use solar power or mains electricity.
- ❏ Use rechargeable batteries rather than non-rechargeable primary cells.
- ❏ Work with your supplier to set up a return scheme for NiCd batteries. Remember they are special waste (see Fabric Maintenance in Chapter 6).
- ❏ Collect spent NiCd batteries for recycling.

surfaces, such as glass, foil and oily metals. These solvents should be avoided unless absolutely necessary.

Lacquers are used to coat wooden pencils and usually contain approximately 15 per cent solvent.

Heavy Metals

Cadmium, used in the manufacture of plastic, can cause serious pollution problems as it does not degrade and cannot be destroyed. It was commonly used in writing materials before its pollution problems were known. Cadmium should be deposited in secure waste disposal sites otherwise it can get into the food chain, where it affects all environmental sectors and can damage the liver, kidneys and brain of humans and fish.

Formaldehyde

Formaldehyde is a toxic organic compound, used in resin glue, which is an irritant to tissue, causing eye, skin and throat irritation, nausea and allergic reactions. At high levels it is believed to be carcinogenic. It is emitted as a vapour and is harmful during both production and use. The UK Health and Safety Executive sets a Maximum Exposure Limit (MEL) of two parts per million (ppm) for an eight hour weighted average time period (see also Furniture section).

Benzene

Benzene is a toxic substance used as a solvent during the manufacture of some products. Persistent exposure to high levels may cause anaemia. It is a carcinogen, particularly linked to leukaemia.

PRACTICAL ACTION

Alternatives to traditional writing instruments are available.

Raw Materials

Reclaimed Wood

Wood that has been salvaged for re-use which might have otherwise gone to waste, it includes reclaimed wooden pallets.

Recycled Cardboard

Recycled cardboard is used in some products instead of the traditional plastic casing for pens and pencils.

Mater-Bi

Mater-Bi is a substitute plastic material developed by an Italian company which can be used to make pens. It is based on maize starch and is said to be completely biodegradable. Tests show that if the pen is buried in the ground, 70 per cent of it will have disappeared after three months, and after a year it will have gone completely.

Recycled Plastics

When choosing writing instruments, consider the type of plastic used in component parts and assess recyclability. There are currently very few schemes for recycling plastic, this is largely due to the variety of plastic types used both singly and in combination. Thermoplastics can be re-melted and reshaped. Some of these which are currently recycled include polypropylene, polystyrene and polyethylene terephthalate (PET). Recycled plastic products available include: pens, paperclip holders, mug stands, rulers and scissors. Save-a-Cup have a range of products made from recycled vending cups. See Chapter 3.

Graphite

Graphite is used in conjunction with clay for the 'lead' in pencils. Some pencils have a solid wooden end and shorter lead helping to save lead, since pencils are often thrown away before they are completely used up.

Use of Chemicals During Manufacture

Ask your stationery supplier for information about the use of the following substances in their products:

❏ Solvents – environmentally acceptable alternatives are water based products.

❏ Lacquers/varnishes – beeswax is an environmentally sound alternative to solvent based varnishes which protects the wood from moisture and prevents it from swelling up and the lead being damaged. Alternatively, non-varnished pencils are widely available.

❏ Heavy metals, formaldehyde and benzene – manufacturers are phasing out the use of heavy metals, formaldehyde and benzene.

Disposal Issues

Packaging

Packaging should be kept to a bare minimum and be made of recycled or recyclable material such as cardboard or tin. Where plastic wallets are used, these should be made from recycled polypropylene. Consider whether the manufacturer takes any action in recovering used packaging for recycling. *It is meaningless to say a product is recyclable if no facilities are available.*

Disposal

The options available for disposal of writing instruments are either landfill or incineration, but by far the most acceptable options in environmental terms are re-use and recycling. Manufacturers of writing instruments are making some progress in devising ways of making their products recyclable and/or re-usable.

Refillability

Refillability promotes re-use. Refillable writing instruments are now available in the form of pencils, highlighters, permanent markers, rollerball and fountain pens. This reduces the amount of casing (plastics, metals) going to landfill. One company issues fountain pens to staff engraved with their name!

Durability

The longer the life-span of a product, the greater the benefit to the environment. Replacement for durable products are needed less often so raw materials are not required as quickly to make a replacement. One significant development in this area is long lasting polymer leads for pencils.

Design

Is the product designed to be re-used or discarded? Are the materials used such that they can be recycled or made from recycled material to begin with?

LASER PRINTER AND DESKJET CARTRIDGES

Environmental Issues

Over six million toner cartridges are used in the UK every year. It is estimated that about 50 per cent of these end up in landfill sites. A toner cartridge is a non-biodegradable product made of durable plastic housing a metal corona wire, selenium OPC drum and residual toner. The bulk of this material will not degrade for thousands of years and represents a significant waste of non-renewable resources. Cartridge consumption is currently rising in the UK by 15 per cent per year and therefore represents a growing environmental issue.

PRACTICAL ACTION

Remanufactured Cartridges

Collect used laser printer toner cartridges for recycling and buy back remanufactured cartridges. Toner cartridges can be refilled or remanufactured which is highly cost effective. There are many companies offering this facility, although quality does vary considerably.

The key issues associated with cartridge recycling are:

❑ Quality – reputable companies completely dismantle the cartridge and replace the drum with a long-life one. This is an important consideration since original

SUMMARY GUIDELINES

❑ Use environmentally preferable products unless there are no alternatives.
❑ Put the necessary bars on all other products.
❑ Negotiate improved rates for the environmentally preferable range.
❑ Work with your stationery supplier to improve the range of products.
❑ Use refillable and solvent-free products wherever possible.
❑ Buy products with minimal packaging.

OPC drums were only designed to produce 3000 A4 copies and long-life drums are guaranteed for 30,000 A4 copies. The cartridge is completely stripped down, and each component is cleaned and inspected for wear and damage.

❑ Type of cartridge – not all toner cartridges are recyclable. Check with your supplier.

❑ Printer warranty – the use of recycled toner cartridges should not affect the printer warranty. Reputable companies guarantee to cover the cost of the repair of your printer if damage is caused by a faulty cartridge.

❑ Recycling – empty toner cartridges should be returned to the supplier for recycling. These have a market value of between £4 and £10 each. Some companies donate this to charities, or it can be off-set against the cost of a remanufactured cartridge. If you are a small organisation, you may not have sufficient cartridges to make collection viable, in this case, use a supplier that provides prepaid return labels or envelopes for you to send the cartridges back to them.

❑ Collection arrangements – most companies offer free collection based on a minimum volume of ten cartridges. Alternatively, they will provide prepaid return labels. Use existing systems such as messengers and internal post to collect used cartridges for remanufacturing.

❑ Cost – recycling and using remanufactured toner cartridges is very cost effective. Average savings against new cartridges are around 20 per cent. Negotiating bulk discounts for remanufactured toner cartridges enabled the Union Bank of Switzerland to reduce their spend and save more than £30,000 per year, with no loss in quality.

Inkjet Cartridges

Inkjet printer cartridges can be refilled. This represents a considerable saving compared to buying the new product, an average of 50 per cent. There have been problems with the quality in the UK, but the process is well established in the USA.

Deskjet refills are supplied in a syringe kit and are promoted as being very efficient and easy to use, but in practice many companies have had problems with them. Although theoretically they can be refilled in-house, it can be very messy and there are potential health and safety risks associated with giving people syringes and spilled toner. Cartridges can be refilled five to ten times and do not affect the warranty on the printers. Cartridge remanufacturing and office supply companies are increasingly providing a refill service for customer companies so source a supplier who will do the refills for you.

United Kingdom Cartridge Recycling Association UKCRA

UKCRA has been formed to ensure the remanufacturing of cartridges to specific standards. UKCRA members have to meet and comply with codes of practice in a number of areas including:

❑ conforming to minimum codes of practice;
❑ conforming to labelling and packaging standards;
❑ meeting standards of general business practice;
❑ having a bona fide warranty system in place; and
❑ accepting arbitration by UKCRA in disputes with customers.

The UKCRA rosette can only be used by fully accredited members of the association who have met, and continue to abide by, the UKCRA codes of practice.

The Federation of European Cartridge Recyclers and Suppliers (FECRS)

An independent manufacturers federation, the FECRS aims to improve the professionalism and integrity of the cartridge recycling industry throughout Europe.

SUMMARY GUIDELINES

❑ Check whether the models of toner cartridge you use are recyclable.
❑ Ensure that the supplier replaces the drum with a long-life one.
❑ Check that the supplier will guarantee to cover the cost of any repair due to cartridge failure.
❑ Ensure that the supplier handles inkjet refills on your behalf.
❑ Look out for the UKCRA rosette or membership of FECRS.
❑ Consider the recyclability of cartridges when buying new printers.

PHOTOCOPIERS

Health, safety and environmental issues should be considered together when you are buying office equipment. Your choice of equipment can affect health and safety within your offices and can reduce the environmental impact of your activities.

Environmental Issues

Environmental issues associated with photocopiers are dealt with in Chapter 6. This section deals with establishing performance standards.

Industry Standards

BLUE ANGEL AWARD

The Blue Angel Award indicates superior environmental performance achieved through low emissions and waste reduction. This scheme is directed by advisory committees of academics in Germany (they also advise the German government on legislation) and has run for several years. The following issues are considered in the assessment of environmental performance:

❑ materials used in photosensitive coatings;
❑ reclaiming and recycling of used selenium-coated drums;
❑ allowable types of copier cartridges;
❑ emissions of dust, ozone and hydrocarbons;
❑ noise emissions;
❑ energy consumption;
❑ ability to accept recycled paper;
❑ toner materials;
❑ disposal of toner wastes;
❑ interference suppression; and
❑ safety.

PRACTICAL ACTION

Environmental Policy

Obtain a copy of the manufacturer's policy and make sure that it has made a continuing commitment to real environmental action (see Chapter 9 for information about environmental policy). A policy on its own can be worth less than the paper it is copied onto!

Ozone Levels

Low level ozone is produced by photocopiers and can cause or exacerbate respiratory illness. Clarify the ozone levels set for equipment, these can vary considerably. Some manufacturers are happy to comply with Health and Safety Executive (HSE) guidelines, whereas others aim for significantly lower levels.

Replacement of Ozone Filters

Check the frequency of filter change. Filters lose their efficiency over time, therefore it is important to have this built in to your service contract. Replacement is generally recommended after a specific number of copies.

Energy Saving Buttons

Most machines have an energy save facility. However, some are manual and some are automatic. This facility is most effective if it operates automatically. In practice staff will not use a manual energy save button.

Acceptability of Recycled Paper

Manufacturers' attitudes to the use of recycled paper vary considerably. It is important to clarify this prior to the purchase of equipment. Some manufacturers recommend specific brands and some also have their own branded papers, whereas others will not recommend its use (see Paper section in this chapter).

Double-Sided Copying

Most machines now have a double-sided (duplex) copying facility, although some cope better with double siding recycled papers than others. For example Oce machines have a short paper path which reduces problems with paper jams.

COMMON PROBLEMS

❑ Some manufacturers use recycled paper as a scapegoat for any problems with equipment which can cause problems with warranty agreements. Make sure that this is resolved before you start.

❑ Servicing companies are often not fully aware of environmental performance of manufacturers. This can lead to problems with the use of recycled paper. However, in a tender situation, most service companies will offer to test recycled papers for suitability.

❑ Some servicing contractors do not recommend the use of recycled papers in photocopiers even when the equipment manufacturer has their own brand or endorse a specific brand.

❑ Preventative maintenance is not carried out, therefore parts will not be running at full efficiency at all times.

❑ Ozone filters are not changed according to the manufacturer's recommendations (also dependent on size, usage and location).

❑ Servicing contractors should not charge call out rates for difficulties arising from the use of recycled paper. Make sure this issue is clarified before contracts are signed.

❑ Consumables are generally included in your contract: if you are purchasing your own consumables, make sure you are not paying for something you do not receive or would rather provide yourselves.

❑ Contractors often try to tie their own choice of paper into deals.

Some copiers may need adjusting before they can deal with recycled paper. Your service engineer should be able (and willing!) to make the necessary adjustments.

SUMMARY GUIDELINES

The key points to consider when buying photocopiers are:

❑ the environmental policy of the manufacturer;

❑ the manufacturer's ability to demonstrate real environmental improvements;

❑ ozone levels set for equipment, and the replacement of ozone filters;

❑ energy consumption and whether machines have energy saving buttons;

❑ compatibility with recycled paper and double-sided copying facility;

❑ recyclability of parts and machines; and

❑ packaging.

Recycling and Disposal of Parts

The main concerns are the correct disposal of OPC and selenium drums and toner bottles. Where selenium drums are used, they should be retrieved and the selenium recovered. OPC drums can also be recycled. Toshiba provides an environmental return scheme to help companies comply with the duty of care. Toner and drums are returned to dealers for correct disposal/recycling.

End-of-Life Disposal

Most manufacturers repair and refurbish machines, re-use and recycle parts. Rank Xerox has moved to a dual product system which offers both new and remanufactured machines, both covered by the same guarantee. Check the life expectancy of the machine you want. Oce, for example, guarantees its machines for ten years.

Packaging

Most manufacturers now use cardboard packaging which is made from 100 per cent recycled material. However, some manufacturers go further and promote the collection of the packaging material for recycling and re-use. Rank Xerox has reduced the amount of disposable packaging used for its equipment. Unwanted packaging is sent back to parts suppliers for re-use. Reductions in the amount of packaging waste left on your premises will reduce your waste disposal costs.

Servicing Arrangements

Ensure that the environmental performance and servicing standards provided by a third party service contractor match up with those of the equipment manufacturer. Make sure you can use your own choice of consumables and paper. Many companies lose flexibility by being tied into a servicing contract which includes paper.

COMPUTERS

Environmental Issues

Disposal

See Chapter 3 for computer disposal issues.

Energy

Electronic equipment currently uses a greater percentage of total office energy than it did in the early 1990s. Equipment based consumption has risen from 10 per cent to 20 per cent and up to as much as 70 per cent of total energy costs in some offices (BRECSU, 1996). As a major area of growth in energy consumption, the environmental impacts of office equipment are growing (see Chapter 6 for further information on environmental issues and energy use).

Studies of the average power demands of computers and other office equipment show substantial differences between similar models by the same manufacturer.

Manufacturing

Heavy metals, solvents and CFCs are used during the manufacturing process. CFCs were used for washing circuit boards but since the 1987 Montreal Protocol, work has been conducted to phase them out (see Furniture Purchasing section for more information). Some manufacturers have replaced CFC use with water and alcohol based solvent cleaners although solvents give rise to volatile organic compounds (VOCs). Further information on solvents and VOCs is given in Chapter 5, Catering and Cleaning section.

Packaging

Most manufacturers now use packaging material with a recycled content. The Producer Responsibility Obligations (Packaging Waste) Regulations make manufacturers more responsible for the packaging they produce and should increase the number of return schemes.

INDUSTRY STANDARDS AND LEGISLATION

US-EPA 'Energy Star'

Energy Star is perhaps the most common energy saving standard currently in use world-wide. The standard is promoted by the US Environmental Protection Agency (EPA) and awarded to units which meet or use less than 30 watts energy consumption when on stand-by mode and which restart quickly from stand-by. An Energy Star can be awarded to monitors and computer equipment.

Not all Energy Star equipment has the same energy rating, on stand-by mode some use less energy than others.

Industry Council for Electronic Equipment Recycling (ICER)

The Industry Council for Electronic Equipment Recycling (ICER) has been created to push for legislation on electronic recycling. ICER, launched in October 1992, draws together suppliers, manufacturers, retailers, recyclers, waste management companies, local authorities and bulk users. It is developing as a centre of expertise, establishing how much is recyclable and looking at product design, methods of recycling collection and markets for recycled material. It seeks to ensure that any legislation is sensible and practical and that consumers are aware of what responsible companies are doing.

ICER has developed a number of schemes which concentrate both on recycling waste electronic products and promoting design for recovery. ICER has been running a pilot collection and recycling trial for electrical and electronic waste in West Sussex since October 1995.

Electronic Equipment Manufacturers Recycling Group (EMERG)

EMERG, launched in May 1995, is a group of 17 electronics manufacturers and the electronics recycling company, the Mann Organisation, which aims to develop environmentally responsible and economically viable electronics recycling.

EMERG is concentrating on collecting high value waste and used equipment from the commercial sector. Collected wastes and equipment are recycled back to raw materials to be used in producing new products.

PRACTICAL ACTION

Choose a manufacturer which is:

❑ Reducing chemical use – manufacturers should be working to eliminate ozone depleting chemicals from the production processes. They should also have an active programme of solvent reduction.

❑ Designing for recyclability – machines can be designed for ease of disassembly to facilitate recycling. For example: steel casings should be separate from plastics and the number of parts within the machine should be reduced; metal inserts, labels and screws should be eliminated. Clear identification of different plastics makes recycling more viable. Plastics can be standardised and the number of different plastics used can be minimised. Refurbished parts and subassemblies can be re-used and equipment can be returned for refurbishment or updating.

❑ Planning for disposal – equipment can be returned to the manufacturer for refurbishment. Computers can be broken down into component parts for re-use and recycling. Copper and silver from cables can be recycled, as can plastic and metal casings. The latter are shredded and broken down into ferrous and non-ferrous metals. The manufacturer can recover precious metals such as copper, gold, silver and palladium on printed circuit boards. Hard disks, printed circuit boards and power supplies can be re-used by the manufacturer internally. Floppy disk drives and various chips can be resold to other manufacturers.

SUMMARY GUIDELINES

Monitors

❑ All monitors should have the EPA Energy Star logo.
❑ Choose low radiation monitors.
❑ Fit screen filters to VDUs to reduce electrical field emissions, glare and reflection. This will reduce visual fatigue and eye strain.

Computers

Purchase computer equipment from a manufacturer which:

❑ has a meaningful environmental policy (see Chapter 9 for information about environmental policy);
❑ has a formal environmental management system or can demonstrate real environmental improvements;
❑ has a programme of reducing solvent and harmful chemical use in the manufacturing process;

❑ has designed for energy efficiency;
❑ designs for ease of disassembly to aid recycling;
❑ collects obsolete equipment for recycling/re-use or is a member of ICER or EMERG; and
❑ uses reusable or recycled packaging.

Use

Purchase equipment which:

❑ has an easily controllable stand-by facility;
❑ has a low average power usage under typical conditions; and
❑ has a quick stand-by recovery time.

❑ Reducing the impact of packaging – manufacturers should be adopting reduction, re-use, recycling and return schemes.

Energy Usage

Energy use varies from machine to machine. Below are some guidelines to follow when purchasing new equipment.

Purchase Computers and Monitors with the Energy Star Logo

US Energy Star accredited units have a fairly low use of energy, whether in use or on stand-by. You can buy energy-efficient models at little or no extra cost.

Consider Energy Cost Savings When Comparing Capital Costs

It may be better to pay more initially. For example, equipment that generates less heat will require less air conditioning, saving money in the long term, even if it is more expensive to buy initially.

The government funded Building Research Energy Conservation Support Unit (BRECSU) has produced guidance for purchasers of office equipment which aims to minimise energy consumption.

For equipment purchases ask your supplier or manufacturer to tell you:

❑ The average power consumed under typical operating conditions (the lower the better).
❑ the peak or nameplate power rating (the lower the better);
❑ power use during stand-by (the lower the better);
❑ the means of setting stand-by mode (the easier the better);
❑ recovery times from each stand-by (the quicker the better); and
❑ whether equipment needs rebooting from stand-by (preferably not).

The most important power ratings to note are not peak or nameplate ratings but how the machine will actually operate when under average conditions or on stand-by. If you can obtain the above information for different potential purchase you can use this information to help in decision making (BRECSU, 1996).

OFFICE FURNITURE

Environmental Issues

The destruction of the world's tropical rainforests in order to supply the timber trade is recognised as a major environmental concern. More than 12 million acres of tropical rainforest are destroyed each year. Particular areas of concern are South East Asia and West Africa. At the current rate of destruction, most tropical forests will have disappeared within 40 years.

The World Wide Fund for Nature (WWF) argues that the international timber trade plays a major role in tropical defor-estation and the loss of old growth rainforests in temperate and boreal areas (WWF, 1995). Careless extraction of timber from forests can cause soil erosion, nutrient loss and the extinction of plant and animal species (reduced biodiversity). Logging also threatens the existence of indigenous forest peoples and communities dependent on the forest.

Less publicised concerns include the use of chemicals in the manufacturing process and the final disposal both of the packaging material and the furniture itself.

Forestry Practice

The main issue in the commercial logging of tropical timbers is the destruction of the biodiversity of rainforests. Tropical rainforests represent valuable resources and are becoming one of the major sources of new medicines, but deforestation is causing the extinction of over 50 different species every day. Forestry practices can also be very wasteful, for every cubic metre of timber removed another cubic metre of useful wood is left to rot. Tree respiration acts to fix carbon dioxide (the most common greenhouse gas) from the atmosphere, so widespread logging results in higher CO_2 levels and an increased threat of global warming and climate change.

The environmental and economic effects of commercial logging on indigenous peoples are often not taken into account. Increases in landlessness and dispossession lead to social problems such as malnutrition and social and economic exploitation.

Claims about forestry practices can be misleading. Terms such 'sustainably managed' may have no independent verifica-tion and can therefore be meaningless. A sustainably managed forest is one where a comprehensive programme of land planning and reforestation is implemented with careful control of the amount of timber removed from the forest, and minimal forest disturbance. Less than 1 per cent of tropical timber comes from truly sustainable sources.

Conservation organisations have identified serious short-comings in management systems in some countries, such as unlicensed felling and failures to observe minimum girths and minimum regeneration periods.

THE FOREST STEWARDSHIP COUNCIL (FSC)

Founded by representatives of the timber trade and NGOs, the FSC aims to support environmentally appropriate, socially beneficial, and economically viable management of the world's forests. To achieve this the FSC accredits and monitors certifiers who audit the quality of forest management against agreed principles. Consumers can then use the FSC trademark as a guarantee that their wood comes from sustainably managed forests.

In the UK, the Soil Association Woodmark scheme is accredited by the FSC, any timber bearing the Woodmark has been produced in forests whose management protects the environment and benefits local people.

WWF 1995 PLUS GROUP

The WWF 1995 Plus Group is a group of companies representing over 25 per cent of the wood and wood products market in the UK with product sales of £2.6 billion and over 20 million customers per week. Signatories include B&Q, Sainsburys and Texas Homecare. They have made the following commitments

❏ Members are committed to supporting internationally applicable, independent systems of forest certification, based upon standards which take full account of environmental, ecological, biodiversity, social and economic needs such as those promoted by the pioneering work of the Forest Stewardship Council.
❏ Members are committed to phasing-in the purchase of forest products from well-managed forests as verified by independent certifiers. These include SCS, Rainforest Alliance, SGS, Soil Association and other independent certifiers when appropriate.

The work of the WWF 1995 Plus Group has raised awareness within the timber and timber products industries that large

TIMBER	SOURCE(S)
TROPICAL HARDWOODS	
African mahogany	W Africa
Afrormosia	W Africa
American mahogany	S America
Limba/Afara	W Africa
Makore	W Africa
Nyatoh	S E Asia
Obeche	W Africa
Ramin	S E Asia
Sapele	W Africa
Teak	Burma, Thailand
Utile	W Africa
Virola	S America
NON-TROPICAL HARDWOODS	
Beech	Europe
Cherry	Europe, N America
Elm	Europe, N America
Maple	Europe, N America
Oak	Europe, N America
Walnut	Europe, N America
NON-TROPICAL SOFTWOODS	
Larch	Europe
Various cedar species	N America
Various pine species	Europe, N and S. America, Australasia
Various spruce species	Europe, N America
Yew	Europe

cale consumers of products are not prepared to accept unsub-
tantiated claims about wood. The Group is likely to raise
tandards of information, performance and management for all
vood uses.

TABLE 4.1

Common timbers used in the production of furniture and region of origin

PRACTICAL ACTION

Refurbish Furniture Where Possible

In comparison with purchasing new office furniture, refurbishment of worn out items can cost about half the price. Renovation can provide an environmentally preferable alternative to purchasing new products as it avoids the disposal of non-renewable resources and reduces costs. Business Seating (Renovations) Ltd provides a refurbishment service for all types of office furniture including chairs, desks and partitions.

Support the Forest Stewardship Council/ WWF Plus Group Initiative

Buy furniture with a recognised label when it becomes available. Demand information from your supplier about the county of origin and forestry practices.

Use Chipboard

Chipboard can be used as an alternative to solid wood in sheet form. Made from the top four feet of softwood timber trees which would otherwise go to waste, it is sometimes faced with melamine or laminate (paper-based and derived from softwoods) and edged in plastic. Low-grade paper waste is also made into chipboard.

Second quality temperate veneers can be substituted for mahogany on chipboard panels.

Use Non-timber Alternatives

Non-timber alternatives such as sheets produced from recycled fibres and agricultural waste are becoming more widely available. Panpro produces a particle board manufactured from straw and other agricultural by-products suitable for the manufacture of furniture. Vending cups can be recycled into wood substitutes and are currently used in the manufacture of garden furniture. Manufacturers can facilitate the recycling of the plastic components in their furniture by marking the plastic according to EC standards so that it can be recognised for recycling.

Case Study

Subject –	**FURNITURE REFURBISHMENT**
Organisation –	**INTERNATIONAL COFFEE ORGANISATION**
Organisation type –	**PRIVATE**
Location –	**LONDON W1**
No. of staff –	**N/A**

BACKGROUND

The International Coffee Organisation (ICO) facilities are used to host conferences for participants involved in the international coffee trade. Seating provision in the conference facility had become worn and damaged. Fabric and foams were dirty and did not conform to current standards.

ACTION

During a three week break in the use of the conference hall, Business Seating (Renovations) Ltd carefully removed 280 seating units from the site. These were taken to its Reading workshop where the unit frames were repaired and refurbished with modern CMHR (combustion modified high resilient) foams and fabrics. The units were then refitted at the ICO site within the three week schedule.

The information in this Case Study was kindly provided by Business Seating (Renovations) Ltd; see Sources of Information.)

RESULTS

❏ The facility was upgraded to all current standards within the tight time scale allowed. Replacement of the seating at the ICO with new furniture would have involved various structural changes and an estimated cost of £40,000. The renovation option utilised all existing metal and wood frames and cost £15,000, a net saving of £25,000.

Recycled Textiles

Synthetic materials and low grade textiles can be used in the manufacture of 'flock', a filling material for upholstery in furniture. Textile collection points, textile banks, are becoming a common sight alongside glass and paper banks at public recycling sites. The use of textiles such as flock reduces the amount of post consumer waste disposed of to landfill.

Recycled Materials

There are a number of products which are manufactured as wood alternatives from a variety of recycled materials. It is not possible to make a blanket judgement over the relative environmental performance of plastic, metal or wooden products as sufficient life-cycle analysis has not been conducted. However, the use of waste products for new materials closes the recycling loop and reduces disposal to landfill.

Tectan

An association between Tetra Pak (carton manufacturers) and Assmann (furniture manufacturers) has resulted in a wood substitute made from recycled drinks cartons. About 1300 waste cartons are used to produce an average desktop. The cartons consist of approximately 75 per cent cardboard, 25 per cent polyethylene and aluminium foil. When milled, heated and compressed, the polyethylene acts as a bonding agent to produce a stable water-resistant material without the need for formaldehyde or other harmful agents.

Durawood

Save Wood Products manufactures a wood substitute made from expanded polystyrene packaging. Packaging is compressed and recycled into a hardwood substitute. It can be used in the same applications as wood but it does not rot, is impervious to water and insect attack and does not require varnishing or oiling. McDonald's is using its polystyrene packaging to make garden furniture for use in picnic areas.

Made of Waste

Made of Waste is an organisation which manufactures

Case Study

Subject –	**RECYCLED WOOD SUBSTITUTES**
Organisation –	**SAVE WOOD PRODUCTS LTD**
Organisation type –	**MANUFACTURING**
Location –	**COWES, ISLE OF WIGHT**
No. of staff –	**20**

BACKGROUND

Save Wood Products Ltd was formed in May 1992 to produce a wood substitute, Durawood, a hard and softwood alternative entirely manufactured from polystyrene waste materials.

During 1992, 1.25 million tonnes of polystyrene were produced in Western Europe alone. The lack of adequate facilities for recycling has meant that the majority of such scrap is disposed of to landfill, a waste of non-renewable resources.

ACTION

Durawood is made by segregating and processing mixed polystyrene scrap to produce a feedstock which is granulated and processed through an extruder which melts the plastic and blends it with colours, fillers and stabilisers. The resulting strands are chipped into pellets. Recognisable products are made by adding a blowing agent to the pellets in an extruder, the molten plastic is then pulled through a series of water cooled formers to achieve the desired size and shape.

Durawood has been used by a number of organisations as a practical and maintenance free alternative to conventional wood products.

Save Wood Products is a specified supplier to McDonald's Restaurants (Europe) Ltd.

(The information in this Case Study was kindly provided by Save Wood Products Ltd; see Sources of Information.)

RESULTS

❑ 1000 Durawood picnic tables have been supplied to McDonald's over three years:

Supply price of Durawood table including parasol	£240.00
Original cost of hardwood alternative	£340.00
Saving	£100,000 over three years

❑ Operational costs will be further reduced because Durawood products need no maintenance.

plastic boards from discarded plastic bottles. Bottles are sorted by hand into five different colour categories to produce boards with differing visual characteristics. Applications for the boards are diverse, the bright colours and random design makes it ideal for shop fittings, kitchen surfaces and children's toys and bowls. Sheets have been used in museums, restaurants and TV studios.

So, when you specify products, be creative and open to alternatives.

Manufacturing

There are a number of chemicals used in the manufacture of furniture which have significant environmental impacts. However, these can be avoided by choosing a manufacturer who uses environmentally-preferable alternatives.

Plastic Foams

CFCs were used in the past as a blowing agent in upholstery foams. The 1987 Montreal Protocol agreed that CFCs would be fully phased out by 1 January 1995. Intermediary replacement chemicals such as HFCs and HCFCs, also ozone depleting substances, are used to blow foam but will themselves be phased out over the next 30 years. Carbon dioxide and air are among the possible replacements for such environmentally damaging chemicals. An alternative to plastic foam is CMHR (combustion modified high resilient) foam. CMHR foam has a better feel than conventional polyether foam and is generally more ignition resistant. It is manufactured using steam instead of Freon gases and is therefore environmentally preferable.

Wood Preservatives

Wood is often treated with preservatives such as pentachlorophenol and lindane which give rise to toxic VOCs (volatile organic compounds, for more information see Catering and Cleaning section in Chapter 5). The use of non-toxic water-based preservatives is preferable.

Formaldehyde

Resin glue used in chipboard furniture contains formaldehyde, a toxic organic compound which is an

	CARLETON FURNITURE GROUP	GYROFLEX OFFICE SEATING	PRESIDENT	KINNARPS
Environmental policy?	Yes	Yes	Yes	Yes
Environmental management system?	Yes Working for BS7750/ISO 14001 by end 1996	No Targeted for accreditation in 1997	No response	No Planning for ISO assessment mid-1997
Sources of wood used?	Veneers – N America/ Europe Chipboard – Europe	N America Europe	N and S America, W Africa, S Asia	N America, Europe
Wood purchased from independently certified sustainably managed sources?	'Sustainable Sources' – currently investigating as part of EMS	Not known	No response	Yes
Energy management programme?	Yes Applied for National Energy Award	Yes	Yes	Yes
Waste management programme?	Yes Recycle over 75% of most wastes	No	Yes	Yes Further initiatives planned
Plastic foams	CFC free	CFC free	CFC free	CFC free
Wood preservatives?	Not used	Not used	Not used	Not used
Formaldehyde?	Yes Surveys show well below MEL limit	No	E1 type board with emissions below MEL limit	E1 type board with emissions below MEL limit
Solvent based lacquer?	Yes Have programme of sourcing alternatives	Yes	Yes	No
Packaging	Recycled cardboard and paper used and reused Recycled once unusable	Recycled packaging	60% recycled fibre board	Blankets used repeatedly
Distribution initiatives to reduce environmental impact?	Subcontracted to Hays distribution Use unleaded and diesel vehicles	Diesel, unleaded and catalysts	Diesel and unleaded	Diesel and unleaded
Disposal: recyclable/repairable parts?	Products easily repairable Encourage users to recycle	Yes	Products easily repairable Some recyclable components	Recyclable and easily repaired

TABLE 4.2

A comparison of the environmental performance of four furniture manufacturers

SUMMARY GUIDELINES

❏ Avoid tropical hardwoods and check raw material sources. Wood products should be from independently certified, sustainably managed sources.
❏ Consider renovation of worn furniture.
❏ Consider wood substitutes made from recycled materials.
❏ Avoid products where ozone depleting chemicals are used as a blowing agent for foams.
❏ Avoid solvent-based wood preservatives, lacquers and adhesives.
❏ Avoid adhesives containing formaldehyde and solvents.
❏ Consider design for re-use and end-of-life disposal.
❏ Investigate packaging recyclable content, recyclability and retrieval.

irritant to tissue, causing eye, skin and throat irritation, nausea and allergic reactions. At high levels, it is believed to be carcinogenic. It is emitted as a vapour and is harmful during both production and use. E1 type boards have low formaldehyde levels and are an acceptable alternative.

Lacquer

In the past lacquer was used which contained approximately 15 per cent solvent, VOCs arising from such solvents are one of the major factors contributing to the depletion of the ozone layer. A more environmentally acceptable alternative has become widely used which involves a totally solvent-free method of rolling on lacquer which is then cured under ultraviolet light.

Packaging and Disposal

There are environmental implications in the packaging and disposal of furniture:

❏ Design – is the furniture designed to be easily repaired or to be discarded? Is it possible to replace worn or soiled items such as textile coverings and foam padding in chairs?
❏ Packaging – 100 per cent recycled fibre board or blankets should be used to protect furniture during transportation. Your manufacturer should also take action to recover used packaging for recycling. Packaging is expensive to dispose of, so it is in your interests to make sure that the manufacturer has taken steps to reduce it.
❏ Disposal – has ultimate disposal been taken into account? Can the product be re-used or recycled? What are the disposal routes?

Comparing Office Furniture Manufacturers

As an example of the kind of questions you should be asking your office furniture manufacturer, see Table 4.2.

PAPER

Environmental Issues

The key environmental issues associated with paper production and use are:

❑ loss of natural habitats to intensive tree farming;
❑ pollution from manufacture;
❑ energy usage; and
❑ waste disposal: landfill and incineration.

In 1995 the UK used over 11 million tonnes of paper and board of which four million tonnes were made from recycled pulp from the UK and abroad, giving a recycling rate of 36 per cent. Paper is a natural resource which is re-usable and can be recycled up to five times. Approximately one third of the world's industrial wood harvest is used by the pulp and paper industry (WBCSD, 1996). This huge market for virgin pulp means that there is pressure on the paper industry to produce trees quickly, leading to intensive tree farming.

Forestry Practice

The paper industry plants more trees than it chops down, but in doing so natural habitats are destroyed to make way for intensive forestry. This is happening in the UK, particularly in Scotland. Some 90 per cent of tree planting in the UK has taken place in the Scottish uplands and covers approximately 15 per cent of the Scottish countryside.

Ploughing of deep peat for forestry in areas such as the Flow country of Caithness and Sutherland contributes to global warming and destroys these unique habitats; an estimated 50 hectares a week are planted with conifers. Peat acts as a sink for carbon dioxide, locking the gas up chemically within its structure. When bogs are ploughed and drained, peat dries and decomposes releasing the trapped carbon dioxide into the atmosphere.

Single species plantations (monocultures), especially those using exotic species, are unable to support the range of plant, insect, bird and mammal life found in more diverse old growth forests. Monocultures provide one basic habitat and food source, if a species is not adapted to that particular niche it will not survive.

The prime source of supply for European paper is Scandinavia, but in recent years there has been an increase in the use of eucalyptus, predominantly from plantations in Brazil and Portugal. Eucalyptus grows eight times faster than pine which contributes to its value for paper making, but it also has significant negative effects upon the environment. The speed of its growth is responsible for lowering the water table in many areas. As the water table falls, top soil dries out and becomes less compacted and is therefore more susceptible to loss through wind and flooding. Soil acidification also occurs as the trees leach nutrients from the soil thereby decreasing its ability to support vegetation without the addition of fertilisers.

In Brazil and Portugal the spread of extensive eucalyptus plantations has lead to the loss of adequate water supplies for farm land, leading to the loss of crops and failed harvests conditions which can precede drought.

Manufacturing Problems

BLEACHING AGENTS

Paper pulp can be bleached with chlorine gas (used to break down lignin, which is a natural glue in wood) and a variety of chemicals including hydrogen peroxide and hypochlorite to achieve whiteness. The resulting effluent, called bleach liquor, has been found to contain over 300 compounds, many of which are dangerous toxins (WWF, 1995). One of the groups of compounds which cause major concern are dioxins. These are highly toxic and accumulate in the fatty tissue of fish where they can pass into the food chain.

EFFLUENT

Wastewater effluent from pulp and paper manufacture can contain up to 1000 organic and inorganic compounds. Waste organic materials which can biodegrade are measured by biochemical oxygen demand (BOD), that is, the amount of oxygen required to break the compounds down to their constituent parts. Effluent discharges from paper mills have been found to cause eutrophication; this occurs when an excess of nutrients enter a watercourse or body and over-enrich the water. This enrichment causes an explosion in the growth of algae (blooming) which consume any available oxygen and threaten plant and animal life. Algal blooms can also lead to the production of foul-smelling substances such as hydrogen

Case Study

Subject –	**CONSUMER PRESSURE – STOPPING CLEAR CUTTING OF CLAYOQUOT SOUND**
Location –	**CANADA**

BACKGROUND

Clayoquot Sound on Canada's Vancouver Island in British Columbia is one of the world's last remaining areas of ancient temperate rainforest. The forests have been the focus of international attention for more than 12 years due to a programme of clear cut logging that has caused extensive damage to the area. Clear cutting is a logging practice of removing all trees and shrubs in a given area. Saleable timber is removed and the remaining wood and leaf material is left on site. The practice not only causes visual blight but devastates the ecological diversity of an area that has evolved over millions of years, leading to soil loss, flooding and ruination of salmon streams. Pulp from Clayoquot Sound was manufactured into newsprint and tissue paper. The UK was the fourth largest importer of British Columbia forest products.

ACTION

A coalition of environmental pressure groups, including Greenpeace, has worked for over a decade to try to prevent the logging which was being conducted by a handful of large companies. Over 900 people have been arrested while protesting at the site and the issue has been the focus of international campaigns designed to exert customer pressure on the companies logging the area.

Information supplied by Greenpeace.

RESULTS

❑ In 1994 international supplier and customer pressure resulted in a number of paper companies cancelling their contracts to take wood products from British Columbia. In October 1996 members of the IUCN (World Conservation Union) voted unanimously to support the designation of Clayoquot Sound as an international UN Biosphere Reserve.

❑ A Biosphere Reserve would provide a greatly enhanced level of protection for the area and would allow a much greater role for the native First Nation inhabitants of the area.

❑ Designation of Clayoquot as a Biosphere Reserve needs to be made by the International Man and Biosphere Committee; this should take place in April or May 1997.

MAJOR RECOGNISED DETERMINANTS FOR PAPER MILL EFFLUENT

❏ Chemical oxygen demand (COD): a measurement of total emissions of organic matter; the prime parameter for emissions to water.
❏ Absorbable organic halogens (AOX): a measurement of chlorinated organics from the bleaching of chemical pulps; the secondary parameter for emissions to water.
❏ Sulphur: the parameter used for emissions to air. Sulphur is a major contributory factor to acid rain. The main source of sulphur emissions is burning fossil fuels.

sulphide and ammonia, the resulting water cannot be used for human consumption and can represent a threat to human life. A Greenpeace Sweden survey identified 21 known or suspected carcinogens (substances causing cancer) and mutagens (substances causing cell mutations) in paper mill effluent (WWF, 1995).

OPTICAL BRIGHTENING AGENTS

Optical brightening agents (OBAs) increase the whiteness of materials by absorbing radiant energy, when added to off-white colours the blue white OBAs create a brighter white appearance. OBAs have been found to be carcinogenic.

MINERAL LOADINGS AND COATINGS

These are added in the paper making process to create an even surface and feel to the end product. Most of the loadings and coatings currently used are china clay (kaolin) and chalk (calcium carbonate). The quarrying of such raw materials creates unsightly areas, dust and heavy traffic movement. In some areas it can also cause damage to important wildlife habitats.

Improvements to the Manufacturing Process

OXYGEN BLEACHING

Oxygen pre-bleaching is designed to reduce the amount of chlorine bleaching necessary in the pulping process; this means fewer organochlorines are formed. Pulp is then washed and oxygen bleached several times to improve the whiteness. The oxygen used in this process can be recycled and, as oxygen is cheaper than chlorine, many mills are changing their operation. Elemental chlorine free (ECF) and totally chlorine free (TCF) pulp is also produced using reduced amounts of chlorine. These are discussed in detail in the Labelling System and Industry Standards section of this chapter.

IMPROVING EFFICIENCY

Many mills have invested heavily in changing their bleaching processes. By improving the efficiency of the pulping process more impurities can be removed prior to bleaching, reducing the degree of subsequent bleaching required and, therefore, the formation of organochlorines.

RECYCLED PAPER

Making paper from recycled pulp uses less energy and, if correctly sorted, no bleach as the pulp was whitened originally when manufactured. The whiteness of recycled paper is achieved by either using unprinted white waste or by de-inking printed white waste paper. The de-inking process is done with detergents, water and compressed air and is not significantly polluting. When bleaching is needed, hydrogen peroxide can be used which is less damaging than chlorine. Optical brightening agents (which have been found to be carcinogenic) are not used in the production of recycled papers.

Waste paper and pulp can be recycled a number of times, although 15–20 per cent of the fibres become too small to use and fall through the paper making screens as a sludge residue. Some uses have been found for such material as a fertiliser and as a spillage control product, sludge is recycled into absorbent granules which can be used to soak up hazardous spillages.

Mill Performance

As shown in the next section, different maximum acceptable levels for mill performance are set by the various labelling schemes. A comparison is shown in Table 4.4 below.

Conservation Papers run a service called EPIC which provides information on paper specification and mill performance for specific brands of paper (see Sources of Information for details).

Disposal

Paper accounts for over a third of our waste and is mainly disposed of to landfill sites or incinerators. Landfill is an unsightly and inefficient land use and can cause contamination sites are poorly managed. There is also a shortage of landfill sites within the UK, for example, some of London's waste is transported to Oxfordshire for disposal.

Incineration has grown in recent years as an alternative method of waste disposal. Such a technique is increasingly combined with recovery of the heat from the incineration process in combined heat and power (CHP) plants. Though incineration recovers more value (as energy) from waste than landfilling, there are still environmental problems associated with it.

Waste disposal is expensive, the introduction of the Landfill Tax in October 1996 increased costs by £7 per tonne (£10 per tonne from April 1998) for most office wastes sent to landfill and also raised awareness about the costs of waste disposal

There is little need for paper to be landfilled or incinerated it can be recycled easily, will certainly reduce your disposal costs as it can represent over 70 percent of total waste, and may even generate revenue (see Chapters 3 and 8 for further information on waste and recycling).

LABELLING SYSTEMS AND INDUSTRY STANDARDS

The environmental classification of paper is a vital consideration when assessing the environmental credentials of particular type of paper. The terms recycled paper or environmentally friendly mean very little without such classification

Recycled Content

There is a system of classification for recycled paper showing the type of waste paper they are made from, as shown in Table 4.3.

A prefix indicates the percentage of each of the groups of waste in recycled papers. For example, 25B/50C means the paper is made from 25 per cent printers' off cuts, 50 per cent post-consumer waste and the remaining 25 per cent virgin fibre. Most high quality office papers contain a small percentage of virgin pulp.

NATIONAL ASSOCIATION OF PAPER MERCHANTS (NAPM)

The NAPM Recycled Paper Mark is a kitemark system for recycled papers. In order to qualify for the Mark, a paper board must be manufactured from a minimum of 75 per cent genuine waste fibre: waste in the B, C and D categories of the

Case Study

Subject –	ENVIRONMENTAL IMPROVEMENTS IN PAPER MANUFACTURING
Organisation –	CURTIS FINE PAPERS
Organisation type –	PAPER MANUFACTURING
Location –	GUARDBRIDGE AND DALMORE MILLS, SCOTLAND
No. of staff –	N/A

BACKGROUND

Concerns have grown in recent years over the environmental performance of the paper making industry. In 1991 the American Environmental Protection Agency reported that the paper industry was the third largest source of toxic pollutants in the USA. Against this background of world-wide concern it important that UK paper manufacturers keen to promote good environmental practice are seen to be reacting positively to customer and commercial pressures.

Curtis Fine Papers (Curtis), part of Crown Vantage Incorporated, is Europe's leading producer of quality uncoated writings, text and cover papers. In 1995 the company produced over 40,000 tonnes of special make, security and branded papers for designers, printers and specifiers world-wide. Curtis brand names include Classic, Conservation, Metaphor, Scotia, Retreeve and Eureka.

ACTION

Curtis has been producing recycled paper since the 1980s. Conservation 100% Recycled was the first ever recycled watermarked stationery paper in Britain. Since then environmental issues have moved beyond the type of pulp used to make paper. More concentration is being given to forestry standards, raw materials sourcing and the way that paper is made.

Curtis Fine Papers produced its first Environmental Report

RESULTS

Changes to practice have been made in the following areas:

❏ stricter standards of forestry practice required from suppliers;
❏ changes in effluent treatment and sludge disposal;
❏ reductions in total energy usage and greater efficiency of use;
❏ reductions in water usage; and
❏ research into the use of effluent sludge as a soil conditioner.

Both Guardbridge and Dalmore Mills have achieved certification to BS 7750 Environmental Management

System with Guardbridge becoming the UK's first fine paper mill to achieve the standard. The standard commits the company to continuous demonstrable environmental improvement.

In 1996 Guardbridge became the first UK paper making operation to achieve EMAS (the European Eco-Management and Audit Scheme). This is a voluntary Europe-wide scheme that recognises companies which have established a programme of continuous environmental improvement through setting targets which can be demonstrated and which will be audited by an independent external body.

in Autumn 1993 and received a positive response from a broad spectrum of interest groups. Curtis were especially encouraged by the support they had received for their policy of open reporting.

Environmental monitoring and management systems have been in place at Curtis for a number of years. The introduction of the British Standard for Environmental Management, BS 7750, enabled the company to adopt a recognised standard at the company's Dalmore and Guardbridge Mills in order to provide an independent assessment of the company's position.

ABCD classification, excluding any mill-produced waste. Although this scheme is widely recognised it does not identify which categories (B, C or D) are used in any given paper. A paper may have a NAPM mark but be predominantly made from category B pulp, sourced from offcuts, which is not post-consumer waste.

HMSO

Her Majesty's Stationery Office (now The Stationery Office) has developed a scoring system to enable comparison of recycled papers. Points are awarded out of 100 according to the source of recycled fibre contained in a paper (0.5 point for pre- consumer and 1 point for post-consumer waste) and the

TABLE 4.3

Environmental classification of waste paper as defined by the British Paper and Board Industry Federation

CATEGORY	TYPE OF PULP
A	Chemically treated unused mill waste (Woodfree Own Millbroke)
B	Unused high-grade printers' offcuts (Woodfree Unprinted)
C	Used high quality white office waste (Woodfree Printed)
D	Low quality waste (Mechanically printed and unprinted)

he percentage use of that fibre type in the paper. The merchant you use to buy paper from will be able to give you he HMSO score of a paper brand.

BLUE ANGEL

This is a German scheme, awarding a Blue Angel label to paper which is 100 per cent recycled, of which at least 51 per cent is post-consumer waste ie categories C or D.

EUGROPA

he European version of the NAPM mark, Eugropa is the European association of paper merchants. In order to qualify for the mark, a board or paper must be manufactured from a minimum of 50 per cent genuine waste fibre in the B, C and D categories.

Environmental Performance

here are also a number of paper labelling systems which look at wider issues of environmental performance.

EU ECOLABEL

Ecolabelling criteria have been set for copier paper and converted paper products (including envelopes) to provide a recognised environmental standard (see Ecolabel section at the start of this chapter). As of November 1996, no paper products had gained the Ecolabel. The development of the copier paper ecolabel has been contentious, and at the time of writing is not supported by the Paper Federation of Great Britain.

ECO-GRADE ASSESSMENT

Eco-Grade is an independent system which assesses the environmental performance of products. Assessments are conducted on individual products which are graded with a system of stars. Star grading is based on five environmental qualifications: energy usage, halogen levels from the bleaching process, chemical oxygen demand, solid waste levels and sulphur emissions to the atmosphere. The system aims to provide a comparable standard by which paper users can assess the relative performance of different papers. Eco-Grade does not look at the recycled pulp content of papers.

BRANDS PAPERS' ECO-CHECK

Eco-Check uses the life-cycle analysis approach. It assesses mills and their products against each of the key environmental issues such as forestry, pollution and recyclability. Eco-Check enables the production of standard papers to be compared with recycled grades and also the same type of paper from different manufacturers.

NORDIC WHITE SWAN

The objective of the White Swan label is to encourage production methods with minimum environmental impacts. Fine papers can be made from virgin pulp or recycled fibres: it is the effect the manufacturing process has on the environment rather than the selection of raw materials, that is assessed.

Chlorine Free

The term environmentally friendly is often used for chlorine free papers as chlorine is now recognised as a pollutant. There are labelling systems for chlorine-free papers and chlorine gas is becoming far less widely used.

TOTALLY CHLORINE FREE (TCF)

Totally chlorine free refers to a pulp bleaching process which does not use chlorine gas or chlorine compounds but uses non chlorine bleaches, such as hydrogen peroxide, oxygen, ozone and enzymes. However, there is disagreement about the definition of 'chlorine-free'. Although it has been defined as maximum of 0.1 kilograms of organochlorine per tonne, Greenpeace insists that chlorine-free should mean 'absolutely no chlorine', while others regard 'low chlorine' as chlorine-free.

ELEMENTAL CHLORINE FREE (ECF)

Elemental chlorine free refers to a pulp bleaching process which does not use chlorine gas (elemental chlorine) but chlorine dioxide.

A recent report has concluded that differences in environmental performance between ECF and TCF pulps are minimal (WBCSD, 1996).

ENVIRONMENTAL MEASURE	ECO-CHECK	ECO-GRADE	ECO-LABEL	NORDIC WHITE SWAN
Energy consumption (GJ/tonne)	25	25.0	30.0	No Standard
Absorbable organic halogens (AOX) (kg/tonne)	0.5	0.5	0.3	0.4
Chemical oxygen demand (COD) (kg/tonne)	50.0	50.0	30.0	65.0
Solid wastes(kg/tonne)	50.0	50.0	No standard	No standard
Sulphur(kg/tonne)	2.5	2.5	1.5	2.0

PRACTICAL ACTION

TABLE 4.4
Comparison of effluent standards under different labelling schemes

Reduce Demand for Virgin Paper

Pressure on natural habitats will be reduced if demand for new timber is also reduced.

❑ Reduce your usage, re-use and recycle your paper. See Chapter 3.
❑ Close the recycling loop by using recycled papers. This will also reduce the volume of waste going to landfill/incineration.

Encourage Recognised Forestry Standards

When purchasing paper with a virgin pulp content you should encourage improved woodland management. For example, planting native species in more sensitive ways and using natural regeneration and selective planting to replace deep ploughing, should be encouraged.

The preservation of biodiversity and the functioning of ecological systems in commercial forests should be made an integral part of efficient, sustainable timber production.

Demand accurate information from your paper supplier about forestry practices. Check the source of the wood pulp used.

Issues outlined concerning forestry in the Office Furniture section of this chapter apply equally to paper. The objectives of the Forestry Stewardship Council scheme and the WWF 1995 Plus Group should be adopted as good practice in paper purchasing. BBC Magazines and Future Publishing are both signatories.

COMMON PROBLEMS

Cost

Due to current fluctuations in the paper market, recycled papers can be slightly more expensive than virgin papers. Negotiate with your suppliers to get a good deal; with bulk purchasing discounts, recycled papers compete with virgin brands. If you are prepared to commit yourself to using it, you should be able to negotiate a competitive price. Be persistent!

Quality

New developments in paper making technology have made possible the production of recycled papers which compare in terms of appearance, quality and performance with virgin grades. Laser printer and photocopier guaranteed recycled papers are now common. It should be possible to match most virgin papers currently in use.

Perception

Changing peoples' attitudes to the use of recycled paper can be a major challenge but it can often be based on prejudice or a failed attempt to use recycled papers some years previously. Modern recycled papers have come a long way, though it may not look it, this book is printed on recycled paper!

Encourage Improvements in Mill Performance

It is important to quantify the environmental standards of the mill which manufactures your paper. It is unrealistic to be able to test these standards yourself; however, reputable paper merchants will be able to provide you with information regarding the measures of effluent from the relevant mill, alternatively this information can be sought from the mill direct. An industry standard such the Eco-Grade described above can give performance figures which you can use to compare with the figures you are given.

Introduce Recycled Papers

Recycled paper uses less energy, and requires less bleaching and chemical use than papers produced with virgin pulp whilst also closing the recycling loop.

Good quality recycled papers are widely available for use as copier, letterhead, presentation and even art and design end uses. Use papers with the highest percentage in the C and D categories. These are environmentally preferable since they are made from genuinely used recycled paper and therefore close the recycling loop.

- ❑ Build in the use of recycled papers at the tender stage of all relevant tender documents and contracts – office equipment, printers and paper supply.
- ❑ Reduce the weight of paper used. Seventy-five g/m copier paper is being introduced by many organisations, saving resources and money. Performance is capable of matching that of traditional 80 g/m paper. Volume users can have 75 g/m paper specially manufactured to their specifications. Ninety g/m letterhead paper is also being introduced in place of the traditional 100 g/m weight.

Ensure Compatibility with Office Equipment

It is important to consider the servicing contract on you photocopiers when considering a suitable brand o copier paper. Check with your copier manufacturer tha the paper you have chosen will not contravene you service contract. Some machines may need adjusting

See the Paper section of the Directory for furthe information.

Recycled Printing Papers

Design For Recycled Papers

Maximise your use of the different textures and finishes available in recycled papers and design to that. Don't design for virgin paper and then print on recycled.

❑ Work with your printer/designer to develop the use of recycled papers. Printing machines may need adjusting.
❑ High-quality, cost effective products are available in recycled fibre. Your choice of paper also affects its ultimate recyclability. The majority of laminated finishes cannot be recycled without the use of chemicals; therefore, we do not recommend their use. Alternative finishes such as water-glaze are available.

Anderson Fraser Publishing produces a detailed manual, *Recycled Paper: A Manual for Printers and Designers*, which gives detailed information regarding the use of recycled papers. Conservation Papers provides a central point for information on all recycled papers and their related environmental issues.

EPIC

EPIC, now a division of PIRA, is a free paper product information and samples service for buyers, specifiers and environmental managers. EPIC holds comprehensive environmental, commercial and technical details on hundreds of different products used in offices.

EPIC Office Technology also provides a similar service for PCs, faxes, copies, laser printers and scanners.

Information is in a standard format allowing comparisons to be made easily and is held on a database enabling EPIC operators to accurately pinpoint suitable products to meet your criteria – environmental, commercial, technical or any combination. When suitable products have been identified, you receive a complete information printout for each one, with suppliers' samples and product literature (see the Directory for further details).

Compatibility with Equipment

Test the paper you intend to use and work with your suppliers. Some manufacturers and service companies blame machine faults on recycled paper and say that this is not covered by the warranty. Test the paper first and check your warranty.

SUMMARY GUIDELINES

❑ Reduce your paper consumption.
❑ Use recycled papers with a maximum of C and D grade pulps.
❑ Make sure that the recycled copier paper you choose is compatible with your office equipment and will not affect equipment warranties.
❑ Use your buying power to negotiate best prices for recycled paper.
❑ Make sure that any virgin pulp content in the paper you choose is ECF or TCF and is from an independently certified, sustainably managed forest.
❑ Request information regarding mill performance and cross check the results against a recognised standard.
❑ Demand accurate information from your paper merchant, and don't be put off.

Case Study

Subject –	**ENVIRONMENTAL SPECIFICATIONS IN CORPORATE LITERATURE**
Organisation –	**BRITISH BROADCASTING CORPORATION**
Organisation type –	**BROADCASTING**
Location –	**NATIONWIDE**
No. of staff –	**N/A**

BACKGROUND

The BBC has a strong commitment to environmental protection and in order that its environmental policy can be reflectein the commissioning a production of corporate publicationenvironmental criteria should be included in all decisioconcerning the production of corporate literature. In orderfacilitate this, guidelines have been drawn up, setting out thspecifications for environmental performance to be followedthe production of all corporate publications.

This report is based on an analysis of environmental impacarising from the stages in production of corporate literaturFor each of the main production stages, a process descriptiongiven, followed by the identification of current best practiceminimise environmental impacts, with recommendminimum specifications to be included in the BBC CorporaLiterature Design Guidelines. In addition, more rigorotargets are given for those departments wishing to exceminimum standards.

All standards recommended are achievable and practicgiven existing products and technologies. The BBC's existienvironmental purchasing policy targets have been incorprated into the recommendations. These targets are:

❑ a 60 per cent use of recycled paper by 1997;

❑ to purchase goods which do not contain solvents other than water; and

❑ to select products which use water based inks and vegetable dyes for colouring purposes.

ACTION

Minimum Standards

The following demanding environmental specifications have been formally adopted and included in the Corporate Literature Design Guidelines. The specifications covered the following issues:

❑ Forestry
❑ Pulping/De-inking and Paper-making
❑ Choice of Paper
❑ Printing Company
❑ Inks
❑ Finishes
❑ Packaging
❑ Enclosures
❑ Designing for Recycled Paper

RESULTS

❑ The standards have enabled the BBC to systematically take into account environmental issues throughout the production of corporate literature. The Corporate Writings Divisions are now meeting these demanding standards and are encouraging other departments to follow suit.

CHAPTER SUMMARY

❑ Follow the standard purchasing principles in the Introduction to this chapter.
❑ Encourage communication between the purchasing and waste management teams.
❑ Look at areas where you can reduce consumption.
❑ Make sure that the manufacturers and suppliers of any product you purchase can provide you with information on the environmentally preferable products that they produce/provide.
❑ Use the information in this *Manual* to help you to identify environmentally preferable products.
❑ Avoid any products that require COSHH sheets or contain hazardous materials.
❑ Avoid disposable products.
❑ Purchase products that can be easily re-used or recycled.

Sources of Information

Furniture Renovations and Wood Substitutes

BUSINESS SEATING (RENOVATIONS) LTD
Units 1 & 2
Wilnecote Lane
Belgrave
Tamworth
Staffordshire B77 2LE
Tel: 01827 261 599
Fax: 01827 261 597

MADE OF WASTE
19 Calthorpe St
London WC1X 0JP
Tel: 0171 278 6971

SAVE WOOD PRODUCTS LTD
Amazon Works
Three Gates Road
West Cowes
Isle of Wight PO31 7UT
Tel: 01983 299 935
Fax: 01983 299 069

Batteries

BRITISH BATTERY MANUFACTURERS ASSOCIATION
Cowley House
9 Little College Street
London SW1P 3XS
Tel: 0171 222 0666

Electronics Recycling Coordinating Bodies

EMERG
c/o Mr Tickner
9 Warnham Manor
Warnham
Horsham
West Sussex RH12 3RN
Tel: 01403 264 699
Fax: 01403 264 619

ICER
6 Bath Place
Rivington Street
London EC2A 3JE
Tel: 0171 729 4766
Fax: 0171 729 9121

General Sources of Help and Information

ANDERSON FRASER PUBLISHING
96 York Way
London N1 9AG
Tel: 0171 833 7700
Fax: 0171 822 7701

BUY RECYCLED PROGRAMME
NRF Administration
Gresham House
24 Holborn Viaduct
London EC1A 2BN
Tel: 0171 248 1412
Fax: 0171 248 1404

UK ECOLABELLING BOARD
7th Floor
Eastbury House
30–34 Albert Embankment
London SE1 7TL
Tel: 0171 820 1199
Fax: 0171 820 1104

Paper Information

PAPER FOCUS
Paper Publications Ltd
Church House
Church Lane
Kings Langley
Hertfordshire WDF4 8JP
Tel: 01923 261 555
Fax: 01923 261 118

PAPER INDUSTRY RESEARCH ASSOCIATION (PIRA INTERNATIONAL)
Randalls Road
Leatherhead
Surrey KT22 7RU
Tel: 01372 376 161
Fax: 01372 377 526

Paper Suppliers

BRANDS PAPERS
Swift Valley
Rugby CV21 1QN
Tel: 01788 540000
Fax: 01788 535 872

CONSERVATION COMMUNICATIONS/EPIC
228 London Road
Reading RG6 1AH
Tel: 0118 966 3281
Fax: 0118 935 1605

CURTIS FINE PAPER
Guardbridge Mill
St Andrews
Fife Scotland KY16 0UU
Tel: 01334 839 551
Fax: 01334 839 332

INVERSK LTD
Kilbagie Mills
Alloa
Clackmannanshire
FK10 4AE
Tel: 01259 455 000
Fax: 01259 455 050

James McNaughton PAPER ADVISORY SERVICE
Jaymac House
Valmar Road
Camberwell
London SE5 9NP
Tel: 0171 501 6002
Fax: 0171 501 6003

PAPERBACK
Unit 2
Bow Triangle Business Centre
Eleanor Street
London E3 4NP
Tel: 0181 980 2233
Fax: 0181 980 2399

Robert Horne HUNTSMAN HOUSE
Unit B
2 Evelyn Street
London SE8 5DL
Tel: 0171 231 9634
Fax: 0171 231 5641

ST REGIS PAPER COMPANY LTD
Silverton Sales Office
Silverton Mill
Hele
Exeter
Devon EX5 4PY
Tel: 01392 881601
Fax: 01392 881607

STEINBEIS TEMMING
(Distributed by John Heyer
Paper)
Chronicle House
Sheldon Way
Larkfield
Aylesford
Kent ME20 6SE
Tel: 01622 790 499
Fax: 01622 882 277

TORA PAPYRUS UK LTD
Im Park Court
Brighton Road
Crawley
West Sussex RH11 9BP
Tel: 01293 616565
Fax: 01293 616 088

Laser Printer and Inkjet Cartridges

THE FEDERATION OF EUROPEAN CARTRIDGE RECYCLERS AND SUPPLIERS (FECRS)
Greencare House
Sharpness
Gloucestershire GL13 9UD
Tel: 01453 511 366
Fax: 01453 511 714

GREENCARE LTD
Greencare House
Sharpness
Gloucestershire GL13 9UD
Tel: 01453 511366
Fax: 01453 511714

TBS CYGMA
Unit 1A, Brookside Business
Park, Greengate, Middleton
Manchester M24 1GS
Tel: 0161 655 3366
Fax: 0161 654 4249

TONERFLOW
Operations and Distribution
Centre,
Unit 3, Sugarhouse Lane,
Stratford
London E15 2QS
Tel: 0181 522 0472
Fax: 0181 522 0475

UNITED KINGDOM CARTRIDGE RECYCLERS ASSOCIATION (UKRA)
PO Box 41
Eccles
Manchester M30 0RT

Furniture

CARLETON FURNITURE GROUP LTD
Monkhill
Pontefract
West Yorkshire WF8 2NS
Tel: 01977 700 770
Fax: 01977 708 740

KINNARPS (UK) LTD
Comfort House
Poyle 14
Newlands Drive
Colnbrook
Slough SL3 0DX
Tel: 01753 681 860
Fax: 01753 683 233

A–Z CORPORATE ENVIRONMENTAL MANAGEMENT

Kit Sadgrove

Is aluminium bad for you? What is an environmental management system? Is there an effective substitute for chlorine bleach? *The A–Z of Corporate Environmental Management* provides the answers and is an invaluable guide to managing a company's environmental impacts.

With over 800 entries, its coverage includes:

◆ Environmental management strategies, such as ISO 14001
◆ UK, EU and international legislation
◆ Toxic substances such as organochlorines
◆ Major environmental issues such as timber production
◆ Waste management problems, including landfill

The A–Z will help you:

◆ Reduce your organisation's environmental impacts
◆ Understand major issues
◆ Assess whether you are conforming to legislation
◆ Communicate better with staff, customers and other organisations
◆ Implement an environmental management system

£18.95 Paperback ISBN 1 85383 330 4 June 1997 356 pages

EARA REGISTER OF ENVIRONMENTAL AUDITORS

Edited by David Thomson, Ruth Bacon, Julie Tarling, and Suzie Baverstock

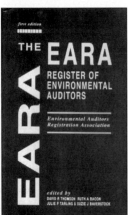

New standards for environmental management systems and a plethora of environmental laws and regulations, are encouraging many businesses and public sector organisations to adopt proactive strategies towards managing their environmental performance.

This is the first ever directory of environmental auditors and contains 730 individuals who have been independently assessed by EARA to carry out a range of environmental auditing tasks, including: establishing an organisation's compliance status, determining liabilities and risks, identifying performance improvements and cost savings, and conducting certification and verification procedures. *The Register* lists full details of each registrant's auditing specialisms, breadth of experience and professional status, together with contact details.

£50.00 Paperback ISBN 1 85383 220 0 1995 320 pages

EARTHSCAN

Earthscan, 120 Pentonville Road, London N1 9JN
Telephone 0171 278 0433 • Fax 0171 278 1142 • email earthsales @ earthscan.co.uk
http://www.earthscan.co.uk

5: Purchasing Services

INTRODUCTION

Dealing with suppliers who are committed to sound environmental performance can make your job easier and help you achieve your purchasing objectives. Equally, poor performance from your suppliers weakens your own environmental position. This is particularly important where you are buying in products with a high environmental impact/profile. Suppliers and contractors can represent significant risks where they are conducting an activity which is covered by environmental legislation. For instance, you may be relying on your cleaning contractors to comply with the Environmental Protection (Duty of Care) Regulations 1991 on your behalf. In such circumstances both your contractor and yourself have responsibilities under the Act (see Chapter 3 for further details).

Consideration of environmental criteria in purchasing decisions reduces the environmental impact of your activities and in many cases has a strong commercial case. But how do you assess environmental criteria? Buyers are confronted with marketing hype from suppliers, and it is very difficult to 'see the wood for the trees'. So where do you start?

This chapter covers a range of services which organisations often contract out, highlighting environmental issues and giving guidance on action you can take to reduce your environmental impacts. It outlines the context for environmental purchasing and describes a way of planning and structuring your initiatives to maximise their effectiveness. The chapter also contains an overview of purchasing structures in different organisations and the points to remember when purchasing services.

The management information in this chapter in the section,

Planning Your Purchasing is equally applicable to planning product purchasing covered in the previous chapter.

Supply Chain Pressure

The increasing importance of the environment to business in recent years has led to a change in the environmental requirements made by companies of their suppliers. Many large organisations, having achieved a recognised environmental standard or decided to manage their environmental effects, have started to apply supply chain pressure to companies that supply them.

SMALL BUSINESSES

Small businesses are the industry sector which is most affected by supply chain pressure and least prepared in response. This is because they are often not big enough to have dedicated staff and do not face the public scrutiny which large or multinational companies find. Many small businesses are still unconvinced by the business case of improving environmental performance which can leave them unprepared if a company they supply sends them an environmental questionnaire.

ETHICS AND THE ENVIRONMENT

The environment has become, along with other issues such as child labour and working conditions, an ethical issue. Consumers in the UK are becoming more concerned about the links that their purchasing has with environmental destruction and wider issues of social conditions in developing countries.

Effective environmental purchasing can reduce your liabilities, promote the sustainability of your organisation, reduce costs, improve control and reduce the impacts that you have on the environment.

Local Authorities and Schools

The Groundwork Foundation has produced a publication *Purchasing and Sustainability* (1996) which is aimed at helping local authorities to integrate environmental concerns with everyday purchasing practice.

Case Study

Subject –	**SMALL COMPANY ENVIRONMENTAL PURCHASING**
Organisation –	**HAPPY COMPUTERS**
Organisation type –	**IT COMPUTER TRAINING**
Location –	**LONDON**
No. of staff –	**12**

BACKGROUND

Happy Computers is a small company which provides IT and computer training. The company has a philosophy of constant innovation, both in the services it provides and in the way those services are provided. It also feels that, as an innovating company, it should minimise the effect of its purchasing on the environment.

ACTION / RESULTS

- ☐ Suppliers with environmental policies are preferred.
- ☐ Plastic cups are not used.
- ☐ Tea and coffee are fair trade goods purchased from Traidcraft.
- ☐ Environmentally preferable cleaning products are purchased.
- ☐ Carrier bags are printed on biodegradable plastic.
- ☐ Recycled paper is used throughout the company's operations and includes: envelopes, copier and letterhead paper, flip charts and toilet rolls.
- ☐ All used paper is collected for recycling.
- ☐ Push bike couriers are used for deliveries.
- ☐ Staff are given a £20 per month allowance if they cycle to work.
- ☐ One acre of rainforest is endowed for every 50 training courses run.

COMPULSORY COMPETITIVE TENDERING

Compulsory competitive tendering (CCT) is based on the principle that local authority staff (including schools) cannot do certain types of work unless their costs have been tested in competition with other potential providers. The legal framework is set out in The 1980 Local Government Act and The 1988 Local Government Act. In addition to UK law, under Article 30 of the Treaty of Rome, local authorities cannot take any action which limits trade between EU Member States.

CCT does not preclude the use of environmental criteria to evaluate tenders, but it does introduce some restrictions. Criteria must be:

❏ appropriate and relevant to the service;
❏ notified in advance to tenderers;
❏ not non-commercial; and
❏ not anti-competitive.

Providing this is the case, local authorities are not required to accept the lowest tender where an alternative offers environmental benefits but this decision must be backed up by a corporate environmental policy which covers purchasing.

PURCHASING STRUCTURES IN LOCAL AUTHORITIES

Purchasing within local authorities falls broadly into three groups: departmental purchasing, central purchasing and purchasing consortia. In any specific local authority all three may be in use at any one time.

Departmental Purchasing

Many local authorities have devolved purchasing within departments where 70–80 per cent of officers have some purchasing responsibilities. Control over purchasing decisions can be weak in these circumstances without strong management and effective communication of environmental policies.

Central Purchasing

Many local authorities have central purchasing units which act within the authority as trading units. These can coordinate purchasing and allow a point of focus for enquiries. Central purchasing units can advise and educate staff on environmentally preferable purchases but they often cannot enforce choices. Central purchasing units can also act as an aid to bulk purchasing, with the following benefits:

❑ control over items stocked – in line with environmental purchasing policy;
❑ monitoring – provides information on purchasing within different departments; and
❑ ensures the best deals – allows bulk discounts through bulk purchasing contracts.

Purchasing Consortia

Purchasing consortia are groups of local authorities that have decided to combine their central purchasing units in order to consolidate their purchasing power. Consortia can use their buying power to promote environmental alternatives and to establish good deals from suppliers. The Central Buying Consortium, a group of nine local authorities has a collective annual spend of £3/4 billion (Groundwork, 1996).

Planning Your Purchasing Strategy

This chapter is mainly concerned with the specific environmental issues associated with purchasing a range of services to help you make informed individual decisions. However, our experience has shown that a systematic approach to environmental purchasing is necessary if real progress is to be made.

ESTABLISH AN ENVIRONMENTAL PURCHASING POLICY

Environmental purchasing should be rooted in an official policy decision endorsed by senior management. An environmental purchasing policy, which commits your organisation to buying goods and services with a reduced environmental impact and sets out objectives by which this will be achieved, should be circulated widely (see Chapter 9 for more details on policy formulation).

IDENTIFY AREAS OF MAXIMUM IMPACT

Review your general areas of purchasing. Concentrate your efforts on the goods and services which have the greatest

Case Study

Subject –	**PURCHASING GUIDE**
Organisation –	**CAMBRIDGESHIRE COUNTY COUNCIL**
Organisation type –	**LOCAL GOVERNMENT**
Location –	**CAMBRIDGESHIRE**
No. of staff –	**N/A**

ACTION / RESULTS

The finished guide included general purchasing principles which can be applied to any product, and specific products which were organised into the following subject areas:

❑ waste disposal;
❑ paper;
❑ general stationery;
❑ toner cartridges;
❑ furniture;
❑ cleaning;
❑ grounds maintenance; and
❑ catering.

Environmental issues relating to these subjects were identified along with a description of relevant industry standards and labelling schemes. The Guide also gave a brief description of the market for environmentally preferable alternatives in each of the subject areas, suppliers selling such products and an indication of their prices relative to normal purchases. Sources of further information were also provided.

BACKGROUND

Cambridgeshire County Council spent £95 million on goods and services in 1995. It recognised the potential environmental impact of this spend and has developed a programme to reduce the impacts of the products and services that it buys in.

Cambridgeshire County Council has an objective to reduce its use of products which damage the environment by contributing to global atmospheric pollution, local pollution, deforestation and the depletion of natural resources.

ACTION

In order to put its objectives into practice, the Council commissioned Wastebusters to develop a Purchasing Guide to be used by approximately 500 budget holders (including 300 schools) within the authority.

The project aimed to provide a simple environmental purchasing guide to officers making general purchasing decisions about items such as office products, furniture, cleaning products and paper. It was intended that the guide would require its users to have little or no environmental awareness and provide them with clear guidance on what to look for when making decisions.

environmental impact. As a rule of thumb environmental impacts can be associated with purchasing spend; identify your ten most expensive items/areas of highest expenditure and start there. Staff or stakeholders may also have issues in mind; it is important to consider their views.

PLAN WHAT TO TACKLE FIRST

Use your review of maximum impacts to prioritise the areas that you will tackle first. It can be a good policy to tackle easy hits early in the process. For instance, paper is a high profile area of purchasing, a decision to purchase recycled paper can be an effective and relatively easy first achievement.

COMMUNICATE YOUR PLANS

Communicate your policy and priorities for change to all staff involved (see Chapter 8 for further details). Many initiatives fail due to a lack of communication, which can leave a pile of nicely presented environmental purchasing policy documents forgotten in a cupboard! Any policy should be a working document.

The implementation of an environmental purchasing policy may require training for staff involved; providing your staff with the best quality information and support is the most effective way of ensuring success (see Chapter 8 for further details).

Partnership Sourcing

Communicate with your suppliers, tell them what you intend to do and ask for their suggestions as to how they can help. The principle of partnership sourcing is to work with your suppliers to jointly develop environmental performance towards a goal of continuous improvement. This approach can be very successful. For example, the development of a partnership approach between Ernst & Young and Bovis Lelliot (fabric maintenance contractors) has resulted in significant waste reduction, cost savings and improved control (see Chapter 6). As an extension of your own environmental policy, it is important to request environmental statements from your suppliers.

INTEGRATE INTO YOUR PURCHASING STRUCTURE

The most effective way of improving the environmental performance of your purchasing is to work within your existing purchasing structure.

COMMON PROBLEMS

Information Overload!

❑ Questionnaires can produce large quantities of information which need to be managed and integrated into existing purchasing structures.

❑ Processing the information you gather can represent a significant cost in terms of staff commitment which should be recognised when deciding on your approach.

Using and Managing Information

❑ Many companies spend time and money gathering information with questionnaires but are then not sure how to use that information. Once the process has started, information needs to be managed, updated and used to inform decision making on an ongoing basis. Before you decide to use questionnaires think how your purchasing decision making will be affected by the results. If you will not use the information you gather, do not gather it.

PURCHASING SERVICES

Where an organisation does not have a formal purchasing structure, design minimum environmental standards for different priority areas and integrate these into tender documentation. Your environmental policy and minimum environmental standards must be included in pre-tender or briefing documents as well as final tender and contract documentation.

Supplier Assessment Questionnaires

Supplier assessment questionnaires are a widely used method of gathering information about the environmental performance of suppliers. Use by several large companies in the UK such as British Airports Authority, B&Q and the Body Shop has led to their adoption by a number of smaller organisations.

Questionnaires can work on two levels: firstly by asking general questions about the environmental management practice of a supplier and secondly by asking specific questions about the environmental performance of products and services. Questionnaires can also serve to send a strong message to your suppliers as to the value of the environment to your organisation and can be used to promote improved environmental performance.

Organisations with a formal quality management standard such as BS 5750 or ISO 9000 are committed to assessing and registering their suppliers. In these cases it is logical to integrate environmental criteria into the normal supplier assessment process so that environmental information can be held on a database along with general supplier information. This information can then be used to evaluate the relative environmental performance of suppliers in order to inform the tender process outlined above. The formal *environmental* management systems (see Chapter 9) have a requirement to assess the environmental impacts of suppliers.

Contract Specification

Another method of integrating environmental information into purchasing structures is to determine minimum environmental standards and write these in to contract documentation. If you integrate environmental criteria into your contracts you have a binding legal agreement that commits suppliers to meeting your environmental standards.

Encouraging suppliers to adopt recognised environmental management systems during the course of a contract can be another way of promoting good practice (see Chapter 9).

SUMMARY GUIDELINES

- ❑ Recognise the importance of purchasing to your environmental performance.
- ❑ Identify areas of purchasing with high environmental impacts.
- ❑ Plan your purchasing strategy to fit within existing structures.
- ❑ Identify the approach that will be most effective for you.
- ❑ Use purchasing tools to help identify environmentally preferable alternatives.

CATERING AND CLEANING

Environmental Issues

There is a strong link between health, safety and environmental issues, all of which must be considered when assessing cleaning contracts. Cleaning substances can represent significant health and safety risks and if released into watercourses in sufficient quantities these substances can harm plant and animal life.

Encouraging your cleaning and catering contractors to select more environmentally benign substances reduces environmental effects and health and safety risks. The major concerns are the use of acids, alkalis, bleaches and solvents (particularly if mixed). All of these cause air and water pollution, so correct disposal is important. Disposal of these substances to drain may require a licence from your local water company (depending on the concentration).

ACIDS

Acids are widely used in cleaning products, most commonly hydrochloric and phosphoric. Dilution of acids with water produces heat as a by-product which can lead to an explosive reaction. Acids should always be added to water, not vice versa. If any acid is mixed with an alkali (also used in cleaning products) a reaction occurs which may be explosive. If acid is added to bleach the poisonous gas chlorine is released which is hazardous to health.

ALKALIS

Alkalis are often found in cleaning products used for dishwashing machines, removing greasy deposits, paint stripping and as concrete cleaners. Common alkalis are: sodium hydroxide (caustic soda), sodium metasilicate and borax (sodium borate decahydrate); and bleach (see below). Alkaline substances can be carefully diluted with water but should not be mixed with acids as this may cause an explosive reaction.

BLEACH

Bleach is a strongly alkaline solution of sodium hypochlorite in water. It can cause harm to human and animal health (if ingested) and to ecosystems if released in a concentrated form. Bleach should not be mixed with any other cleaning compounds and should only be diluted with water.

SOLVENTS

Solvents cause the emission of volatile organic compounds (VOCs) which contribute to photochemical smog, are low level air pollutants and also act as ozone depleters. Solvents retain their hazardous properties when mixed with other substances, they are used in many cleaning preparations and pose special problems – their volatility can lead to skin damage and rapid absorption into the body. Some are highly flammable and most can be decomposed by heat into highly toxic products. They are used in pure form for specialist tasks, for example, chewing gum removal.

PHOSPHATES

Phosphates are an environmental concern, but do not have health and safety implications. They are used in dishwasher powders, multipurpose cleaning agents and scouring cleaners. Phosphates can cause eutrophication, this occurs when an excess of nutrients (such as phosphates) enter a water course or body and over-enrich the water. This enrichment causes an explosion in the growth of algae (blooming) which consume any available oxygen and threaten plant and animal life. Algal blooms can also lead to the production of foul-smelling substances such as hydrogen sulphide and ammonia; the resulting water cannot be used for human consumption and can provide a threat to human life.

NTA AND EDTA

NTA and EDTA are phosphate substitutes. NTA (nitrolotri acetate) is carcinogenic and teratogenic (causing foetal abnormalities). NTA combines with toxic metals already in the environment and remobilises them, which can result in them being passed into drinking water or food, especially fish and shellfish. EDTA (ethylene diamine-tetra-acetate) causes similar problems.

PACKAGING AND DISPOSAL

In addition to the products used, packaging material relating cleaning products also has an environmental impact.

PRACTICAL ACTION

Alternative Cleaning Products

Cleaning contractors often provide their own cleaning products, but it is important to establish the following:

❑ Material type and selection – find out which substances are used on-site and the environmental criteria used for product selection. The range of products should be kept to a minimum to reduce health and safety risks and administration under COSHH (Control of Substances Hazardous to Health).
❑ Hazard identification – replace hazardous materials with less hazardous alternatives such as water based products to reduce environmental impact and health and safety risks.

Reducing the Impact of Packaging

❑ Use concentrates.
❑ Use refillable containers.
❑ Use packaging material made from recycled material.

Washroom Consumables

❑ Use toilet paper and hand towels made from recycled material.
❑ There is no consensus on the life-cycle assessment of hot air dryers versus using towels, on balance, the overall environmental impact is similar.
❑ Use refuse sacks manufactured from recycled plastic.

Catering Supplies

Disposables

There is a problem with the use of recycled materials for food hygiene products due to the risk of residual contamination. On average, disposable catering products contain 30 per cent recycled material, but this tends to be recycled at source, that is, at the production stage. Plates can be manufactured from recycled paper and card, but need to be given a thicker coating of plastic which rather defeats the object of recycling. A more practical option is to reduce the usage of disposables and extend the use of recycled products.

There are a number of products commonly used within catering which can be replaced with environmentally preferable options:

- ❑ Individual milk and cream cartons (jiggers), designed for single use, create unnecessary packaging. Phase them out and use jugs where possible. Coasters can also be dispensed with.
- ❑ An in-house water purification system is a cost-effective alternative to buying in mineral water and can produce still and sparkling water. This means bottles can be re-used instead of being recycled.
- ❑ Takeaway bags can be manufactured from recycled Kraft paper. This is acceptable since they are secondary packaging and not in direct contact with the food. Encourage re-use: for example, you could credit staff for returned takeaway bags.
- ❑ Serviettes are available manufactured from recycled material.

PRINTING

Legislation

Printworks come under local authority air pollution contro under the Environmental Protection Act 1990 because of th potential for solvent emissions to air. The Act introduced a ne system of pollution control which recognised that emissions t one medium (air/water etc.) can have an effect upon anothe The Act authorised a range of 'prescribed processes an substances'; highly polluting industries are covered by Part and regulated by the Environment Agency via Integrate Pollution Control. Part B processes are regulated under loc authority air pollution control. Printing is a prescribed proce under Part B if 20 tonnes or more of printing ink or met coatings, or 25 tonnes or more of organic solvents are used any 12 month period.

Environmental Issues

PRINTING PROCESSES

The main environmental issue associated with printi processes is the use of organic solvents. Organic solvent u gives rise to the release of VOCs, major ozone depleti substances (see Solvent section in Catering and Cleanir

Case Study

Subject –	**WASTE REDUCTION**
Organisation –	**ROWE & MAW**
Organisation type –	**SOLICITORS**
Location –	**LONDON**
No. of staff –	**360**

BACKGROUND

Approximately 6750 bottles of mineral water for client use in junction and meeting rooms were being purchased per annum, at an estimated cost of £3614. Approximately 1200 bottles of wine were purchased per annum. All this glass was sent to landfill.

A water purification system had already been installed for staff use only. This is plumbed into the local water supply and provides still and sparkling water on-site. The bottles used are supplied with lids and can be sterilised and re-used.

This had resulted in savings of £1,886 per annum on mineral water and substantially reduced the volume of glass going to landfill.

ACTION / RESULTS

The system has now been extended to include in-house bottled water for client use resulting in:

- ☐ further cost savings of £3,614 on bought in mineral water;
- ☐ a substantial reduction in glass going to landfill: wine bottles are also being collected and recycled;
- ☐ reduction in waste disposal costs;
- ☐ the opportunity to promote a strong environmental message to clients;
- ☐ efficient use of resources; and
- ☐ total savings due to the introduction of the in-house water purification system are in excess of £5,500.

Case Study

Subject –	**PURCHASING AND WASTE REDUCTION**
Organisation –	**ROYAL ORDNANCE DIVISION – BRITISH AEROSPACE DEFENCE**
Organisation type –	**DEFENCE**
Location –	**CHORLEY, LANCASHIRE**
No. of staff –	**180**

RESULTS

- ❏ Reduced wastage and volume of waste sent to landfill.
- ❏ Reduced demand for raw materials in manufacture.
- ❏ Reduction in waste disposal costs and re-use of resources.
- ❏ Improved perception for staff and visitors.
- ❏ Saving in purchase of packs of £990 pa.

BACKGROUND

The Royal Ordnance site at Chorley consists of office building spread out across a large site, making the provision of caterin difficult. The catering department is housed in a separat building, and meals for functions were transported in airlin packs to the various meeting rooms. Approximately 250 airlin packs were used per month for serving buffet lunches at certai functions. These cost 33p each, a total of £990 pa.

The multi compartment food trays:

- ❏ create unnecessary packaging;
- ❏ are unappealing and perceived as extremely wasteful by many employees – many staff visit the head office for meetings;
- ❏ are disposed of after use as general waste;
- ❏ are not made from recycled material and are not recyclabl and
- ❏ come in packs which contain disposable cutlery, also thrown out as general waste.

ACTION

The airline packs were replaced with china plates/platters a non-disposable cutlery. Crockery used is returned for washi up to the central kitchen.

PROCESS	DESCRIPTION	TYPICAL USE	VOC SOURCES
Flexography (includes letterpress)	Relief letterpress printing using rubber rollers or photopolymer plates on presses	For packaging, eg print on cartons and labels	VOC forming solvent based inks
Lithography (offset)	Flat surface process where only image areas of printing plate attract the ink. Uses alcohol or water based fountain solution	Corporate print: brochures, annual reports. Magazine and newspaper production	VOC forming solvent based cleaning products Isopropyl or other solvent in fountain solution – magazine printing VOC forming solvent based inks
Gravure	Recesses on a printing cylinder are filled with ink which is then 'lifted' by contact with the paper	Long run printing eg magazines and catalogues (This process is only used by a few large magazine printers who are already capturing and recycling solvent emissions)	VOC forming solvent based inks
Screen	Ink is squeezed through a stencil and applied to the printing substrate	Posters, fabrics/textiles	VOC forming solvent based inks

hapter 4). Printworks account for approximately 10 per cent
the 379,000 tonnes of VOCs emitted in 1995 by industry.
he UK is committed to cut its VOC emissions by 30 per cent
 1999 from an 1988 baseline. The Department of the
nvironment estimates that emissions from the printing sector
ill fall from 41,000 to 21,000 tonnes by 1999 (ENDS, 1996a).
 Volatile organic compound emissions arise in printing from:
ks and ink thinning, press cleaning and washing, pre-print
ess cleaning and reclamation processes and the use of alcohol
sed solvents (see Table 5.1). Organic solvents are also used in
her printing processes to clean ink off the presses after print
ns. Ninety per cent of lithographic printers still use isopropyl
:ohol in fountain solutions (ENDS, 1 1996).

▪KS

ks are comprised of pigments, solvents and oil. Solvent based
ks are a source of VOCs. Some inks have been especially
:mulated to resist dispersion in water which can cause
blems when printed material is de-inked as part of the

TABLE 5.1

Printing processes and sources of VOC emissions

recycling process. Pigments may also contain heavy metals such as lead, which can be harmful to human health and the environment. Other metals are also used in printing inks; in sufficient quantities, these metals can be harmful to flora and fauna

Lithographic inks are traditionally based on mineral oils, a non-renewable resource.

Any product which relies on evaporation for drying purposes is a potential source of VOCs, this includes heatset, flexographic, gravure and screen printing inks.

PRACTICAL ACTION

Ask Your Printer for Environmentally Preferable Alternatives

Printing involves a series of complex interactions between inks, processes and specific outputs. It is therefore difficult to draw together specific environmental best practice standards for inks and printing as these may not apply to the specific job you may require. Nevertheless, the following sets out the types of products that are currently available. It is important to discuss environmental issues with your printer; they should:

❑ be aware of the environmental effects of their business;
❑ be making steps to minimise and manage their effects; and
❑ be able to demonstrate an ongoing commitment to using non- solvent based solutions and inks.

Many printers who comply with legislation will already be demonstrating good practice. Make sure that you encourage them to push the boundaries to develop best practice (see Beacon Press Case Study in Chapter 9).

As a consumer of a service you have buying power. Printers should be keen to respond to enquiries and customer requests. If you feel that they are not keeping you abreast of the latest developments you do not have to continue using them. The BBC has integrated environmental specifications into its design guidelines for corporate publications. This includes the introduction of minimum performance standards for external printing companies.

Printing

Press Washes

In the past year interest has been shown in citrus fruit based solvents. However, they have not been widely used because their smell becomes sickly with ongoing use and they have been implicated as possible carcinogens.

Chemically modified vegetable oil based washes are available from most suppliers, they are effective but can be disliked by press operators. Such products are widely used in Germany, Scandinavia and the USA but it may take legislative pressure to force their use in the UK.

Low viscosity solvent washes provide an environmentally preferable alternative to traditional products as they emit few or no VOCs. A solvent free water based cleaner is also available (ENDS, 1996a).

Fountain Solutions

Used in lithographic printing, fountain solutions are the largest source of VOCs. Vegetable oil based alternatives have not sold well to date because printers feel they do not perform as well as alcohol based solutions. Solutions containing high boiling alcohols which do not evaporate as easily as traditional solutions and thus release less VOCs are widely used in Denmark and Italy.

Waterless litho technology, which uses high viscosity inks and results in a reduction in waste paper production and ink use is widespread in the USA (ENDS, 1996a).

Inks

Environmentally preferable inks exclude heavy metals and have low solvent content (most water based products contain only 5–8 per cent of organic solvent). Water based and UV curing inks emit no VOCs, either during manufacture or when used by the printer. Inks are also available based on rape seed or soya bean oil in place of mineral oil, thus maximising use of renewable resources.

VOC control can be avoided with the use of flexographic inks formulated for drying using ultraviolet light. However, UV curing lamps give rise to low level ozone emissions which can cause or exacerbate respiratory illness.

SUMMARY GUIDELINES

- ❏ Obtain details of the environmental policy of your printer or any printer you expect to use.
- ❏ Ensure that your printer has a policy for reducing VOC forming solvent use and can demonstrate achievements.
- ❏ Integrate a requirement to use the most environmentally preferable processes, inks, solutions and washes in tender documentation.
- ❏ Encourage your printer to maximise the use of non-solvent based fountain solutions, press washes and inks.
- ❏ Encourage your printer to maximise the use of inks that do not contain heavy metals where available.
- ❏ Encourage your printer to communicate with their suppliers to ensure that they are kept up to date on, and supplied with, the latest environmentally preferable products and raw materials.
- ❏ Ensure that your printer keeps you up to date with the latest developments in solvent reduction and replacement.
- ❏ Remember that as a consumer of a service you have buying power.

GROUNDS MAINTENANCE

Developing good practice for the management of grounds, parks, and playing fields promotes a strong environmental message to the public, staff and pupils. Enhancing the wildlife value of grounds, and plants, whether indoor or outdoor, can provide a useful way of making people think about their connections with the environment. Though many offices do not have large areas of grounds, many have indoor plants and may even have small outside areas that could be enhanced with a pond or wildlife area. Encouraging wildlife value is also increasingly important to schools and local authorities; as the guardians of areas of park, grounds and countryside, they have a responsibility to develop and promote best practice.

Environmental Issues

CHEMICAL USE

The main environmental issue associated with purchasing products for grounds maintenance is chemical use. Herbicides and pesticides, if inappropriately chosen and used, can provide a major threat to plant, animal and bird species. The use of pesticides such as DDT earlier this century passed poisons into the food chain, from grass and vegetation to insects, mice and rabbits and eventually to higher predators. Such chemicals have been blamed for the decline in populations of peregrine falcons and other birds of prey. Poisons were passed to the bird through eating prey that had eaten crops and vegetation sprayed with DDT. Although its effects were not immediately fatal, DDT acted by weakening the birds' egg walls so that eggs were frequently broken before the chick had fully developed.

Pesticides and herbicides can wash into watercourses through surface water drainage during rain and can damage both water quality and biodiversity.

The World Wide Fund for Nature (WWF) has recently (September 1996) called for a phase-out of several chemical pesticides which are thought to mimic oestrogen in the environment and contribute to: reproductive cancers, declining sperm counts and retarded child development. Chemicals specifically mentioned include permethrin, linuron, lindane and endosulfan, which are agricultural chemicals but may have been used in rare cases for grounds maintenance. The WWF report 'Pesticides posing hazards to reproduction' highlights the danger of all chemical use: long term and contributory effects are regularly discovered and concerns have been raised about the long term effects on the human endocrine system.

PEAT

The use of peat for horticulture and grounds maintenance has become an issue of major environmental concern; lowland raised peat bogs are those which are most threatened at present. Many bogs, including those being actively used for peat extraction, are sites of national and international wildlife importance. Extraction of peat for commercial purposes is the single biggest threat to peat bogs in Britain.

Groups such as Friends of the Earth and conservation bodies such as English Nature have made progress in protecting sensitive areas of peatland but the main opportunity to reduce the threat is to find alternatives and to encourage their use.

Do it yourself stores such as B&Q have also made progress in introducing growing media utilising peat free alternatives and have had some success at encouraging customer take up through education and competitive pricing. The quality of peat free compost has grown dramatically since the early 1990s. Alternatives to peat compost include:

- bark chips;
- cocoa shell mulch;
- coir (derived from coconuts);
- spent mushroom compost; and
- composted green waste.

The Government's White Paper *Making Waste Work* (DoE, 1995) estimates that between 2.5 and 5 million tonnes of green waste is produced in England and Wales each year. The Government has set targets for composting green waste, some of which will involve the participation of local authorities and all of which will increase the availability of non-peat based compost.

NATURAL FEATURES

Hedgerows

In wildlife conservation terms, hedgerows provide two main functions for the animals which are associated with them: they

THE GOVERNMENT'S TARGETS FOR COMPOSTING

- ❑ 'To recycle or compost 25% of household waste by the year 2000.
- ❑ 40% of domestic properties with a garden to carry out composting by the year 2000.
- ❑ All waste disposal authorities to cost and consider the potential for establishing central composting schemes by the end of 1997.
- ❑ Easily accessible recycling facilities for 80 per cent of households by the year 2000.
- ❑ One million tonnes of organic household waste to be composted by the year 2001' (DoE, 1995).

provide a place for nesting and a place for feeding. Birds and invertebrates will nest in the hedge itself but equally important are the associated banks, ditches and verges which provide a home for small mammals, amphibians, reptiles, birds, insects and other invertebrate groups.

Hedges also provide a refuge for plants. Some of our older hedges contain plants that are usually only found in woodlands such as bluebells and wood anemones. Verges and ditches may also contain plants that are relics of the flower-rich pastures that were once commonplace in the UK.

Weeds

Weeds can be a nuisance and in certain circumstances a safety hazard. However, they are often a valuable resource for wildlife. Ragwort is the food plant of the cinnabar moth, and the caterpillars of four of our most popular butterflies feed on nettles (comma, peacock, small tortoiseshell and red admiral). Patches of nettles in sunny, sheltered spots are particularly valuable.

Trees and Shrubs

Although beds of exotic plants can look extremely attractive in urban areas, choice of appropriate species is extremely important, particularly in rural areas. Non-native tree and shrub species can be invasive and take over areas of ground, pushing out existing species. Native species also support more types of insects than non-native ones because insects have evolved with those trees and shrubs over time. The more insects a species supports, the more types of birds and animals are also supported. Planting carefully selected trees and shrubs will give great benefits to wildlife and the landscape.

Mowing Road Verges

Repeated cutting of vegetation tends to produce a sward (vegetation cover) of fairly uniform structure and composition with an excess of bulky, competitive perennials. If cuttings are left on site then smaller plants may be smothered. Furthermore, as cuttings rot down, the soil becomes enriched with nutrients which increases the cover of a few of the bulkiest, most competitive plants at the expensive of the variety of less competitive ones.

Grasslands, however, provide more than just a home for plants. Birds may nest on the ground between March and July

Butterflies such as the marbled white will feed on nectar plants such as scabious and knapweed in the summer but the caterpillars rely on long grass during the winter and spring. Rough grass, especially in the winter, is a valuable habitat in its own right.

Parks and Recreation Grounds

The issues surrounding management practice on parks and recreation grounds combine all the activities detailed above.

Safety and amenity should also always be combined with conservation and public enjoyment.

As with mowing grass verges, the value of grass often lies with both its structural diversity and species composition. Many species, such as the marbled white mentioned above, rely on different components within grassland during different times of year. Areas of long grass are vital in the winter for over-wintering insects (including butterfly eggs and larvae) and in the summer for ground nesting birds. Shorter areas in which flowers are promoted will provide valuable nectar sources for butterflies, bees and other insects. In order to promote this a relaxation of mowing during the spring and summer is all that is required – even raising the cutter bar will allow some plants to flower. This may also save a great deal of money, one city council spends an estimated £500,000 per year on grass cutting.

LEGISLATION

Chemical Use

Chemicals for use within grounds maintenance have become more tightly controlled in recent years. The Control of Pesticides Regulations 1996 covers the advertisement, sale, storage and use of pesticides and two statutory codes of practice under the Regulations define procedures for pesticide suppliers for their safe use.

Management Practice

The following list of legislation covers work which may come within grounds maintenance contracts; some legislation covers work within different areas. It should not be taken as an exhaustive list:

IDEAL PARKS WILL HAVE
☐ thick, tall hedges; ☐ plenty of mature trees (which should keep rotten hollows and fissured bark); ☐ borders of long grass; and ☐ patches of native scrub and an abundance of nectar-producing plants in areas where fertilisers and herbicides are not applied.

❏ 1979 Wildlife and Countryside Act – protects certain species (eg badgers and nesting birds) from disturbance.
❏ 1994 European Community Species and Habitats Directive – protects breeding or hibernation sites of certain species.
❏ 1959 Weeds Act – requires landowners to control creeping and spear thistle, broadleaved dock and ragwort, where they pose the threat of spreading on to neighbouring land. Always clear away treated or cut ragwort where livestock are grazing – this poisonous plant becomes palatable when dead or dying.
❏ Plant Protection Products Regulations 1995 (incorporates EC Directive 91/414/EEC 'Authorisations').
❏ Control of Substances Hazardous to Health Regulations (COSHH) 1988.

PRACTICAL ACTION

GOOD PRACTICE IN GROUNDS MAINTENANCE

Chemical Use

Non-residual chemicals are essential to avoid the build up of harmful chemicals on the ground or within plants and animals.

A contact weed wiper, through which herbicide is directly applied to specific plants, is an accurate method of herbicide application and avoids the danger to other plants, animals and humans that can occur through the drifting of chemicals from spraying. If spraying does take place, the wind should never be above force 2.

The Ministry of Agriculture, Fisheries and Food recommends that, because the use of pesticides involves risks to human health and wildlife and may also lead to pesticide resistance and damage to crops, they should only be used when absolutely necessary. They also suggest that these steps should be followed:

❏ The weed and its potential impact are properly identified.
❏ The possibility for alternative forms of control have been considered.
❏ An assessment of how effective pesticide application will be – can it be applied at the right time? Is it likely to cause pesticide resistance?

Management Practice

The following suggestions for good practice concentrate on maximising the ecological value and biodiversity of ground features.

Hedgerows

❑ Trimming: never cut before the end of July, you may be prosecuted under the Wildlife and Countryside Act if nesting birds are disturbed. Preferably cut in January/February after berries have gone. Ideally, unless there is a specific pest problem, trim every second or third year – try to leave sections uncut, especially at hedge junctions.

❑ Verge cutting: never cut or spray underneath the hedge. Always try to leave a 2 m verge along the length of the hedge. Unless safety implications necessitate regular cutting always cut reasonably high as soil disturbance often perpetuates problem weeds. If weeds are a problem, cut two or three times a year, but never between March and July. Where weeds are not a problem leave some parts rough as over-wintering or hibernation areas for species such as frogs, toads, hedgehogs and butterfly larvae.

❑ Management of standards: remember the value of dead wood. If large trees become a safety hazard – is it possible to pollard or trim rather than remove them? If there are no standards (trees which are larger than the surrounding vegetation), can some hedge plants be marked and left to grow on?

❑ Regenerating hedgerows: eventually, with time and in the absence of management, hedges can become leggy and gappy at the bottom – some bushes grow into trees, others die. At this stage, it is often better to rejuvenate the hedge by coppicing or laying. This sort of management can appear quite destructive to the inexperienced eye but it promotes vigorous new growth. It is therefore always best to tackle small areas at a time, and leave some trees as standards. Make sure the local community is informed as to why the work is being done.

Weed Control

Ask the following questions before taking action:

❏ Do the weeds really present an eyesore or a safety hazard?

❏ Can a strimmer or brush-cutter be used?

❏ Where herbicide must be applied (eg to maintain safe pathways), use non-residual, translocated herbicides. Can you use a contact weed-wiper rather than a spray?

Trees and Shrubs

Select species to match those in the local area. Many nurseries are now providing mixtures of native trees – if you can't find one, try the British Trust for Conservation Volunteers (BTCV). Some shrubs (eg buckthorn) can harbour cereal pests and ideally should not be planted in abundance close to arable land. Slow growing shrubs such as crab apple, field maple and hawthorn require less maintenance than fast growing trees.

Establishment maintenance is important in the first year or two. Saplings suffer from competition with other species (root competition is particularly severe) and will establish much more readily in bare ground. Mulch mats (plastic or natural straw mulch) provide an alternative to herbicide use and help to protect the young trees from being shaded out by weed and bramble growth. Strips of polythene are available for hedge planting.

When planting new hedgerows, the Royal Society for the Protection of Birds (RSPB) recommends planting on a bank 1 m wide and 0.3 m high (as it will eventually become a better habitat for ground nesting birds). A staggered double row will give denser growth, providing better cover for wildlife. Regular topping in the first few years helps to promote bushy growth.

If you are considering removing a tree ask yourself the following questions:

❏ Does the tree pose a genuine threat to safety?

❏ If so, can careful trimming by a qualified tree surgeon remove any danger?

❏ If the tree is an old pollard with a hollow trunk, can the tree be re-pollarded? (Remember that if a tree has not been pollarded for many years, the shock of re-pollarding can often kill it. The risk is reduced if some of the limbs are left on and removed two or three years later.)

Mowing Road Verges

❑ Safety first: obviously, some verges have to be cut regularly to maintain visibility.

❑ Remove nutrients: wherever possible (and it isn't often possible) remove the cuttings to prevent smothering and nutrient enrichment (as this will favour the more competitive species which will slowly push out weaker ones). This is particularly important on verges that have a number of flowering plants. Never apply fertilisers or herbicides of any kind. Green waste removed from mowing and maintenance can be composted and used in areas where nutrients are required (see Chapter 3).

❑ Delay cutting: try not to cut between March and July whilst birds are breeding and butterflies are on the wing. Some verges will be fertile and produce vast amounts of coarse growth – these may need to be cut more regularly. Verges on poor soils (eg sand, chalk or very wet areas) usually contain more plants and will need cutting less frequently – perhaps only once or twice a year.

❑ Avoid disturbing the ground: although some annual species are becoming rare and rely on a continual supply of bare ground, accidental soil disturbance by mechanical cutting usually causes soil compaction and often promotes the growth of vigorous annual and biennial weeds. If adjustable, set the cutter high – at least 10 cm.

❑ Create structural diversity: many birds, small mammals, butterflies and other invertebrates need long grass, particularly during the winter. Always try to leave some reasonably large areas uncut each year (these can be left as strips or patches). If areas are being cut early, can the half on the side away from the road be left, then both halves cut later (after July)?

❑ Special cases: in certain areas distinctive regional floras have developed under particular management regimes. Specific examples include hedgebank verges in Devon where woodland-type flora is maintained by early cutting, or on sandy, coastal areas where unusual plants such as heath and common spotted orchids flourish in drainage ditches on the verges. If you have specialist communities (almost always associated with poor soils – either very wet, very acid or very calcareous) – then you

SUMMARY GUIDELINES

- ❑ Avoid the use of chemicals.
- ❑ Avoid the use of peat.
- ❑ Encourage organic methods.
- ❑ Where chemical use is necessary follow good practice guidelines.
- ❑ Promote biodiversity by removing nutrients from site, encouraging native species and avoiding soil disturbance.
- ❑ Use the advice of experts such as your local Wildlife Trust or County
- ❑ Ecologist for specific sites.
- ❑ Integrate best practice standards into your grounds maintenance contracts.
- ❑ Avoid trimming and cutting between March and July.

CHAPTER SUMMARY

- ❑ Conduct training seminars for staff purchasing goods and services with significant environmental impacts, in most offices this will be waste management and purchasing teams.
- ❑ Integrate environmental criteria into all purchasing decisions.
- ❑ Include environmental criteria in tender documents.
- ❑ Include environmental criteria in contractors' specifications.
- ❑ Include environmental criteria in performance targets.

should always seek advice from the County Council Ecologist or your local Wildlife Trust.

Parks and Recreation Grounds

Try working with the County Ecologist – perhaps producing a brief management plan for the best sites (which need be no more than two pages and a map). These should detail the conservation work planned over the forthcoming five to ten year period. Sites where this extra effort will bring greatest benefits include those adjacent to existing nature reserves or woodlands, and historic sites where relict flora often holds on in discreet corners or even on the walls of crumbling ruins. Promote organic methods; further information on organic gardening can be obtained from the Henry Doubleday Research Association, details can be found in the Directory.

Sources of Information

General Sources of Help and Information

ASSOCIATION OF METROPOLITAN AUTHORITIES (AMA)
35 Great Smith Street
Westminster
London SW1P 3BJ
Tel: 0171 222 8100
Fax: 0171 222 0878

THE CHARTERED INSTITUTE OF PURCHASING AND SUPPLY
Easton House
Easton on the Hill
Stamford
Lincs PE9 3NZ
Tel: 01780 56777
Fax: 01780 519610

ENDS
Environmental Data Services
Finsbury Business Centre
40 Bowling Green Lane
London EC1R 0NE
Tel: 0171 278 4745/7624
Fax: 0171 415 0106

THE GROUNDWORK FOUNDATION
Groundwork National Office
85–87 Cornwall Street
Birmingham B3 3BY
Tel: 0121 236 8565
Fax: 0121 236 7356

LOCAL GOVERNMENT MANAGEMENT BOARD (LGMB)
Layden House
76 Turnmill Street
London EC1M 5QV
Tel: 0171 296 6600
Fax: 0171 296 6666

WORLD BUSINESS COUNCIL FOR SUSTAINABLE DEVELOPMENT (WBCSD)
160 route de Florissant
CH-1231 Conches
Geneva
Switzerland
Tel: +41 22 839 3100
Fax +41 22 839 3131

Grounds Maintenance and Composting

HENRY DOUBLEDAY RESEARCH ASSOCIATION
Ryton Organic Gardens
Ryton-on-Dunsmore
Coventry CV8 3LG
Tel: 01203 303517
Fax: 01203 639 229

ECO COMPOSTING LTD
Chapel Lane
Parley
Christchurch
Dorset BH23 6BG
Tel/Fax: 01202 593601

Printing

ANDERSON FRASER PUBLISHING
96 York Way
London N1 9AG
Tel: 0171 833 7700

BEACON PRESS
Beacon Print Ltd
Brambleside
Bellbrook Park
Uckfield
East Sussex TN22 1PL
Tel: 01825 786611

GIBBON INKS AND COATINGS
3 High View Road
South Normington
Derbyshire DE55 2DT
Tel: 01773 813704

6: Building and Energy Management

INTRODUCTION

Buildings are responsible for about 50 per cent of the UK annual emissions of carbon dioxide. Therefore, your office represents a significant proportion of the environmental impacts of your organisation, particularly if you are in the service sector, where the core business is office based. Sound office practice needs to be considered in the assessment of overall corporate environmental performance. The Building Research Establishment recognises the environmental impact of buildings in their environmental assessment method – the Building Research Establishment Environmental Assessment Method (BREEAM).

You should be aware that there are legislative requirements which apply to the management of your building. These include: the Duty of Care and Special Waste Regulations, the Montreal Protocol and the COSHH Regulations. Many areas of the building management function are frequently contracted out; you must make sure that your contractors are complying with these regulations on your behalf.

A refurbishment programme provides an excellent opportunity to invest in new technology for an energy-efficient building. Office equipment is an area of high energy use. It also has health and safety risks which need to be minimised. Energy efficiency measures have clear commercial and environmental benefits.

There is often room for improved management control

An A-Z of Employment Law
A Complete Reference Source for Managers
Second Edition
by Peter Chandler

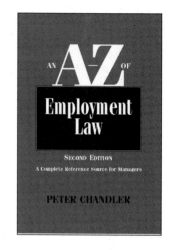

With all the new EC directives coming into force lately, employers are raising questions such as:

- Can employees agree to work more than an average 48-hour week?
- How must an employer accommodate disabled employees?
- What are the new rules for employing under-18's?

For the answers to these - and hundreds of other questions - employers need look no further than the new edition of *An A-Z of Employment Law*. This established reference guide is now in its second edition and has been updated to include all recent regulations and laws as well as giving valuable advice on important topics such as: disciplinary rules; contracts of employment; redundancy; sexual harassment; strikes and many more relevant issues.

With an index of useful address and advice about alternative sources of information within its pages, *An A-Z of Employment Law* is a reference book which must be the desktop companion of every UK employer as well as students of industrial relations law.

An A-Z of Employment Law
£45.00 Hardback 600 pages
ISBN 0 7494 2443 5
Published 1997
Order No: KT443

Available from all good bookshops or direct from the publisher:
Kogan Page
120 Pentonville Road
London N1 9JN
Customer Services Tel: 0171 278 0545 Fax: 0171 278 8198
e-mail: kpinfo@kogan-page.co.uk

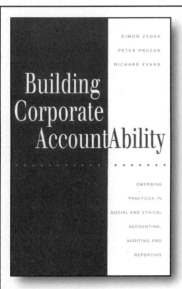

particularly in the areas of fabric maintenance and refurbishment programmes. You may have a purchasing policy in which the use of unsustainably produced wood for your furniture requirements is banned, but has this been communicated to your fabric maintenance contractors? Fabric maintenance can represent significant loopholes in your overall environmental policy. Be aware of what is purchased on your behalf (see Chapter 5).

Improved control is cost effective both for yourselves and your contractors. The introduction of effective waste reduction measures, such as donating obsolete furniture to charity, can reduce the volume of material going into the builder's skip. Accurate assessment of the volume of raw materials needed can reduce waste.

INDUSTRY STANDARDS

Building Research Establishment Environmental Assessment Method (BREEAM)

BREEAM is a method of assessing the environmental quality of buildings. It is operated by the Building Research Establishment (BRE) and takes into account the large environmental impact of buildings and the potential for reducing environmental damage by improving their design. BRE have a number of versions of BREEAM including one for the environmental assessment of existing office designs.

The environmental impact of buildings can be radically reduced by the application of cost-effective technology. A certificate is provided by the BRE, based on an independent assessment; builders will be able to use assessments in their publicity and buyers will have a record of the way in which their building has been designed according to environmental criteria. BREEAM is a very useful structure for assessing the environmental impact of your building.

The Office Toolkit

The Office Toolkit is produced by BRE, in partnership with PA Consulting Group. The Toolkit is designed to help the busy facilities, building or office manager to improve environmental performance and save money. The Toolkit is divided into review sections that guide you through the analysis of your environmental impacts based on an 'ecopoint' system and action sections that outline the actions you can take in each area.

BSRIA

The Building Services Research and Information Association (BSRIA) published a strategy for environmental care in building design, construction and ultimate demolition in May 1994. Entitled *The Environmental Code of Practice for Buildings and their Services*, the guidance document provides a common language for all concerned in the building process – client, architect, quantity surveyor, designer, services and facilities manager. The Code spans the life-cycle of any building, whether commercial, industrial or residential, from concept to demolition. It asserts that, with skill and foresight, environmental impact can be reduced at little or no increase in overall cost.

LEGISLATION

Hazardous Waste

The legislation on general waste is detailed in Chapter .
There a number of everyday materials which many office will have for maintenance or cleaning purposes which have hazardous properties. Hazardous materials are those which their storage or use are considered to be potentially harmful human health or the environment. Under the duty of care outlined in Chapter 3, care must be taken to make sure these are properly disposed of. In addition a number of these materials are covered by the new Special Waste Regulations.

1996 SPECIAL WASTE REGULATIONS

The Special Waste Regulations set out the provisions for the keeping, treatment and disposal of controlled wastes that a dangerous or difficult to manage. Their main purpose is to provide an effective system of control that ensures that special waste is soundly managed from its production until final destination for disposal or recovery. They replace the Control of Pollution (Special Waste) Regulations 1980 and implement European legislation on hazardous waste. The DoE have published guidance on the Regulations (1996).

Waste is defined as 'special' if it appears on the European Hazardous Waste List and it possesses certain hazardous properties or it is a prescription only medicine. The exception to this is that household wastes are not special. Examples of special wastes include widely used products such as oils, lead and NiCd batteries, acids, flammable liquids, and solvents. Those commonly used in the office are covered in more detail below.

If you are dealing with special wastes you must pre-notify the local or area Environment Agency office in the area to which the waste is being taken, by filling in a consignment note. You must keep a copy of all consignment notes. A fee is charged for each consignment.

Breaking the regulations is punishable by a fine of up to £5000 and/or two years in prison.

CLINICAL WASTE

Most healthcare wastes come under the Special Waste Regulations. However some may not meet the hazardous thresholds in the Regulations and in these cases the duty of care provisions of the Environmental Protection Act should be followed (see Chapter 3). Clinical waste is defined in the Controlled Waste Regulations 1992 under the Environmental Protection Act as:

'Any waste which consists wholly or partly of human or animal tissue, blood or other body fluids, excretions, drugs or other pharmaceutical products, swabs or dressings, or syringes, needles or other sharp instruments, being waste which unless rendered safe may prove hazardous to any person coming into contact with it; and

Any other waste arising from medical, nursing, dental, veterinary, pharmaceutical or similar practice, investigation, treatment, care, teaching or research, or the collection of blood for transfusion, being waste which may cause infection to any persons coming into contact with it.'
(NSCA, 1995)

Guidance on the treatment and management of clinical waste is given in Waste Management Paper No 25 available from the Environment Agency.

Water

WATER INDUSTRY ACT 1991

It is an offence for occupiers of trade premises to discharge trade effluents into a public sewer unless authorised by the sewerage undertaker.

To obtain a consent to discharge, occupiers of trade premises must make an application to the sewerage undertaker. The consent may impose conditions such as the rate, quantity and composition of effluent.

WATER RESOURCES ACT 1991

It is an offence to cause or to knowingly permit any poisonous noxious or polluting matter or any solid waste matter to enter any controlled waters. Application for a consent to discharge to controlled waters must be made to the Environment Agency. If consent is granted the Agency will set conditions to ensure compliance with statutory water quality objectives.

Ozone Depleting Substances

THE MONTREAL PROTOCOL

In 1987, an agreement on substances that deplete the ozone layer was reached in Montreal. The Montreal Protocol was ratified by 60 countries, who committed themselves to reducing the production and use of ozone depleting substances such as CFCs and halons. This protocol was amended in June 1990 and November 1992 to bring forward phase out deadlines. The EU has implemented the protocol through Regulation 3093/94/EC that sets tighter deadlines for some chemicals. Table 6.1 shows the phase out dates for the manufacture of the main ozone depleting substances.

	MONTREAL PROTOCOL	EC REGULATION
CFCs	100 per cent phased out by 1996	100 per cent phased out by 1995
Halons	100 per cent phased out by 1994	100 per cent phased out by 1994
HCFCs	On 1989 levels 35 per cent cut by 2004 65 per cent cut by 2007 90 per cent cut by 2015 99.5 per cent cut by 2014 Phase out by 2030	On 1989 levels 35 per cent cut by 2004 60 per cent cut by 2007 80 per cent cut by 2010 95 per cent cut by 2013 Phase out by 2015

Office Equipment – Health and Safety

DISPLAY SCREEN EQUIPMENT REGULATIONS 1992

This Regulation aims to make sure that employers provide well designed and safe equipment, workstation furniture, conditions and practices for display screen users. Workstation assessments need to be conducted for any employee spending over 25 per cent of their working day using a VDU.

TABLE 6.1
Phase out dates for the manufacture of ozone depleting substances (DoE, 1995)

ENERGY

Environmental Issues

From oil spills to radioactive waste, the impacts of energy use are some of the key environmental issues we face. The extraction, generation and use of energy can all have a major impact on the environment. Energy efficiency can provide an immediate and cost effective response to these impacts.

EXTRACTION AND TRANSPORT

The extraction and transport of oil can cause disastrous pollution. Oil spills like those from the *Exxon Valdez* in Alaska and the *Sea Empress* off the coast of Wales have done enormous damage to sensitive habitats.

BURNING OF FOSSIL FUELS

When fossil fuels such as gas, oil and coal are burnt to produce electricity or heat, a number of gases including carbon dioxide, nitrogen oxides and sulphur dioxide are released into the atmosphere. These emissions are major contributors to acid rain and the greenhouse effect.

Greenhouse Effect (Global Warming)

Certain trace gases (for example water vapour, carbon dioxide methane, nitrous oxides) form an insulating blanket around the Earth. This blanket allows the sun's rays through, but prevents some of the heat radiated back from the Earth escaping. This heat retention can be likened to the role of glass in a greenhouse. These gases are a natural phenomenon, without their effect the Earth would be uninhabitable, with an average temperature over 30 degrees lower than now.

Emissions from human activities are increasing the atmospheric concentrations of several important greenhouse gases, in particular carbon dioxide. The 1995 report by the International Panel on Climate Change (IPCC) concludes: 'the balance of evidence suggest that there is a discernible human influence on global climate'. The Panel warns that if current trends persist we may see a warming of the globe by 2 degrees Celsius by 2100. Climate change on this scale will have wide ranging impact. For example the rise in sea level will flood low lying areas.

The UK is a signatory to the 1992 Climate Change Convention that was agreed at the Rio 'Earth Summit'. This commits the UK to reduce carbon dioxide emissions to 1990 levels by the year 2000 to help combat the greenhouse effect. At the Kyoto Climate Change Summit in December 1997 the government agreed to a target of 20 per cent reduction in UK greenhouse gas emissions (from 1990 levels) by 2010.

Acid Rain

Acid rain consists of acid substances that fall as dry deposit which are washed out in the rain, mist or snow. The main constituents are sulphur dioxide and nitrogen oxides. Acid rain results in loss of plant nutrients – threatening the long-term productivity of forests. Tree damage is widespread throughout Europe as a result of acid rain and the direct effects of gaseous pollutants. Water becomes more corrosive to a variety of materials including metals and concrete, which can cause damage to piping systems. In the UK, acid rain's main effect is building corrosion.

The 1994 Helsinki Protocol commits the UK to reduce sulphur dioxide emissions (on 1980 levels) by:

❑ 50 per cent by 2000;
❑ 70 per cent by 2005; and
❑ 80 per cent by 2010.

NUCLEAR POWER

Over 20 per cent of our electricity is generated through the use of nuclear power. Although nuclear power does not contribute to the greenhouse effect it creates a legacy of radioactive waste that will be potentially lethal for thousands of years. The costs associated with managing this risk have contributed to making nuclear power uneconomic and no new power stations are planned in the UK.

RENEWABLE ENERGY

The Government is encouraging the development of alternative energy sources such as wind and solar power through the Non-Fossil Fuel Obligation (NFFO). There are now a large number of wind farms operating. These technologies do not use non-renewable resources such as coal and oil and have no emissions of carbon dioxide or other air pollutants. The Body Shop has invested in a wind farm in Wales to offset its use of fossil fuels.

INDUSTRY STANDARDS

Make a Corporate Commitment

The Government Energy Efficiency Office (EEO) runs a campaign 'Making a Corporate Commitment'. This aims to encourage organisations to include energy efficiency as part of positive environmental management. Those supporting the campaign make a board member responsible for developing an energy efficiency strategy and make sure this becomes a regular item on the boardroom agenda.

The central feature of the campaign is the Declaration of Commitment that the chairperson or chief executive can sign and prominently display in the company's headquarters. The declaration commits the company or organisation to the steps outlined below.

❏ Publish a corporate policy. This sets out the standards and objectives for the company and those who work in it. Obviously, energy efficiency may already be a part of a company's published environmental policy.

❏ Establish an energy management responsibility structure. A board member should be responsible and may wish to appoint an energy manager. Other key employees should have responsibility for their particular areas and know how they relate to each other.

❏ Monitor and evaluate performance levels. By monitoring and evaluating performance, targets can be assessed and reviewed. At least once a year, such a performance review is desirable at board level.

❏ Set performance improvement targets. Targets need to be quantified and publicised.

❏ Increase awareness of energy efficiency among employees. There are immediate benefits by making all employees more energy conscious and by giving them practical advice on energy efficiency that they can use at work and home.

❏ Hold regular reviews. Reviews to assess energy consumption and performance should be held regularly.

❏ Report performance changes and improvements to employees and shareholders. Announce improvements and changes in performance figures to employees and shareholders, perhaps through the annual report.

PRACTICAL ACTION

Energy is the largest controllable outgoing in running office buildings. Consumption can be reduced by at least 10 per cent (heating and lighting) at no cost. With investment, further reductions are achievable. Energy can be saved in many ways. A refurbishment programme can be the ideal time to make environmental and cost saving changes. The Department of Environment, Transport and the Regions's Energy Efficiency Best Practice programme has published a wide range of guides on energy efficiency. Some of the information in this section is based on these publications (ETSU, 1995b).

Manage Your Energy Use

Energy efficiency can be a major cost factor as well as an environmental issue. Often companies see it simply as a technical problem; however the key to efficient energy use is good management. The aim of energy management is to minimise cost while maintaining high standards of service. It is important to give responsibility for energy management to a named person who can coordinate your approach. The Making a Corporate Commitment campaign provides a structure that you can follow whether or not you actually sign up to the campaign.

To encourage senior management commitment you need to present the business case by establishing the energy costs. Find out what you paid for all your energy sources over the previous year. This may come as a shock. A good way of highlighting the costs is to relate the savings of a small reduction in energy costs to the equivalent increase in sales that would have the same impact on the bottom line.

Assess Current Position

Information as to where you are is essential to motivate and monitor progress. Using the charts below you can use your meter readings to calculate your carbon dioxide emissions and your performance against benchmarking figures.

A key part of energy management is regular continued metering of your consumption on a monthly (or even weekly) basis. This information will help you to assess the success of measures implemented. It will also allow you to monitor and report progress to senior management and staff so as to build commitment to energy efficiency.

More detailed analysis of energy consumption can also be carried out by, for instance, relating heating use to weather. For further information see *Introduction to Energy Efficiency in Offices* (BRECSU, 1995).

Calculating your emissions

The information you need to make these calculations can be obtained from your fuel bills. These should cover a full year and be the actual cost, not an estimate by the utility.

Treated floor area is the gross floor area without plant

rooms and other areas not heated (eg stores, covered car parks and roof spaces). An estimate of treated floor area can be made by multiplying the gross floor area by 0.9 or the net floor area by 1.25.

Motivate your Staff

When examining energy use most people start by gathering information, such as meter readings, and move on to consider investment in new equipment. These are both important. However, unless you encourage a culture

FIGURE 6.1

Calculating your CO_2 emissions

	Annual kWh		Treated floor area(m^2)		Annual kWh/m^2		CO_2 Conversion factors		Annual CO_2 emissions kg/m^2
Gas		x		=		x	0.20		
Oil		x		=		x	0.29		
Coal		x		=		x	0.32		
Electricity		x		=		x	0.70		

Total CO_2 emissions kg/m^2

TABLE 6.2

Carbon dioxide performance assessment

(Reproduced from the Department of the Environment's EEB6 © Crown Copyright 1994)

	LOW EMISSIONS KG/M²	MEDIUM EMISSIONS KG/M²	HIGH EMISSIONS KG/M²
	Less than ⟶	Between ◀ ⟶	Greater than ◀
Smaller office	44		74
Naturally ventilated open plan	62		100
Air conditioned open plan	112		186
Headquarters (computer room and catering)	209		307

change amongst your staff in the way they use energy, any amount of technology will have little impact.

Few people are excited by energy management. This provides a challenge for the energy manager trying to involve staff. A guide from the EEO *Managing and Motivating Staff to Save Energy* (ETSU, 1995a) gives ideas including the following ways of encouraging people.

❑ *Ask* people what they know, think and suggest about your use of energy and how they could contribute to reducing it.
❑ *Agree* objectives, targets and monitoring duties with your staff.
❑ *Give* incentives, rewards, feedback on results and thanks.

Chapter 8 suggests techniques for involving people in environmental actions.

Space and Water Heating

Check the Room Temperature

Reducing the temperature of a room by one degree can cut the heating bill by as much as 10 per cent. Check that thermostats are set correctly (minimum 16 degrees – maximum 19 degrees). Turn off heating in unused rooms.

Check When Heating is on

Make sure that heating is off or reduced outside working hours. Fit sensor switches and timer controls in places not in constant use. The use of these devices can have a dramatic effect on fuel consumption.

Check Windows And Outside Doors

All windows and outside doors should be closed when heating is on. Install automatic door closure devices on external doors to cut down heat loss.

COMMON PROBLEMS

Lack of Knowledge of the Cost of Energy

Establishing your energy costs is an essential starting point to identify potential improvements from improved efficiency. Small reductions in controllable costs such as energy can result in the same improvement to your profitability as a large increase in sales.

Lack of Management Responsibility

Energy can fall between different people's responsibilities and never be managed effectively. Give responsibility to a specific member of staff.

No Board Level Support

If the board is not initially interested in energy efficiency you need to make an effective presentation of the business case. This can be more powerful if you have had success with some small scale initiatives before looking to the board for support.

No Money

Many of the actions outlined in this section require little or no investment. If you have no capital at the start use the returns on the low cost measures to finance investment. This will enable a comprehensive energy efficiency programme to be managed with no initial funding.

Boredom

Few people are excited by energy management. This can be overcome by good management that involves staff; encouraging their ideas and commitment; and linking the process to energy use in the home and reduction in fuel bills.

Recover Waste Heat

The heat produced in a computer suite can be used for heating hot water services within the building.

Install Insulation and Draught Proofing

The insulation of boilers and pipes will help prevent heat loss. The most important pipes to wrap are the hottest ones and the ones in the coldest places. Draught proofing can prevent heat loss from roofs, doors and walls.

Reduce Temperature of Stored Hot Water

Hot water is often too hot and needs to be mixed with cold water before use. The thermostat should be turned down to a minimum of 60 degrees. Any lower than this can increase the risk of Legionnaire's disease.

Air Conditioning

Use Natural Ventilation

Minimise areas of air conditioning by using mechanical or natural ventilation. You do not need to provide air conditioning for all areas of your office. Most people like to be able to open their window. Air conditioned buildings use about twice as much energy as naturally ventilated buildings.

Make Sure Your Air Conditioning is Not Overspecified

The amount of heat that computers generate is frequently calculated using maximum power demand figures. This gives a distorted figure since it is based on the peaks of energy use rather than an average figure. This leads to many buildings being overspecified in terms of air conditioning needs. See Office Equipment section below for more information.

Make Sure Cooling and Heating Are Not on Together

They often are!

Check Air Conditioning Times

Any need for air conditioning outside office hours will only be for small areas of your office.

Case Study

Subject –	**LIGHTING**
Organisation –	**BIG BEN**
Organisation type –	**CENTRAL GOVERNMENT**
Location –	**WESTMINSTER**
No. of staff –	**ESTIMATED AT 3000**

BACKGROUND

The Government signed up to a target of reducing Britain's CO_2 emissions to 1990 levels by the year 2000 at the Rio Earth Summit. To meet this target as the economy grows it is essential that energy, a key source of carbon dioxide emissions, is used more efficiently. In order to contribute to this and to demonstrate what can be achieved the Government has set energy efficiency targets for government departments.

The Parliamentary Works Department, in common with other government departments, is aiming for a 20 per cent energy saving on all fuels in government buildings. Savings of over 10 per cent have already been achieved. As part of this commitment the Works Department has installed energy efficient lighting at one of the nations most distinctive landmarks, Big Ben.

ACTION

New high energy efficient lamps were installed behind the four clock faces of Big Ben at a cost of £20,000. These came into operation on 19 January 1995.

The new fittings were developed by Phillips and are a special type of fluorescent bulb with a lamp life of 60,000 hours (ie about 13 years of normal use). The output of each 55 watt bulb equivalent to a 250 watt conventional incandescent lamp. The new lamps replaced cold cathode tubes which lasted some 0,000 hours and together consumed 11.2 kilowatts of electricity.

Other energy saving measures that have been implemented in the parliamentary estate include the replacement of 300 watt lamps with 55 watt lamps in the chandeliers at Westminster Hall and the Royal Gallery.

(Contributed by the Parliamentary Works Directorate.)

RESULTS

The use of energy efficient lighting in Big Ben and the rest of the parliamentary estate has significant environmental benefits. It also saves tax payers money, the initial cost will be recovered from savings in just six years. The benefits of the new lighting include:

❑ a reduction in emissions of global warming gases;

❑ savings of £1000 in electricity; and

❑ savings of £2500 in maintenance costs each year.

Set Temperature Controls To At Least 24 Degrees

Do not set the air conditioning to come on before the temperature gets to at least 24 degrees. Even a slight increase in temperature setting can give a substantial reduction in your energy bills.

Make Sure Windows Are Shut When Air Conditioning Is On

Office Equipment

Investigate Energy Consumption

Calculate the true energy consumption of equipment. The nameplate rating is often based on maximum power demand. In practice, energy usage can be substantially lower. You should also take into consideration the energy used during power-up time and when the equipment is on standby. Contact the manufacturer for detailed information on actual power demands. This information will help you calculate your air conditioning requirements (see Air Conditioning section above).

Launch a Switch Off Campaign

One third of all PCs are left on overnight or over the weekend. Prevent this waste of energy by implementing an energy-saving policy to switch off machines when they are not in use. Turning off machines for any lengthy breaks during the day can achieve up to 60 per cent energy savings. To avoid residual background power consumption, switch equipment off at the plug when it is not needed.

A switch off campaign will reduce the costs of air conditioning by reducing the heat generated by office equipment. One major bank that had computers switched on in its trading floors 24 hours a day, found that the costs of cooling during the night were approximately £120,000 pa.

The Department of the Environment, Transport and the Regions (DETR) provides free posters and stickers to encourage switching off office equipment and other energy saving tips.

Share Printers Wherever Possible

This will reduce the energy demands of printers standing idle.

Use Monochrome Monitors Where Possible

Monochrome monitors have a lower energy usage.

Technology

There are a number of technologies that you should consider installing in your building, particularly if you are refurbishing or moving to a new location.

Combined Heat and Power (CHP)

CHP plants generate both heat and power and can achieve high levels of efficiency in reducing carbon dioxide emissions. CHP is not cost effective in all buildings and needs to be evaluated on a case by case basis. The BBC has installed a CHP scheme at Television Centre in London which was predicted to reduce annual CO_2 emissions by 12,553 tonnes.

Building Energy Management Systems (BEMS)

These offer the most sophisticated energy control by using micro-electronics to automatically monitor and control the buildings' services.

Condensing Boilers

Condensing boilers recover more heat from flue gases which leads to a 15 per cent gain in efficiency. New boilers you install should be of the condensing type.

SUMMARY GUIDELINES

- ❏ Set up a management structure for energy.
- ❏ Investigate your current energy costs and carbon dioxide emissions.
- ❏ Motivate staff by involving them in the project and providing feedback on progress.
- ❏ Check that your heating and air conditioning are only on in the right areas at times when they are needed and at the most efficient temperatures.
- ❏ Investigate energy saving technologies such as condensing boilers.
- ❏ Review your progress.

LIGHTING

Environmental Issues

ENERGY

Inefficient lighting systems use more energy. This contributes to global warming and acid rain (see Energy section earlier in this chapter). You can save energy and money simply by introducing efficient lighting. Your choice of lighting can also affect staff productivity levels.

DISPOSAL

There are approximately 80,000,000 fluorescent tubes disposed of annually in the UK. Fluorescent lighting tubes contain mercury (as much as 30 mg), cadmium and lead. Crushing used tubes produces dust and vapour emissions that present a health hazard. Disused sodium lamps are a potential fire risk until they are correctly broken and the sodium neutralised.

Choice of Lighting

Your choice of lighting can have a significant effect on energy consumption. The normal domestic tungsten bulb lamps produce light by passing an electrical current through a fine wire filament, which becomes 'white hot'. Ninety five per cent of this light is turned into heat, which can add to the workload of an air conditioning system. Long usage results in brittle filaments which break due to vibration or heat expansion when the light is turned on.

Fluorescent lamps produce light by applying electrical energy to either end of a tube containing inert gas plus a little mercury, creating an electrical arc. This method of lighting is cost and energy efficient. Fluorescent lamps produce very little heat compared to tungsten bulb lamps. The useful life span of fluorescent lamps is approximately 7500 hours; they lose efficiency after this time.

TYPE OF LAMPS AVAILABLE

Tungsten Bulbs

The standard tungsten bulb is very cheap to purchase but has short life span and is very inefficient in its use of energy.

Tungsten Halogen Lamps

These can be used to replace tungsten spotlights for desk and display lighting with energy savings of about 50 per cent.

Compact Fluorescent Lamps (CFLs)

CFLs are a relatively new form of lighting which can replace standard tungsten bulbs and use about 20–25 per cent of the electricity for a similar lighting level. They have a lifetime up to eight times as long as tungsten bulbs and are now common for domestic use.

Fluorescent Tubes

Fluorescent tubes are widely used in offices. They use about

18 per cent of the electricity of a tungsten bulb and less energy than a CFL. Fluorescent tubes have become steadily more efficient over recent years.

One advance has been the development of more sophisticated electronic control gear for tubes. Control gear is necessary for fluorescent tubes to start up and maintain light output, and modern electronic controls are more efficient.

Slimline Fluorescent Tubes

Slimline fluorescent tubes are thinner in diameter and shorter than standard fluorescent tubes. With the reduction in size they produce an instant saving in the amount of energy required to give off light. Replacing standard fluorescent tubes with slimline fluorescent tubes will produce approximately 8 per cent energy savings.

Triphosphor Fluorescent Lighting

These tubes last longer and are more energy efficient than a standard fluorescent tube particularly when used with modern electronic control gear. They typically use 16.5 per cent of the energy of a tungsten bulb.

Daylight Fluorescent

Daylight fluorescent tubes simulate the full colour and beneficial ultraviolet spectrum of natural daylight. These daylight tubes help to create a more healthy working environment by reducing fatigue. They may help seasonal affective disorder (SAD) sufferers, who suffer a cyclic form of depression linked to the reduced light levels of the autumn and winter months. These lamps use the same amount of energy as a standard fluorescent. They are particularly useful in areas with no natural light such as basements, which can be depressing to work in, in print and design studios.

Metal halide and Sodium Discharge Lamps

These are suitable for lighting large areas such as car parks. They are usually more efficient than fluorescent lights although this varies by type.

LIGHTING CONTROLS

There are a number of controls that can be used to make your lighting more efficient.

❏ Time controls – these allow you to set lights to switch off automatically at set times.

❏ Presence detection controls – these will switch the lights on or off automatically when somebody enters or leaves an area. It is important to set the timing correctly on these, particularly in toilets!

❏ Daylight detectors – these can switch off or dim lights according to the levels of natural light in the office and so maximise the use of natural light.

PRACTICAL ACTION

Action on lighting will be a key part of your overall energy efficiency programme.

Install Low Energy Lighting

Modern fluorescent tubes are vastly more efficient than tungsten lamps and are continuing to improve in efficiency. The low energy consumption and longer life of modern lamps will mean they show a good return on their initial investment. Whenever lighting is upgraded use the opportunity to install the most efficient option available.

Improve Lighting Efficiency

All types of lamp lose efficiency with time (less light is given off and more energy used). Introduce a relamping programme where all lights are replaced at the same time, so that all fittings are running to full capacity. This programme will save on maintenance and disposal costs and will ensure consistent lighting levels.

Use Natural Light

Maximise your use of natural light. Keep all windows clean and make sure lights can be switched off manually, particularly near windows or have daylight sensors.

Install Presence Detector Lighting Controls

Fit presence detector switches in places not in constant use, for instance, lavatories and meeting rooms. Consider investing in a building management system that controls lighting levels.

Run a 'Switch Off' Campaign

Increase staff awareness of energy efficiency – encour

Case Study

Subject –	**ENERGY EFFICIENCY**
Organisation –	**TECHNICOLOR LTD**
Organisation type –	**FILM INDUSTRY**
Location –	**WEST DRAYTON, MIDDLESEX**
No. of staff –	**230**

BACKGROUND

The Technicolor site at West Drayton is a large site comprising of film storage, cutting/processing/assembly rooms, administration, workshops, customer services, corridors and a restaurant.

In 1992, Technicolor Ltd evaluated several energy savings projects. As part of the programme, a decision was made to convert the lighting to energy efficient lamps.

ACTION

Over the past three years Energy Solutions Ltd have been designing, supplying and installing energy efficient lighting in the Technicolor buildings. Besides the installation of new high frequency luminaries, existing luminaries have been retrofitted with high frequency ballasts and triphosphor tubes.

(Contributed by Energy Solutions Ltd)

RESULTS

Technicolor has recorded savings on lighting electricity costs of between 30 to 50 per cent, dependent on areas and usage. The lighting in the assembly areas is being monitored by a Hawk Analyser. It showed that in addition to the reduction of electricity consumption, the triphosphor tubes had been operating in excess of 21,000 hours and still maintained an average lighting level in excess of 600 lux. As standard fluorescent tubes rapidly deteriorate in light output and only last on average 7500 hours, further savings were obtained due to less maintenance requirements.

Technicolor is pleased with the results of energy efficient lighting as its overheads have been considerably reduced and there is an improved working environment for its staff.

COMMON PROBLEMS

Turning off Lights

It is a common misconception that a burst of energy is required each time lights are switched on, when in fact this is not the case.

Fluorescent Tubes

Going into Skip

Fluorescent tubes are often simply put into a skip as this involves no extra cost. It is more responsible to have a bulk change of lamps and either recycle these or dispose of them through a specialist contractor.

Lack of control of contractors

If maintenance contractors are disposing of your lamps on your behalf then you should talk to them about responsible disposal methods and consider including disposal requirements in the maintenance contract.

age staff to be diligent and turn lights off whenever possible. It is a common misconception that a burst of energy is required each time lights are switched on, when in fact this is not the case.

Dispose of Fluorescent Tubes Responsibly

Fluorescent tubes do not currently come under the Special Waste Regulations. They are categorised as Difficult Waste under the Environmental Protection Act 1990. However the hazardous nature of the mercury they contain means that particular care should be taken over waste fluorescent tubes.

Introduce a Relamping Programme

All bulbs should be replaced together, at a fixed time, to maintain consistent lighting levels. This will reduce your maintenance costs, the tubes can be disposed of by a hazardous waste contractor or recycled in bulk and you will maintain consistent lighting levels throughout your building(s).

Recycle Fluorescent Tubes

Recently facilities have been developed to enable fluorescent tubes to be recycled. These are competitively priced with specialist disposal facilities. Lamps are crushed and sieved in a closed dry recycling process. Mercury can be extracted from the fluorescent powder once separated from the glass and metals. All the materials can be recycled, including the mercury which is used in new lamps. Details are available from Mercury Recycling and EC Recycling.

Check the contractors' and the intended waste site's licences to make sure that they are licensed to handle fluorescent tubes and that they are being recycled.

It will help to know how many tubes you dispose of when considering the feasibility of recycling. The Benefits Agency uses the following figures to estimate the number of tubes on its estate:

❑ One tube per 9 square metres of office space.
❑ Each tube lasts about two years.

Dispose of Fluorescent Tubes Safely

The DoE recommends that special arrangements should

be made if more than one tube is disposed of to six bags of general waste. If quantities of 20 or 30 tubes are to be disposed of at any one time a waste contractor with appropriate disposal facilities should be identified. The DoE recommends that the contractors' and the intended waste site's licenses should be checked to make sure that they are licensed to handle such waste.

SUMMARY GUIDELINES

- ❑ Maximise use of natural light.
- ❑ Introduce energy efficient lamps and controls.
- ❑ Implement a switch off campaign.
- ❑ Introduce a relamping programme.
- ❑ Recycle your fluorescent tubes.

OFFICE EQUIPMENT
Health, Safety and Environmental Issues

Your choice of office equipment manufacturer and servicing contractor has important implications for your environmental and health and safety policies. The main environmental concerns are the disposal of spent toner cartridges, emissions of ozone and dust, and the end of life disposal of the machine and component parts. Symptoms of air pollution caused by laser printers and photocopiers include headaches, catarrh and an unpleasantly dry working environment. The dry working environment is exacerbated by high room temperatures.

OZONE

Photocopiers and printers, especially when they are inadequately maintained or used in small rooms, can release dangerous amounts of ozone. The ozone layer protects the Earth's surface from ultraviolet radiation. However, in the office, ozone is a toxic gas with a distinctive odour. It is produced naturally from oxygen whenever ultraviolet radiation of high voltage electrical discharges occur. Copiers and printers rely on high voltages to make the toner powder stick temporarily to a print drum, before its transfer to paper. This process generates ozone.

Exposure to ozone can irritate the eyes, nose and throat, and cause lethargy, lassitude, loss of concentration, headaches and upper respiratory tract illnesses. This has considerable implications for asthmatics and for general staff welfare.

The Health and Safety Executive (HSE) guidelines for occupational exposure limits for ozone are set at 0.2 ppm (parts ozone per million parts air) over a 15 minute weighed average. Most laser printers and copiers have a built-in filter to extract the ozone from the exhaust fumes. They contain activated carbon to break down ozone and, when new, reduce ozone to well below the HSE levels. However, the filters are small and lose efficiency with time, especially if clogged with dust from paper, toner powder or room air. Clogging is faster if ventilation is poor, and ozone becomes more dangerous.

TONER AND DUST

Dust is given off by paper and toner. The amount of dust from the toner varies from machine to machine and is also dependent on the type of paper used. Methacrylate and styrene are chemical constituents of toner powder which are potentially harmful. During the printing process, as these substances are being heated, a process of decomposition occurs which releases acids. In large quantities, these acids are known to be capable of penetrating the skin resulting in various degrees of skin irritation commonly manifested as rashes or eczema.

Substances Used

Toner contains several substances that are known to be skin irritants and even allergenic. The quantities however are so small that they themselves are not seen to be of any importance. Once fixed on the paper, the toner gives rise to little risk of skin irritation.

Dust Particles

Toner consists primarily of a binding agent that, when heated fixes the colour particles to the paper. This binding agent is either called resin or polymer. Toner may also contain carbon black and iron granules. Carbon particles in toner used in photocopiers are normally no smaller than 0.005 mm, making them too large to cause bronchial disorders. However, carbon particles used in toner for laser printers and colour photocopiers are smaller than 0.005 mm. If these particles are inhaled they can cause damage to the bronchi.

Waste Disposal

All types of toner for copier systems consist of coarse and fine particles. The components of toner do vary depending on the manufacturer. Carbon dust may contain minute quantities of nitropyrenes or PAH (polyaromatic hydrocarbons) which are carcinogenic. Most manufacturers remove these pollutants from their toner. The health implications of toner dust are more significant.

Health and Safety

Copiers can give off electrostatically charged toner dust – this can cause irritation in the respiratory tract when inhaled. When the air is thick with dust, stress intensifies, aggressiveness increases and the ability to concentrate is reduced. Toner can be hazardous to health. Manufacturers must produce COSHH hazard sheets with details on the components, the health hazards associated with them and how toner should be handled. This includes special requirements for exposure control.

COMPUTERS

VDUs emit various types of radiation. A significant proportion of the radiation consists of pulsed EMFs (electromagnetic fields) of between 15 kHz and pulsed 50 kHz fields. The exposure to electrical fields and the expected damage to the operator depends on the strength of the field, the distance from the field source and the length of exposures over a long period of time. Static electricity is generated from high voltage tension in a VDU screen. The electrostatic field created disturbs the normal balance of ions in the air causing it to be positively charged. Headaches, irritability, tiredness and skin complaints can result from this static electricity.

PRACTICAL ACTION

Ventilation

Photocopiers used by a number of people should be located in a specific, well ventilated room. If large quantities of printed material are produced, extractor fans should be fitted on the machinery, and the air conducted directly out of the building.

Ozone Filters

Make sure copiers are fitted with filters. Verify the frequency of filter change recommended by the manufacturer and make sure that filter changing is included in the service agreement. In areas of poor ventilation or heavy usage, supplementary filters should be fitted. They are more powerful and remove ozone, toner and paper dust from the laser printer and clean the office air in the immediate vicinity.

Enclosed Cartridge System

Use toner in cartridges to reduce the risks of spillage. Stipulate a toner cartridge system when purchasing new machines and check that the cartridges can be recycled. (See laser printer and deskjet cartridges in Chapter 4.)

COSHH

Ensure correct handling of toner under COSHH and obtain detailed assessments from the manufacturer. Use toner with minimal hazardous materials (details will be on the COSHH sheets) to minimise health and safety risks. Use disposable gloves when replacing toner – clean up any spilt toner and wash your hands thoroughly. Use protective clothing and possibly a mask when replacing loose toner (plan to change over to cartridges). Toner must not smudge or be released into the surroundings.

Duty of Care

Ensure correct disposal of toner. Some manufacturers such as Toshiba have collection schemes for empty cartridges which are then recycled.

Handling

Avoid handling large quantities of printed or photo-copied material immediately after it is produced. The shorter the time between printing or copying and staff handling the paper, the greater the risk.

Plants

Research by NASA (National Aeronautical and Space Agency) found that up to 87 per cent of poisonous substances found in office buildings can be absorbed with the right selection of plants. By breathing in carbon dioxide and contaminated air, they help to improve the air quality in an office by providing a natural filtering system. Mother-in-law's tongue is found to be particularly effective!

Monitor Air Quality

Air quality should be monitored on a quarterly basis to minimise the impact of indoor pollution.

SOURCES OF HELP

The Business Equipment Users Association

Each year the Business Equipment Users Association (Europe) conducts hundreds of benchmark tests on photocopiers, fax, printers, multifunctional devices and consumables. Tests cover performance, productivity, noise levels, energy consumption, life expectancy of parts and longevity and performance of consumables. The information contained in this section is based on research conducted by Wastebusters for the Association and has been reproduced by kind permission of the association.

Workstation Health and Safety

Workstation design should consider health and safety issues and the efficiency of the working environment. It is important to consider the positioning of VDUs, since EMFs are at their highest at the sides, rear and tops of VDU terminals, rather than the front. Therefore the number of hours at a terminal may not be a reliable indicator of exposure. Ideally, operators should not work within one metre of the sides or back of adjacent VDUs unless the machines have been tested and confirmed to emit only low levels of non-ionising radiation.

Mainframe Machine Rooms

Space

Machine rooms are often run unmanned, therefore, false ceilings may not be necessary. Fewer building materials are needed and valuable, naturally-lit office space can be kept for employees.

Raised floors

Consider environmental criteria when selecting the raw material used. They are primarily made from metal, woodchip or plywood. Refer to Life-cycle analysis, in Chapter 4, for further information.

Lighting

Machine rooms are not office environments; therefore, lighting levels can be minimised. They are often run unmanned, in which case no lighting is needed. Alternatively, lighting can be arranged in blocks so that it can be switched on where needed and left off elsewhere. Windows are not needed. Note that vertical illumination may be necessary for maintenance purposes.

Cabling

The cable management system should be flexible to accommodate changes in machines. Flexibility is also needed in power distribution and communication cable systems.

Heat Recovery

Machine rooms generate a lot of heat. This can be recovered to help heat the remainder of the building. There needs to be sufficient filtered fresh air to pressurise the machine room to prevent the ingress of contaminants (dust, for example).

Energy Efficiency

Power saving devices can be fitted to give flexibility. They can be used to make sure that only those machines which are necessary to run the system remain on at all times. This permits other machines to be turned off which will consequently reduce power demands and heat generation. Decide which machines will have to stay on for 24 hours and turn the others off when possible.

Fire Protection

Traditionally, halon flooding equipment has been installed as fire protection in computer rooms. Under the Montreal Protocol halon production has been phased out since it is a very powerful ozone depleter. An acceptable alternative is the use of a sprinkler system, with an automatic cut-off of electricity in an emergency, or passive detection, for example, smoke alarms.

FABRIC MAINTENANCE

Most organisations contract out the fabric maintenance of the building(s). Implementing sound environmental controls ca reduce costs and make sure your environmental position is n weakened by your subcontractors.

Environmental Issues

PLASTERBOARD

Plasterboard is manufactured from gypsum. The quarrying of raw materials destroys areas of the countryside, damages wildlife habitats and creates dust and heavy traffic movements.

Industrial gypsum can also be used in plasterboard, this is produced in power stations during the desulphurisation process; activity in this process may cause concentrations of heavy metals to build up. There is concern that the resulting materials may have health risks.

PAINT AND VARNISH

The major environmental issue with paint and varnishes is their use of solvents (See Writing Materials in Chapter 4 for information on the environmental issues of solvents). In 1993 the DoE calculated that paint manufacture and use accounted for 3.4 per cent of emissions from solvent use in 1988. Solvent based paints can be replaced by low solvent or water based alternatives.

Certain types of paint are now covered by the European Ecolabelling scheme, see Chapter 4 for details.

Solvent based paints are also hazardous in disposal and come under the Special Waste Regulations.

BATTERIES

Around 600 million batteries arise in the UK per year. Chemical reactions continue in old batteries that can result in hazardous metals leaching into the environment causing adverse effects to humans and wildlife, and vegetation damage. Wet batteries containing both lead and acid can be particularly damaging if disposed of in an uncontrolled way. Batteries used to contain low levels of toxic metals, particularly mercury. This has been almost eliminated from batteries since 1994.

NiCd and lead acid batteries can be recycled, there are currently no facilities for recycling other batteries. NiCd and lead acid batteries are hazardous in disposal and come under the Special Waste Regulations. (For further information on purchasing batteries see Chapter 4.)

OILS

The biggest oil incidents have been spills by tankers such as the *Sea Empress* off the coast of Wales in 1996. However small quantities of oil can also cause major damage to watercourses and groundwater if it is spilt or inappropriately disposed of. Oil forms a film on the surface of rivers and lakes that makes it difficult for fish to breathe by reducing the amount of oxygen in the water. Five litres of oil can cover a small lake. Oil will also coat animals and plants that come into contact with it.

In 1994 6354 substantiated water pollution incidents due to oil were dealt with by the National Rivers Authority (NRA), more than 25 per cent of the total number of incidents that year. Common types of oil dealt with by the NRA, that could arise from office use, included central heating oil, diesel and petrol.

INDUSTRY STANDARDS

Environment Agency Oil Care at Work Code

❑ Site your storage tank within an oil tight bund wall on an impervious base. Make sure that valves and pipes are contained within the bund.
❑ Make sure that the bund has no drain which would allow oil to escape.
❑ Don't overfill your tank, check the amount of oil already in the tank before receiving a delivery.
❑ Supervise all deliveries, stop the delivery if there are any leaks or overflows.
❑ Clearly mark all pipework to show the type of oil and where it leads, and lock all valves and gauges securely after a delivery.

If an oil spill occurs:

❑ Try to stop the oil from entering any drains or watercourse using earth or sandbags to absorb it. Never hose it down.
❑ Call the Environment Agency Emergency Hotline free on 0800 807060.

The National Household Hazardous Waste Forum

The forum is a multi-sectoral organisation that engages i

dialogue with the government, industry associations and non-governmental bodies, particularly on the future impact of waste regulations and on the national waste strategy. The information they provide focuses on household waste but is also relevant to offices.

PRACTICAL ACTION

Materials

Make sure environmental criteria are considered in the selection of materials on-site. For example, plywood may be used on-site – some of this is made from tropical hardwoods. Wallpaper is now available with a recycled content. The choice of water based rather than solvent based paints reduces disposal problems and the environmental impacts of your activities. Make sure your environmental policy extends to subcontractors.

Usage

Obsolete materials may go into the skip due to lack of storage. Efficient project planning can facilitate re-use. There may be scope to reduce the quantities of materials ordered to minimise wastage. The choice of materials can also affect re-use. Plasterboard frames are often demolished during office moves. There are modular systems for plasterboard which facilitate re-use.

Disposal

Find alternative disposal routes for materials currently going into the skip. Typically these will be timber, metals, furniture and carpets. There are a number of charities who will match donations to organisations. This can significantly reduce the costs of disposal of building waste. For example, when the Union Bank of Switzerland had a large number of obsolete desks it gave them to the charity Elephant Jobs for distribution to other charities. This saved money on waste disposal costs as well as being environmentally preferable. Another example is the Bournemouth International Conference Centre which donated carpets from the stage set of the Conservative Party Conference to the Wessex Heart Foundation.

Contractors

Make sure contractors are complying with the Duty of

SUMMARY GUIDELINES

❏ Consider environmental criteria in selection of materials.
❏ Introduce waste reduction measures for building waste.
❏ Re-use or recycle building waste where possible.
❏ Ensure contractors are complying with the Duty of Care and Special Waste Regulations on your behalf.
❏ Maximise opportunities for energy improvements in refurbishment programmes.

Care Regulations, Special Waste Regulations and COSHH on your behalf. This includes the disposal of hazardous and special waste. Check the training procedures of the supplier: the environmental controls need to be understood at all levels of the organisation.

Refurbishment Programmes

The practical action outlined above is equally applicable to refurbishment programmes, where the quantity of materials both purchased and disposed of is substantial. You should:

❏ Purchase environmentally sound products. Build environmental criteria into the purchasing process. Refurbishment programmes provide an excellent opportunity to develop environmental purchasing objectives through the sourcing of raw materials. In the case of a large refurbishment programme, there will be a structured tender process: environmental criteria should be built in at the tender stage.
❏ Re-use or recycle obsolete materials. There are a number of organisations that will take obsolete materials; for instance in Bristol, Sofa Project will take old furniture and sell it at low prices to those on benefits, or students. Contact local charities and the recycling officer at your local authority.
❏ Manage energy. Introduce energy efficiency measures, efficient lighting and building management controls (see Energy section earlier in this chapter).
❏ Phase out CFCs, HCFCs and halons. Review the use of CFCs and halons on-site and develop a planned replacement programme (see Refrigerants: CFCs and HCFCs, and Fire Protection: Halon, later in this chapter).

Case Study

Subject –	**FABRIC MAINTENANCE**
Organisation –	**ERNST & YOUNG**
Organisation type –	**ACCOUNTANTS**
Location –	**LONDON**
No. of staff –	**3200**

BACKGROUND

Ernst & Young has a comprehensive environmental programme. This has included examining fabric maintenance in cooperation with Bovis Lelliot who handle all fabric maintenance work for Ernst & Young (London).

ACTION

Discussions with Bovis Lelliot have resulted in a number of initiatives to reduce the environmental impact of both operations. A number of potential areas for improvement were identified:

- Volume of waste going into the building skip.
- Lack of storage was a major obstacle to the re-use of materials.
- Lack of effective communication of the Environmental Policy.
- Control procedure.

RESULTS

- Improved project planning to facilitate the re-use of materials.
- Introduction of environmental criteria in product selection by Bovis Lelliot. For example, Bovis Lelliot is investigating the possibility of using wallpaper with a recycled content.
- Increased purchase of re-usable partitioning.
- Alternative disposal routes for skip contents. Obsolete carpets have been sent to charity; glass is being recycled.
- Bovis Lelliot has introduced a more stringent system of monitoring its environmental impact which includes environmental controls.
- Reduced costs hve been achieved by cutting the amount of waste sent to landfill.

DISPOSING OF HAZARDOUS MATERIALS

PRACTICAL ACTION

Do Not Purchase Hazardous Materials

Materials that are hazardous to humans or the environment require much greater control during use and disposal. They are therefore expensive. Wherever possible you should seek to use an alternative material, such as water based paints. (See Chapter 4).

Identify Special Wastes

To identify whether you have any materials that require disposal as special waste you will need to follow the steps outlined in the Special Waste Regulations 1996 and the Department of Environment Circular 6/96 (see Legislation section earlier in this chapter). The Environment Agency will also help you with any queries you have.

Follow Special Waste Consignment Note System

In addition to the provisions of the duty of care for special waste you must follow these steps:

1 Before any special waste leaves your site you must pre-notify the local area Environment Agency office in the area to which the waste is being taken. This is done by completing parts A and B of a five copy consignment note.
2 You must send one copy to the regulator for the area where the waste is going. This must be done at least three working days, but not more than one month, before the waste is to be moved.
3 When the waste is removed the carrier must complete part C to the form. You must then sign part D. You must keep a copy of the consignment note and give the other three to the carrier.

There is a fee charged by the Environment Agency for each consignment.

Waste Oil

All oil waste is considered as special waste.

Case Study

Subject –	**BATTERY RECYCLING**
Organisation –	**BRITISH TELECOMMUNICATIONS PLC**
Organisation type –	**TELECOMMUNICATIONS**
Location –	**UK-WIDE**
No. of staff –	**130,700**

BACKGROUND

British Telecommunications (BT) is one of the largest users of nickel–cadmium (NiCd) rechargeable batteries in the UK. In line with its environmental policy to minimise waste and promote recycling, BT decided it was time to cut down on the environmental impact of sending batteries to landfill.

ACTION

BT has established a collection scheme for NiCd batteries used in operational equipment including payphones, testers and hand tools used by technicians. Recycling schemes have also been established for collecting lead–acid batteries used in vehicles and lead–acid batteries used in telephone exchanges.

RESULTS

❏ In the year 1995/96 10.5 tonnes of NiCd batteries were collected, a 0.5 tonne increase from 1994/95.

❏ Quantities of lead–acid batteries sent for recycling also significantly increased from 4690 batteries collected in the year 1994/95 to 21,921 batteries in 1995/96. This was due to an upgrade of the entire Ford Transit fleet.

❏ Recycling of lead–acid exchange batteries has also increased by 13 per cent from 1994/95 to 1995/96 to 3800 tonnes.

Recycle Waste Oil

Never pour waste oil down the drain; this is illegal as well as environmentally damaging. Waste oils can be recycled. Oil can be re-refined into new lubricating oil, laundered and returned to the company that supplied it for re-use or cleaned to produce a fuel product. Used car engine oil can be taken to an oil bank for recycling. Large quantities of waste oil, generated at sites such as a garage, should be collected by a registered contractor who will buy it from you.

Follow the Oil Care Code

See Industry Standards earlier in the chapter.

Use a Reputable Garage

Make sure any garage you use to maintain your vehicles follows the Special Waste Regulations when disposing of waste oil and the Oil Care Code. Encourage them to look at recycling waste oil.

Paint

All paint waste containing halogenated solvents is special waste. This will include old paint tins which contain some waste paint. To minimise your special waste you should purchase water based paints. B&Q labels all paints it sells with the solvent content. Some decorative paints now have a European Ecolabel indicating a low solvent content (see Chapter 4).

Minimise Paint Waste

Only purchase the quantity of paint you need; any surplus should be stored and used. This will save money on paint purchasing and on expensive special waste disposal.

Make sure Contractors Remove Waste Paints

If you have contractors working on your site make sure they remove their waste paint from your site for re-use or proper disposal.

Batteries

Only lead, mercury dry cells and NiCd batteries are covered by the special waste requirements. For other batteries large quantities should not be concentrated in disposal but diluted with other wastes. The normal duty of care procedures should also be followed.

Recycle Lead–Acid Batteries

Ask your supplier for information on returning lead–acid batteries for recycling. Facilities for recycling lead–acid batteries are well developed and the vast majority are recycled at three plants in the UK. Recycling must be done under tightly controlled conditions because of the risk to the environment from battery acid and the lead salts it contains (DoE, 1995).

Recycle NiCd Batteries

Some collection schemes for NiCd batteries are in place. You can check with your supplier for details. The lack of facilities in the UK means they will be sent to France for recycling. These include mobile phone batteries. For further information contact the British Batteries Recycling Association or the UK NiCd Battery Recycling Group.

SUMMARY GUIDELINES

- ☐ Assess your wastes to see if they require disposal as special waste.
- ☐ Follow the Special Waste Regulations for wastes, such as paints and oils, that you have identified as special wastes.

REFRIGERANTS: CFCS AND HCFCS

Environmental Issues

CFCS

Chlorofluorocarbons (CFCs) derive from methane and ethane, where one or more of the hydrogen atoms are replaced by chlorine or fluorine. Over the past years, scientists have realised that CFCs are destroying the stratospheric ozone layer that protects the Earth's surface from ultraviolet radiation. Increased ultraviolet light near the Earth's surface can increase the incidence of skin cancer and damage plants, animals and whole ecosystems.

The manufacture and import of new CFCs was banned in the European Union on 1 January 1995.

HCFCS

HCFCs (hydrochlorofluorocarbons) are also ozone depleting substances but have one twentieth of the ozone depletion potential (ODP) of CFCs. They are being used as transitional substances. The widely used refrigerant R22 is an HCFC and is still being manufactured.

HCFCs are currently due to be phased out in 2015; this date may come forward. Usage in new systems should therefore be avoided.

COMMON USES

CFCs and HCFCs are found in a variety of applications, from flexible and rigid foams – as used in furniture, bedding, carpet underlay and packaging – to refrigerants and dry cleaning. The major application of CFCs and HCFCs in offices is as refrigerants in air conditioning systems and catering fridges. When you are looking for an alternative, it should have zero ODP.

GLOBAL WARMING POTENTIAL (GWP)

CFCs are also greenhouse gases, so you should consider alternatives with the lowest possible global warming potential (GWP). The global warming potential of a gas is usually expressed relative to carbon dioxide where carbon dioxide has a GWP of one. HFCs (hydrofluorocarbons) are a popular alternative to CFCs and have zero ODP. However these chemicals are very powerful global warming gases: HFC 134a has a GWP of 1300. The efficiency of the refrigeration plant should also be taken into account when selecting a refrigerant because electricity consumption will also contribute to global warming.

INDUSTRY STANDARDS

Criteria for refrigerators and freezers to be eligible for an EU Ecolabel were agreed in October 1996. (See Chapter 4 for further information.) Those relevant to ozone are:

❏ Ozone depleting potential (ODP) – chemicals used as refrigerants or as foam blowing agents must have zero ODP. This means no HCFCs can be used.
❏ Global warming potential (GWP) – the maximum level of GWP for coolant is 15. This includes hydrocarbons such as butane but excludes HFCs that have GWPs of over 1000.

PRACTICAL ACTION

Plan for Alternatives

If you are still using CFCs your environmental policy must contain a commitment to phase them out if it is to be credible, and therefore plans for alternatives should be under consideration.

Minimise Leakage

Design and operating procedures need to minimise leakage of the new refrigerant. Lack of maintenance is the common reason for coolant escaping into the atmosphere. When equipment is not serviced regularly leaks go undetected, CFCs escape and equipment has to be topped up all the time. The availability of CFCs will become increasingly limited and expensive, although some is available from reprocessing facilities.

Find an Alternative Substance

Your alternative should fulfil the following environmental criteria:

❏ zero ODP;
❏ zero or very low GWP; and
❏ energy efficient.

The hydrocarbons propane and butane meet all these criteria.

You may need to use an HCFC or HFC that does not meet these criteria as a transitional substance that is retrofittable (can be used with your existing equipment). If your chosen substance is not retrofittable, it is probably best to replace systems in stages. You will also need to consider price and availability. Note that some alternatives are only available from one source.

Alternative Fluids

There are two types of replacement: pure fluids and blends made up of two to three fluids. Some of the information below is taken from the DTI guide *Refrigeration and Air Conditioning* (1995). The DTI can be consulted for more detailed information.

Pure Fluids

HFC (eg R134a)

HFCs are a family of halocarbons that contain no chlorine and hence do not damage the ozone layer. However they are powerful global warming gases. For instance R134a has similar properties to the CFC R12. It is often retrofittable and is suitable for new installations. R134a is not compatible with existing lubricating oils and you will probably have to change to a polyol ester oil. It does not have zero GWP and efficiency drops for refrigeration below −15°C.

Ammonia

This has been available for a long time and has a zero ODP and zero GWP. It's both cost effective and efficient. It is toxic and flammable so safety is very important when using ammonia. It is not retrofittable due to incompatibility with copper pipes, but if you are installing a new system consider ammonia. A number of supermarkets, including a Cactus Store in Luxembourg, use ammonia-based cooling systems.

Hydrocarbons (Propane and Butane)

Some hydrocarbons make excellent refrigerants. Propane and isobutane can be used as pure fluids. Hydrocarbons can also be used in blends. They do not damage the ozone layer or contribute to global warming potential. Hydrocarbons are therefore the best environmental option. They have been promoted by Greenpeace under the name 'Greenfreeze' as an alternative to HCFCs and HFCs in refrigeration.

The main concern with hydrocarbons is that they are highly flammable. In small applications such as domestic fridges this is not a major concern. However in all applications appropriate safety precautions must be taken in design, delivery, storage, handling and disposal.

Blended Fluids

R12 substitutes

R12 substitutes that can be retrofitted include the HFC R134 which has a high GWP and the hydrocarbon blend Care 30 that has a negligible contribution to global warming.

Case Study

Subject –	**REFRIGERATION**
Organisation –	**DEPARTMENT OF THE ENVIRONMENT**
Organisation type –	**CENTRAL GOVERNMENT**
Location –	**LONDON**
No. of staff –	**5000**

BACKGROUND

International agreement was reached in the Montreal Protocol to ban production of CFCs in order to preserve the ozone layer which shields the Earth from the sun's harmful rays. Two solutions were offered at the time by the refrigeration industry: HCFCs which are now also being phased out because they damage the ozone layer; and HFCs which do not harm the ozone layer but are very powerful global warming gases. In 1992 Greenpeace launched 'Greenfreeze' technology with a German fridge manufacturer. This was based on relatively inexpensive hydrocarbons which do not deplete the ozone layer and have virtually zero impact on global warming. Despite the suspicion of chemical companies and initial caution of fridge manufacturers this technology is now making major inroads into the European market.

ACTION

In August 1993 the then Department of the Environment, Transport and the Regions (DETR) decided to purchase 13 table top refrigerators. The DETR's green housekeeping policy to purchase products free of ozone depleting substances and, where feasible, to control other gaseous and non-gaseous pollu-ants which contribute to climate change.

The only refrigerators which met this policy requirement were those using the Greenfreeze technology and so the decision was taken to specify fridges with hydrocarbon blown foam and coolant. This limited the choice to three German

RESULTS

This is an example of good practice from an office based organisation which has recognised that one of its major impacts on the environment is through the purchase of goods and services. By keeping abreast of technological developments the DoE was able to meet its policy requirements ie to buy a fridge free of ozone depleting substances and using a refrigerant having virtually no potential impact on global warming. Furthermore, by choosing the model with the lowest energy consumption the DoE achieved value for money and helped to conserve electricity – the generation of which also contributes to global warming.

NOTE: Copies of the DETR's green housekeeping policy statement are obtainable from its Publications Despatch Centre, Blakmore Road, London, SE99 6TT. Tel: 0181 691 9191. Fax 0181 694 0099. Or look it up on the Department's site on the World Wide Web for Greening Government Operations. The address or Universal Resource Locator (URL) is: http://www.open.gov.uk/doe/gre ening/gghome.htm.

manufacturers who had only just begun selling this type of fridge in Britain. The DoE then checked to see which was the most energy efficient.

The energy consumption of Liebherr's fridge was found to be 0.13 kWh per 24 hours lower than its nearest rival. But did it provide value for money – a requirement of government policy on public procurement? The fridge cost more than the others but a calculation of its running costs revealed savings in excess of the extra cost over five years. The decision was therefore taken to set up a call-off contract for the Liebherr refrigerator and the first purchases were publicised by the Department's Green Minister to encourage other manufacturers to invest in more environmentally preferable technology.

The DoE issued a green housekeeping note to its property managers alerting them to the call-off contract and, also, copied it to other government departments encouraging them to follow suit.

(Contributed by the Environmental and Energy Awareness Division of the Department of the Environment, Transport and the Regions.)

R502 Substitutes

There are various blends on the market with zero ODP, many of which are retrofittable. Some are compatible with mineral lubricating oils; others may require the oil to be changed.

R22 Substitutes

These are blends using HFCs and can mostly be retrofitted into existing equipment.

Alternative Technologies

Desiccant dehumidification uses chemicals to absorb moisture from the air rather than using refrigeration.

Absorption refrigeration is a heat-driven technology that does not use CFCs.

Refrigerant Management Programme

Any existing CFC in stock is a valuable resource. Set out below is a cost-effective way of introducing an alternative to CFCs gradually. A transitional fluid may be used until an alternative with zero ODP is found.

❑ Invest to minimise leaks.
❑ Establish your annual requirements for CFCs.
❑ Identify which plants can be converted or replaced most easily/cheaply and which plants are old and due for replacement.
❑ Year 1: convert or replace enough equipment to supply sufficient recovered CFC for the annual servicing requirement of your remaining equipment.
❑ Year 2 and beyond: continue the process.
❑ Make sure that no refrigerant is being vented to atmosphere.

SUMMARY GUIDELINES

When replacing CFCs and HCFCs the following key issues should be considered:

❑ Switch to a fluid with zero ODP and GWP.
❑ If possible, find a retrofittable replacement.
❑ Clarify any safety issues arising from the new fluid.
❑ Maximise your use of existing equipment.
❑ Minimise leakage in your current system and make sure it is regularly maintained.

FIRE PROTECTION: HALON

Environmental Issues

Halon is an excellent fire extinguisher that unfortunately destroys the ozone layer. When contained, providing there are no leaks, it is harmless to man and the ozone layer. In the past it has been released into the atmosphere via leakage during training exercises and through lack of maintenance.

Halon begins decomposition at 480°C so, at the point of extinguishing a fire, it is harmless to the ozone layer. However, with a system such as computer flooding, because the halon literally floods the system, not all of it reaches 480°C.

There is no definitive solution to halon replacement and additional alternatives are likely to be developed. Some of the information in this section is based on the DTI guide *Halon Phase Out: Advice on Alternatives and Guidelines for Users*. The DTI can be consulted for further information.

PRACTICAL ACTION

Plan For Alternatives

An environmental policy must contain a commitment to phase out halon use if it is to be credible, and therefore plans for alternatives should be under consideration. You should consider the following issues when selecting an alternative to halons.

❏ Fire fighting effectiveness.
❏ Damage to equipment from use.
❏ How easy it is to install.
❏ How suitable the area is for a gaseous system.
❏ The hazards it presents for occupants.
❏ Environmental performance.

Recycle

Halon can be recycled very effectively and since production ceased, recycling has become an important source of supply. Your current halon system can continue to be used until it runs out or until the supply of recycled halons is no longer available. However, this is an expensive and unreliable option. The Halon Users National Consortium (HUNC) collects halon for recycling for companies who have changed their system and companies who wish to continue using halon.

Establish Compatibility With Existing Equipment

When considering an alternative, establish whether it is compatible with your existing equipment. Some replacements tend to take up more space than halons, therefore you would need larger extinguishers.

Contact Your Insurers

It is vital to discuss this with your insurers. They will need to test the alternative system you intend to use to check quality, capability and effectiveness compared to your existing system. They will need to be satisfied that your alternative meets all their required standards for fire protection. If it does not meet with their requirements, your cover may be affected.

Current Alternatives

There are a range of alternatives to halons in fire fighting which are detailed below. Whichever system you choose it should have zero ODP and have the same quality, capability and effectiveness that halons have.

Carbon Dioxide

Carbon dioxide has zero ODP, is colourless, odourless and clean. As its density is greater than oxygen, in a flooding system it will quickly take over the oxygen in the area making breathing extremely difficult. Carbon dioxide takes up more room than halon (more equipment may be needed) and works by providing a blanket of heavy gas that reduces oxygen to a point where combustion is no longer possible. Systems can be automatic or manual; however, when an area is occupied it needs to be switched to manual. On a manual setting your company needs to have excellent detection systems allowing the system to be set so evacuation can take place before the CO_2 is turned on.

Water Sprinkler Systems

These are the most common type of fixed fire protection. Do not use this system on live electrical equipment fires and flammable liquids. Compared to halon, water is slow to react to fires, and machinery may be subject to some damage.

Fine Water Spray Systems

These are relatively new to fire fighting. Since the application rate is less than that of a sprinkler system, some of the water damage possible is avoided, making it suitable for computer rooms. Fine sprays can be used on flammable liquids and live electrical equipment but not on substances such as reactive metals.

SUMMARY GUIDELINES

- ❏ Advise your insurance company that you intend to change your fire fighting equipment.
- ❏ Clarify the health and safety issues.
- ❏ Maximise use of existing equipment.
- ❏ Decide on the timescale of the change over.
- ❏ Minimise leakage in your current system and make sure there is regular maintenance.
- ❏ Replace and recycle your halon.

Foam Systems

Low, medium and high expansion foams act by forming a barrier between fire and the supply of oxygen. They are not effective against running or spray fires. Foam can be destroyed by some liquid fuels (alcohol, for example) by chemical reaction, so make sure the right foam is chosen.

Dry Powder Systems

These are capable of rapid extinguishment, but provide very little cooling. Once the powder has settled it becomes ineffective. There are different powders suitable to different applications. All types of powder are unpleasant to breathe and are not recommended for occupied areas. They also settle after use and add to the post-fire clean up.

Detection Only

This is a method of fighting fires manually with extinguishers, hose reels or by the fire brigade with the introduction of a highly sensitive smoke detection system.

Alternative Gaseous Agents

These are direct alternatives to halons that are electrically non-conductive and leave no residue. They fall into two categories: inert gas systems and halocarbon gas agents. When considering these you should seek further information from The British Fire Protection Systems Association which produces a code of practice for gaseous fire fighting systems.

TABLE 6.3

Gaseous agents and their GWP (Based on material from DTI, 1995)

TRADE NAME	CHEMICAL DESIGNATION	CHEMICAL NAME/ GAS BLEND	GWP
CEA–410	FC–3–1–10	Perfluorobutane	7900
FM–200	HFC227ea	Heptafluorobutane	3300
FE 13	HFC23	Trifluoropropane	12100
Argonite	IG–55	Argon, nitrogen	0
Inergen	IG–541	Argon, nitrogen, carbon dioxide	0
Argon	IG-01	Argon	0

Inert Gases

Inert gas systems are natural gases from natural sources. They have zero ODP and no global warming potential. Inert gas systems include:

❏ Argonite;
❏ Inergen; and
❏ Argon.

Halocarbon Gas Agents

Hydrofluorocarbons (HFCs) and perfluorocarbons (PFCs) have an important role in fire fighting. They do not harm the ozone layer and are not therefore covered by the Montreal Protocol. These gases are, however, powerful greenhouse gases. They should therefore only be used where careful analysis shows them to be the best alternative.

❏ FM200;
❏ CEA–410; and
❏ Fe 13.

CHAPTER SUMMARY

❏ Implement an energy saving programme.
❏ Communicate energy efficiency initiatives and encourage staff participation.
❏ Consider the health and safety issues of office equipment.
❏ Maximise the opportunities of refurbishment programmes to invest in energy efficiency measures.
❏ Make sure your environmental policy and purchasing policy is communicated to subcontractors.
❏ Follow Special Waste Regulations for disposal of hazardous materials.
❏ Replace CFCs, HCFCs and halons with chemicals that do not damage the ozone layer and, where possible, do not contribute to global warming.

Sources of Information

Industry Organisations

BRITISH BATTERY MANUFACTURERS ASSOCIATION
Cowley House,
9 Little College St
London SWIP 3XS
Tel: 0171 222 066
Fax: 0171 233 0335

BUSINESS EQUIPMENT USERS ASSOCIATION
BEUA Research and Test
Laboratory
Unit 22b, Horseshoe Park
Pangbourne RG8 7JW
Tel: 01189 844999
Fax: 01189 844998

BRITISH FIRE PROTECTION SYSTEMS ASSOCIATION
48a Eden Street
Kingston Upon Thames KTI IEE
Tel: 0181 549 5855

HALON USERS NATIONAL CONSORTIUM (HUNC) & REFRIGERATION USERS GROUP (RUG)
46 Bridge St, Godalming
Surrey GU7 IHL
Tel: 01483 414147
Fax: 01483 414109

NATIONAL HOUSEHOLD HAZARDOUS WASTE FORUM
74 Kirkgate,
Leeds LS2 7DJ
Tel: 0113 246 7584
Fax: 0113 234 4222

UK NICD BATTERY RECYCLING GROUP
c/o International Cadmium
Association
42 Weymouth Street
London WIN 3LQ
Tel: 0171 499 8425

Government Bodies

BUILDING RESEARCH ESTABLISHMENT
Garston
Watford WD2 7JR
Tel: 01923 894040
Fax: 01923 664010

BUILDING SERVICES RESEARCH AND INFORMATION ASSOCIATION
Old Bracknell Lane West
Bracknell
Berkshire RG12 7AH
Tel: 01344 426511
Fax: 01344 487575

BUILDING RESEARCH ENERGY CONSERVATION SUPPORT UNIT
Garston
Watford WD2 7JR
Tel: 01923 664258
Fax: 01923 664787

DEPARTMENT OF THE ENVIRONMENT, TRANSPORT AND THE REGIONS
Publications Dispatch
Blackhorse Road
London SE8 5JH

DEPARTMENT OF TRADE AND INDUSTRY
Environment Directorate
151 Buckingham Palace Road
SWIW 9SS
Tel: 0171 215 1018
Fax: 0171 215 1691

ENERGY TECHNOLOGY SUPPORT UNIT
Harwell, Didcot
Oxfordshire OX11 0RA
Tel: 01235 436747
Fax: 01235 433066

ENVIRONMENT AGENCY
Your local office general
enquiries line
Tel: 0645 333111

Suppliers

EC RECYCLING LTD
Brookfield Business Centre
333 Crumlin Road
Belfast BT14 7EA
Tel: 01232 745241
Fax: 01232 748025

ENERGY SOLUTIONS
Castle House
Bear Lane
Farnham
Surrey GU9 0NR
Tel: 01252 717133
Fax: 01252 717155

MERCURY RECYCLING LTD
Canalside
Unit 6
Off John Gilbert Way
Trafford Park
Manchester M17 1DP
Tel: 0161 877 0977
Fax: 0161 877 0390

7: Transport

INTRODUCTION

The road protests at Newbury and Twyford Down and fears about the health impacts of air pollution have made everybody aware of the environmental costs of the car. The eighties vision of a great car economy has been replaced with a broad acceptance that we need to reduce our car dependency. Transport, however, is an area that many people do not think about when considering the environmental effects of their office. Offices can be heavy users of transport, both in commuting and business travel. Company car sales account for half of all new cars purchased and have a higher mileage than privately registered cars. The environmental effects of your transport needs may therefore be a significant part of the overall environmental impact of your offices.

Transport has a range of effects that have made it a key environmental issue. Surface based transport contributes 21 per cent of Britain's carbon dioxide emissions and this figure is rising. This makes increasing transport demand a major obstacle to meeting Britain's international commitments to reduce emissions of carbon dioxide in order to combat the greenhouse effect. At a local level the pollution from vehicle exhausts is linked to a range of health effects, in particular respiratory ailments. These problems are made more pressing by the fact that the number of vehicles using the roads is forecast to double over the next 30 years (DoT, 1993).

Efficient use of transport will also improve business effectiveness and profitability. A recent guide *The Company, The Fleet And The Environment* (ETSU, 1995) written jointly by the DoE, DoT and CBI concludes that:

Experience shows that effective fleet management releases typical savings of 10. per cent. With fleet cars costing £5,000 or more each year, an average fleet of 100 cars could save £50,000. For many companies, turnover would have to increase by £0.5 million or more to make a comparable contribution to profits!

These benefits are certain to increase. The Government is committed to raising the price of fuel by 5 per cent above the rate of inflation each year as part of its strategy to reduce carbon dioxide emissions. Efficient transport is a win-win solution for profits and the environment.

The chapter is divided into commuting and business travel. It explains how your organisation can provide facilities and encouragement to allow staff to reduce their car dependency when travelling to work. The chapter also looks at ways of reducing the impact, and cost, of the company car. To enable you to prioritise the key areas to target, the chapter also includes a hierarchy of transport solutions.

Transport Hierarchy

FIGURE 7.1
Transport hierarchy

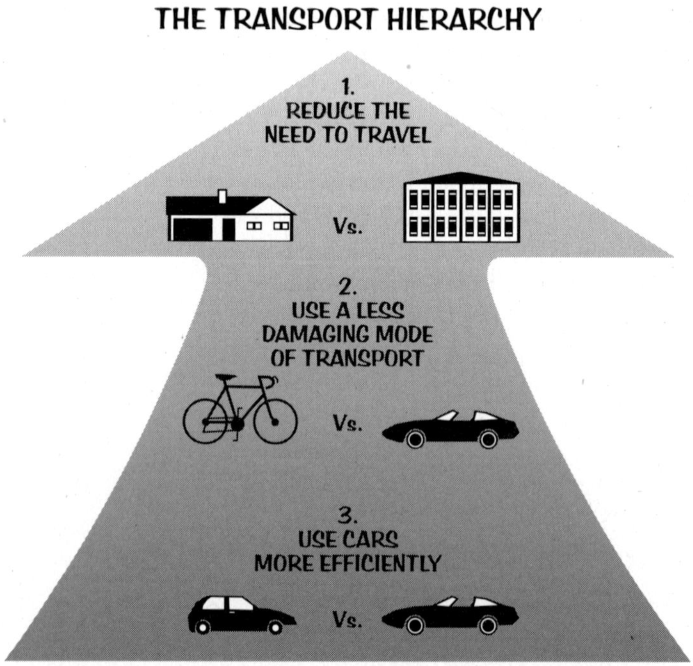

The environmental issues surrounding transport can be complex and make approaching the issue confusing. In Chapter

THE TRANSPORT HIERARCHY

1.
REDUCE THE
NEED TO TRAVEL

Vs.

2.
USE A LESS
DAMAGING MODE
OF TRANSPORT

Vs.

3.
USE CARS
MORE EFFICIENTLY

Vs.

3 we looked at the Government's waste hierarchy which provides a guide to dealing with your waste. We have developed a transport hierarchy (Figure 7.1) that provides a simple rule of thumb to reducing the environmental effects of your transport.

1) Reduce the need to travel at all, better planning and communication technology can play a part in this.
2) Switch from energy intensive and polluting vehicles to more efficient transport modes such as public transport, cycling and walking.
3) Make sure your car is efficient and well maintained.

The guidance given in this chapter follows this hierarchy. Within the two main sections of commuting and business travel, subjects are covered in order of their level in the hierarchy.

Board Level Commitment

Company cars are heavily linked to remuneration. Vehicle allocation, free fuel and parking are policy areas that will require board level agreement. Senior managers are often very reluctant to lose their Jaguar! Equally, significant expenditure on video or teleconferencing to reduce the need to travel will require board agreement. It is therefore important when tackling transport to make sure top level commitment is there to back initiatives.

Senior management need to understand the business case. The main benefits are: the potential for significant savings; and that tackling a sensitive issue such as transport will show that the organisation has a genuine commitment to environmental improvement. You are also likely to receive more support if transport initiatives are linked with the organisation's overall environmental programme. An environmental programme which ignores transport will lack credibility.

LEGISLATION

Emissions and Maintenance

The Road Vehicles (Construction and Use) Regulations made under the Road Traffic Act 1988 set emission requirements for cars and light goods vehicles. These have been amended a number of times, partly to comply with European Union Directives setting maximum emissions levels. The Regulations now require vehicle users to keep engines in tune and to make sure that any emission control equipment, such as catalysts, work efficiently. It is an offence to use a car on the public highway if it fails to conform to the prescribed emission standards. Roadside checks are regularly carried out by the Department of Transport; owners failing the tests can be fined up to £5000.

ROAD TRAFFIC REDUCTION ACT

This law, passed in March 1997, requires local authorities to report on local traffic levels and to set targets to reduce them or their rate of growth.

The National Air Quality Strategy

The 1995 Environment Bill contains provisions for a national air quality strategy that will set standards for air quality and the measures to be taken by local authorities and other bodies to achieve these standards. The standards for air quality are much tighter than previous limits and are based on the Department of Environment's Expert Panel on Air Quality Standards.

Vehicles are accepted to be the main air polluters in most areas. They are therefore targeted for action. Local authorities will receive greater powers to manage air quality that could include powers to tax non-residential parking, carry out roadside emissions tests and introduce a congestion pricing scheme.

Fuel Tax

There is an increasing legislative trend to use economic instruments to promote environmental good practice. The Chancellor of the Exchequer has pledged that the Government will raise road fuel duties by at least 5 per cent above the rate of inflation each year to discourage road traffic. This commitment was restated in the April 1996 Green Paper *Transport The Way Forward* (DoT, 1996).

The costs of road travel could rise dramatically in the future. The Royal Commission on Environmental Pollution (RCEP) report *Transport and the Environment* (1994) recommended doubling the price of fuel by 2005.

Environmental Issues

The environmental effects of transport are primarily caused by aeroplanes, cars and lorries. Public transport using rail, tram and bus is considerably less damaging but can still have significant effects. Walking and cycling have the least impact on the environment, create little pollution or noise, use little space and cause few accidents. They also, according to the British Medical Association, have a strong positive impact on health through increased exercise.

AIR POLLUTION

Greenhouse Effect

In 1993 surface based transport accounted for 21 per cent of UK carbon dioxide emissions, the main greenhouse gas. This level is rising as traffic growth continues to climb and is even higher if air travel is included. Other exhaust emissions such as nitrous oxide also contribute to the greenhouse effect. Reducing pollution from transport is therefore a key factor for Britain to meet its international commitments to help combat the greenhouse effect.

FIGURE 7.2
Diagram of emissions of pollutants by transport mode. (Figures from Whitelegg, 1994)

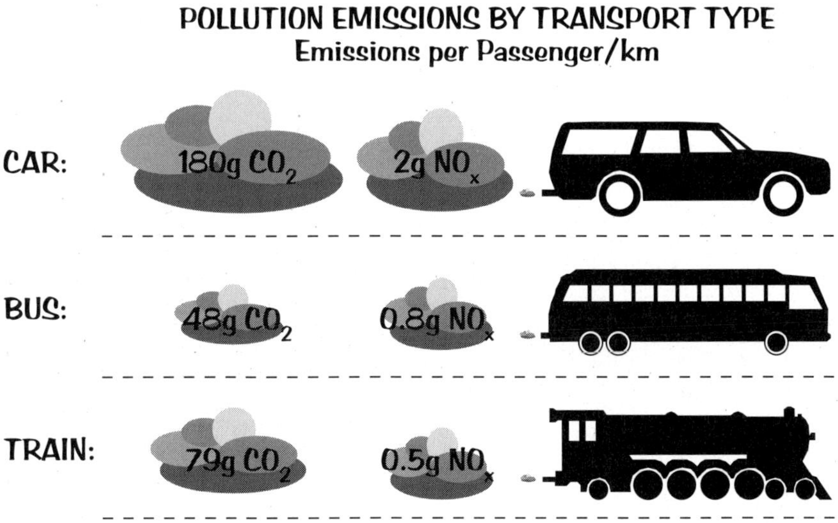

POLLUTION EMISSIONS BY TRANSPORT TYPE
Emissions per Passenger/km

CAR: 180g CO_2 2g NO_x

BUS: 48g CO_2 0.8g NO_x

TRAIN: 79g CO_2 0.5g NO_x

Polluting Emissions

All types of transport emit air pollutants; however the internal combustion engine is the main culprit pouring a wide range of gases into the atmosphere. Over recent years there has been increasing concern over the impacts of these gases on human health, particularly, though not exclusively, in built up areas where traffic is concentrated. These were highlighted by the RCEP report *Transport and the Environment* in October 1994.

Among the health issues raised are lead poisoning, particularly in children, and the carcinogenic effects of chemicals such as benzene. Recently however, most concern has focused on links between air pollutants and respiratory illness. There has been an increase in the incidence of respiratory illness over recent years, particularly amongst children. Between 1976 and 1987 acute attacks of asthma more than doubled in England and Wales. Pollution from vehicles has been suggested as one factor in this. In December 1991 weather conditions resulted in unusually high concentrations of nitrogen dioxide in London; 160 additional deaths were recorded by the Department of Health that week (RCEP, 1994).

Particles of matter such as carbon and unburned fuel and oils that are found in exhaust gases (known as particulates) are especially implicated in the causes of respiratory problems. Emissions from diesel engines contain higher levels of particulates. Smaller particles, known as PM10s, cause the greatest concern for health as they can penetrate the body's defences. An American study has suggested that particulates may be responsible for as many as 10,000 extra deaths a year in England and Wales (RCEP, 1994).

Petrol, Diesel or Alternative Fuels

Until recently diesel cars were promoted as greener due to their greater efficiency which leads to lower carbon dioxide emissions. However, the Committee on Medical Effects of Air Pollution recently stated that on health grounds in the current state of knowledge, diesel engined cars should not be recommended over petrol engine cars with catalytic converters (London First, 1996). The RCEP (1994) took an optimistic view in its report on the potential of diesel but recommended caution at this stage. At present it is safest to regard petrol and diesel as equally polluting.

In the near future the comparison between petrol and diesel may alter and will also be complicated by a range of alternative fuels, the use of which is increasing. The Royal Mail is currently trialing twenty light vans running on biodiesel while Boots the Chemist has converted a VW Transporter van to liquefied petroleum gas (LPG). LPG and natural gas both have significant net benefits over petrol in the reduction of air pollution and carbon dioxide emissions. Gas based fuels are much closer to being economically viable than alternatives like hydrogen and so look the most likely to increase in the short term.

OTHER IMPACTS

Road Accidents

Whilst the health impacts of air pollution are much disputed there is no arguing with road accident figures. In 1993 road accidents killed 3820 people; caused 44,890 serious accidents and involved over 250,000 other casualties (RCEP, 1994). While these are amongst the lowest in Europe they represent nearly two fifths of all accidental deaths in Britain.

Noise

For the majority of people in the UK, road traffic is the main source of noise (RCEP, 1994). At a local level airports and aircraft flight paths can create serious problems. Although it has received less attention than air pollution there is a growing body of evidence on the effect of noise on health. In particular it is linked to stress related conditions such as raised blood pressure.

Noise is also a major reason why people avoid walking or cycling on busy roads and therefore acts as a deterrent to using more environmentally preferable modes of transport.

Space

Different modes of transport require different amounts of space to accommodate them. In a city, or indeed almost anywhere in a heavily populated country like Britain, this has a major impact.

There simply is not the space in a city centre for large numbers of people to travel by car without severe congestion. Outside cities the building of new roads to accommodate the increasing use of cars and lorries has wreaked havoc on the remaining unspoilt countryside. The fierce opposition to this process has been demonstrated at the recent Newbury and Twyford Down protests.

Maintenance and Disposal

Disposal of worn out car parts and final disposal of cars as scrap presents a major waste problem. Cars contain many hazardous or contaminated materials such as batteries, exhaust systems and oil that need to be carefully dealt with. Tyres are a major waste stream that is difficult to dispose of and wastes natural resources. To manufacture a new passenger car tyre takes on average 7 gallons of oil and 7 kg of rubber compound.

Environmental Effect Ready Reckoner

To work out the impact of your office travel on the environment you can use Table 7.1 to estimate the carbon dioxide emissions arising from your business mileage. Use this figure to measure and report on progress and to help gain commitment from staff.

First, calculate the total business car fuel use, this should be held by the accounts department. If you only have the total mileage available you can estimate the fuel use from this figure and an estimate of fuel efficiency. Then multiply this by 2.5 to give total carbon dioxide emissions (ETSU, 1996).

Emissions are different for petrol and diesel cars so if you wish to make the calculation more accurate you can divide your fuel use into petrol and diesel, multiply petrol by 2.3 and diesel by 2.7 and add the results together to arrive at your total CO_2 emissions.

As an example we have estimated the amount of carbon dioxide emitted from British Telecom's commercial fleet from the figures given in its 1995/1996 Environmental Report (Table 7.2). The units are scaled up by a million due to BT's large fuel consumption.

The ready reckoner can also be used for commuting if you have carried out a survey of how staff travel to work and the distance they travel.

TABLE 7.1

Ready reckoner of CO_2 emissions from business travel

Business fuel use (litres)	x 2.5 = Total CO_2 emissions (kg)

FUEL USED BY BT'S COMMERCIAL FLEET 1995/96 (MILLION LITRES)			CO$_2$ EMISSIONS (1000 TONNES)	
Petrol	15	x 2.3	=	34.50
Diesel	58.6	x 2.7	=	158.22
Total				192.72

TABLE 7.2
Example ready reckoner from BT

COMMUTING

Environmental Issues

Commuting to work creates a huge demand for transport. British Telecom's Environmental Report for 1995/1996 records that:

> the combined weight of vehicles carrying drivers, and occasionally passengers, to work in both Europe and the US is 379 million tonnes with an average commuting distance of 24km. This is equivalent to lifting a third of Mount Everest, carting it 24km before 9.00 am then carting it back again every evening!

While no organisation can, or would wish to, control the way staff get to work in the way it controls business travel, it is possible to provide facilities and encouragement to reduce this burden.

INDUSTRY STANDARDS

TravelWise

TravelWise was launched by Hertfordshire County Council in 1993. The aim of the TravelWise campaign is to change people's attitudes towards the use of their cars. It is now supported by over 30 local authorities and has a quarterly newsletter, 'Changing Tracks'. There are a wide range of local initiatives taking place under the TravelWise umbrella including Walk to School Week, staff car sharing schemes and park and ride sites. A contact point for further information is given at the end of the chapter.

GREEN COMUTER PLANS: KEY FEATURES

- ❑ senior management commitment, including leading by example and appointment of a senior member of staff as the Staff Travel coordinator;
- ❑ staff travel survey to provide a baseline;
- ❑ a target to monitor and encourage progress;
- ❑ extensive consultation with staff to overcome resistance to change and gain commitment; and
- ❑ use of work area travel plans in larger organisations.

Green Commuter Plans

Nottingham City Council has been at the forefront of promoting 'green commuter plans' for the city's employers. These plans help companies to set up a comprehensive approach to reducing the environmental impact, and often cost, of commuting. Green commuter plans are intended to be developed and implemented over a three year period with a target to cut car commuting journeys by 30 per cent.

PRACTICAL ACTION

Establishing a Baseline

An important first step is to have an accurate idea of how your staff currently get to work. This will provide you with a baseline figure from which to monitor improvements and allow you to target initiatives on areas with the most potential for improvement.

Survey Staff Travel

A survey of all staff, or of a representative sample, will allow you to gather information on current commuting patterns. For example Unilever International carried out a simple survey of its staff at its Bristol office that asked all staff whether they drove to work, took public transport, walked or cycled.

Use Survey to get Staff Involved

A survey presents an opportunity to find out what measures would encourage staff to cycle or take public transport to work. This will yield useful information and will develop staff interest in the project.

Encourage Participation

Organise a prize draw for those who have been involved in the survey to encourage participation. For example Boots in Nottingham carried out a staff travel survey with a response rate of 85 per cent. Respondents were entered into a prize draw of a 'family of bicycles'.

Minimising Commuting

For commuter travel – meeting the top level of the transport hierarchy – reducing the need to travel, demands radical thinking. Can you bring the office closer to staff or even let staff work from home so that they rarely need to come to the office?

The development of new communication technologies has meant that many people now spend at least a part of their time working from home. Studies have found that teleworkers produce more work and have lower support and property costs. This has been calculated as a 45 per cent gain in efficiency. The overall environmental effects of the teleworking trend are complex, however it is likely to reduce the amount of travel per person by at least two trips a day. Trips which would be in congested areas at peak times.

Plan Relocations

When moving to a new office make sure it is near to residential areas and has good public transport access to minimise the distance staff have to commute.

Book Accessible Conference Venues

Hold conferences at venues with good public transport links rather than those located at motorway junctions. Include instructions as to how to travel by public transport as well as by road. This might be the first impression of your company and it can promote your environmental awareness.

Encourage Home Working

To develop home working focus on one major benefit and use that to sell the idea. For instance, if the sales force of a company is hardly ever at their desks, could they work from home and save office space and costs?

Cycling

Cycling has great potential for implementing the second level of the hierarchy – using a less damaging mode of transport. The Department of Transport has recently issued *The National Cycling Strategy* (1996) which highlights this potential ,'In Switzerland there are more hills, Sweden has colder winters and Germany higher

COMMON PROBLEMS

Resistance to Teleworking

Some organisations still see teleworking as an easy option. However many companies have found that, in the right situation it can save money and increase the efficiency of staff time.

Attachment to the Car

Many people have never dreamt of using anything but their car for commuting. Measures to encourage less damaging modes of transport are therefore potentially controversial.

If staff see the initiatives as a management cost cutting exercise, imposed from above, they will fail; you cannot force staff to use the bus or cycle. Make sure you involve staff from the beginning and that your programme is seen positively, offering benefits to staff and the environment. In this context measures such as charging for car parking will be easier to introduce.

Poor Image of Public Transport

Many people see public transport as inefficient and expensive. Where reasonable services do exist, encouraging staff to try public transport or cycling may overcome this

car ownership; yet each has five times the share of bicycle trips than the UK'.

The Strategy urges all companies to provide facilities for cyclists to increase the proportion of staff cycling to work. It also suggests providing financial incentives for employees to encourage cycle use and that 'Consideration be given to reallocating car parking space to cycle parking as a potentially cost efficient use of land by commercial concerns'.

There can be a direct benefit to organisations from encouraging staff to cycle. The British Medical Association states that cycling has considerable health advantages, particularly for preventing heart disease. Healthier staff means fewer days off sick.

Provide Storage and Changing Facilities

Providing a secure, dry place to store bicycles is crucial to encouraging staff to cycle to work. Risking your bicycle being stolen is a major deterrent.

The other facility needed is showers and changing areas. Neither the cyclist nor their colleagues will be keen on cycling miles to work if they have to wear the same clothes all day!

Promote the Benefits of Cycling

Use the health and environmental benefits of cycling to promote cycling to work to your staff. Further information on these benefits can be obtained from your local council or health authority.

Guarantee a Taxi For Emergencies

Giving staff the reassurance of a guaranteed taxi ride in the case of an emergency will overcome many of their concerns about doing without their car.

Provide Loans for Purchasing Bicycles

National Savings at Durham is one organisation that encourages staff to cycle to work by providing loans to purchase bicycles.

Public Transport

Public transport may already be a widely used alternative to driving if your office is in a town centre. In thi case simple measures such as providing timetables may be very successful. If you are out of town most staff are likely to be unaware of the train station down the road or the bus route past the office and more high profile ideas will be needed to encourage a culture change away from the car.

Provide Season Tickets Loans

Staff may be put off public transport by the initial cost of a season ticket, particularly if they are commuting into London. Some organisations such as British Telecom and Friends of the Earth offer their staff an interest free loan for the ticket which enables the cost to be spread out.

Provide Maps and Timetables

Good information is a key to encouraging use of public transport. There should be points in the office where local public transport information, such as timetables and route maps, is held. Some of this information may be available on computer; London Transport has a guide to its services available on the Internet. Large companies may be able to obtain tailored information from bus companies.

Provide Dedicated Services

Another option for large companies is to build on existing public transport by providing company transport for local employees or a shuttle service to the local train or bus station. For example: Ernst and Young in the City of London provides a daily shuttle from its main offices to Waterloo station.

Work with the Council and Transport Operators

Large organisations can accomplish a great deal by working with their local authority, who will be trying to encourage more use of public transport and cycling, and transport operators who have an interest in attracting more passengers.

An example of this partnership approach would be an employer working with a local bus operator to provide: discounted tickets for staff, services that fit in with the times staff want to travel and travel information targeted at staff. For instance, Nottingham City Council provides

barrier. One way of doing this is by running a leave your car at home day (see Public Transport section).

Lack of Public Transport

Where services are poor large organisations can work with a transport operator and local authority to provide a better service. Hewlett Packard worked with a bus company to put a bus stop on its site (see Case Study).

Poor Cycling Facilities

On your own site you can provide changing and storage facilities for cyclists. You can also work with your local authority to develop better cycle paths in the local area (see Hewlett Packard Case Study).

a staff discount travelcard scheme. Travelcards for the city's buses are sold to staff at a discount and sent directly to the workplace. The cost is then automatically deducted from the payroll. Park and ride season tickets for staff can be negotiated along the same lines.

Leave Your Car at Home Day

One of the barriers to switching from car to public transport is habit. An initiative to overcome this is to hold a leave your car at home day. Many local authorities have run these successfully and linked them to Green Transport Week, which is held in June. The day will need to be publicised well in advance. Publicity such as a picture of the chief executive on a bicycle will help! The reward is that some of those staff who switch to a bus or bicycle for the day may decide to do so regularly.

Parking

Free parking spaces are an expensive perk that encourage staff to commute by car. Southampton University Hospitals has calculated that an average of £300 a year is spent on maintaining each of its parking spaces (including maintenance and opportunity costs). This figure is higher in expensive town centre areas. To encourage staff to use less polluting modes of transport you need to tackle this subsidy, as well as implementing the positive measures outlined above.

The cost of providing parking is likely to rise further as the Government is considering giving local councils powers to tax non-residential parking to help curb air pollution. Reducing the need for car parking spaces will minimise direct costs and allow the opportunity cost of that land to be realised by using it for another purpose. Some of the profits can then be put back into encouraging other forms of transport to work.

Assess the Cost of Your Car Park

The first step to efficient car park management is to assess how many spaces you have available, who is using them, when they are used and how much they cost. The real cost of the parking should be allocated to specific work areas so it can be managed rather than hidden in overheads. The real cost includes the land, laying out, maintenance and management and loss of alternative uses.

Case Study

Subject –	**COMMUTING**
Organisation –	**CAMBRIDGESHIRE COUNTY COUNCIL, HEALTH AUTHORITY AND CAMBRIDGE UNIVERSITY**
Organisation type –	**PARTNERSHIP OF DIFFERENT SECTORS**
Location –	**CAMBRIDGE**

BACKGROUND

One city in which employers are working to 'green' commuter travel is Cambridge. Here are three organisations creating options for reducing car dependency.

ACTION

Cambridgeshire County Council

Cambridgeshire County Council uses the travel awareness initiative TravelWise to promote the case for sustainable transport. The two key messages are to encourage the use of the alternatives to the car and to use the car more efficiently. The three-stage process of generating awareness and understanding to bring about a change in attitudes is firmly underway with recent research showing some 15 per cent of Cambridge people being aware of TravelWise.

Provision has been made to encourage and enable County Council staff to reduce their reliance on cars. Staff receive a business mileage allowance for using their own bike or pool bike and cycle facilities have been upgraded to include showers and more sheltered cycle racks. The County Council is looking for other opportunities to broaden the range of options to reduce the need to travel and allow more sustainable travel for staff and has introduced projects such as teleworking and a free park and ride pilot scheme.

Cycle Friendly Employers Scheme

Both Cambridgeshire County Council and Cambridge University are in a partnership with others supporting the Cycle Friendly Employers Scheme. The scheme aims to increase the number of cyclists in Cambridge through promoting the benefits of cycling and encouraging employers to install or upgrade facilities and incentives for cyclists. A Cycling Promoter has been appointed and has achieved early success in signing up companies and improving facilities for cyclists.

Notable achievements include installation of cycle facilities, eg 200 extra covered cycle parking spaces at Addenbrooke's Hospital; Pool Bikes at Cambridge and Huntingdon Health Authority; Cycling Training Scheme for adults; and voluntary cycle coordinators in member companies.

Cambridge University

The University has an Environmental Policy which actively encourages environmentally sustainable forms of transport. For example, many staff and students already cycle but the University recognises the potential to increase the number of cyclists. The University is a key member of the Cycle Friendly Employers Scheme and individual departments and college have cycle coordinators promoting the case for cycling. The University has a strong focus on safer cycling with good practice advice being spread from the trained cycling coordinators

(Contributed by Cambridge University, Cambridgeshire County Council and the Cycle Friendly Employers Scheme

---

Prevent Unauthorised Access

To prevent unauthorised access there is a range of equipment such as automatic card systems that allow quick entry and exit.

Assess Who Needs a Parking Space

Only staff who genuinely need to bring their cars to work should be given a parking permit.

Charge For Parking Space

Charge for parking spaces at a market rate and use the money to provide support for other modes of transport such as facilities for cyclists and loans towards public transport season tickets. Encourage staff to car share with lower parking charges.

Car Sharing

Car sharing is a relatively simple way to achieve more efficient use of the car, the final level of the transport hierarchy. Some of your staff may already be car sharing and this, along with the savings, means resistance is likely to be lower than to some of the measures described above.

Provide a Noticeboard

The simplest way to promote sharing is a dedicated noticeboard or computer bulletin board where staff can exchange information to enable them to link up (you could publicise it as a dating agency for car sharing!). This also provides a focal point for publicising environmental initiatives and reporting progress back to staff.

Organise a Database

To provide more active support for car sharing an organisation can develop a database of those wishing to car share and the locations from which they commute. The database should have a designated member of staff responsible for updating or it will swiftly become out of date.

Guarantee A Taxi In Emergencies

A guaranteed ride home by taxi in the event of an emergency should be made available to all staff who are car sharing.

SUMMARY GUIDELINES

- ❏ Plan new developments that minimise the need to travel and are accessible by public transport.
- ❏ Promote home working where it is appropriate.
- ❏ Provide secure facilities for bicycles.
- ❏ Provide changing facilities for cyclists.
- ❏ Offer loans for season tickets or other incentives to encourage staff to use public transport.
- ❏ Charge for car parking spaces and use the proceeds to support cycling facilities, season ticket loans and car sharing.
- ❏ Support car sharing by maintaining a database of those wanting to participate and details of their journey.

BUSINESS TRAVEL AND THE COMPANY CAR

Environmental Issues

Business travel and the company car fleet can be a major expense for an organisation. Maximising the efficiency of the car fleet and business travel is sound business practice. It can also produce substantial environmental improvements.

Company cars cause a major part of the environmental damage done by vehicles. A recent report by the Institute for European Environmental Policy (IEEP) (Transport 2000, 1996) found that company car owners used their cars for commuting and leisure more than private owners paying the full cost for running their vehicles; 80 per cent more where the company meets the fuel bills. The tax system also encourages greater mileage as tax liability is reduced by a third if a company car is used for business miles of more than 2500 a year and by two-thirds if for more than 18,000 miles a year.

Company cars tend to be larger engined models than privately registered vehicles. Most company cars are eventually sold on to the private market and so the supply of large engined cars has a knock on effect on the private car fleet. Company car drivers are twice as likely to break motorway speed limits as private motorists. Large engined cars travelling at higher speeds for greater mileage entail greater pollution and a higher accident rate.

The IEEP concluded that the current state of the company car market undermines government policy in a number of ways, by:

❏ limiting the effectiveness of price mechanisms on fuel;
❏ exacerbating urban congestion and air pollution;
❏ undermining the Government's aim of curbing the growth in transport demand; and
❏ working against accident reduction targets.

INDUSTRY STANDARDS

London First Clean Air Charter For Fleet Best Practice

The London First Clean Air Charter encourages businesses t contribute to an industry-wide effort to improve the enviror mental performance of their fleets. While the Charter focused on London its aims and guidance are relevant natio wide. The guidance picks up on may of the recommendatio given in this section. Signatories to the charter are required t

❏ nominate a senior manger to take forward the Charter;

❏ establish a baseline by monitoring the environmental impact of current corporate transport policy;

❏ write an action programme to decrease the environmental impacts of corporate fleet practice, including targets for improving performance. One of these should be a three year target for increasing miles per gallon; and

❏ submit annual reports of progress against the action plan to London First.

Companies will be de-listed if they fail to fulfil the requirements. The Charter is sponsored by the RAC and the Department of the Environment. Companies who have endorsed the Charter include London Electricity plc, J. Sainsbury plc, and BAA plc.

PRACTICAL ACTION

Reducing the Need to Travel

New technology has provided a growing number of ways to reduce the need to travel. Whilst face to face meetings remain important to all organisations the growth of communication technologies such as video conferencing provides an alternative to the traditional business meeting.

A phone call still consumes energy and resources but at a far lower level than a vehicle. These savings multiply as the distance increases. This is reflected in the relative price of a phone call against an international flight.

There is also an effective and low technology way to reduce business travel. Better planning and logistics have been shown to have a major impact on the efficiency of freight transport and the same will be true of business travel.

Use Video Conferencing

Following the initial capital cost there is potential for considerable savings on travel costs and staff time, particularly where conferencing replaces international travel. Modern video communication products offer a wide range of facilities. For instance two screens can be used to maintain face to face contact while working with graphics and slides.

Coordinate Meetings

Make sure that meetings and travel are coordinated by efficient journey planning. For instance schedule meetings near to each other on the same day so only one trip is required or share a car with other staff going to the same location. This is particularly important to large organisations with a number of sites and frequent travel between them.

Plan Staff Commitments

Planning of staff commitments can also cut travel demand, particularly where staffs work is split between two or more sites. When staff are seconded to other sites, providing hotel accommodation will avoid them having to make long round-trip journeys

Using Other Transport Modes

Use Public Transport for Business Travel

Make sure that, wherever practical, all business travel is by public transport. This can result in a more efficient use of staff time since it is possible to work on the train.

Encourage Visitors to Use Public Transport

One simple step you can take is to make sure that standard directions you provide to visitors cover access by public transport as well as by car. This may be one of the first things a visitor sees about your organisation and is therefore important in communicating your environmental commitment. Some companies with an environmental policy fail to give directions for travel by public transport.

Provide Information on Public Transport

To encourage staff to use public transport the provision of good information is crucial. For business travel the information needs to cover the whole country. An IBM initiative in this area is a good example of a simple idea that can help bring about improvements. To encourage staff to use public transport it provides on-line guides to bus and rail services to help journey planning.

Alternatives to the Company Car

Do your staff need a company car? Many companies

now offer alternative packages that can save the company money, reduce environmental impact and satisfy their staff.

Provide an Alternative Package to the Company Car

An attractive and realistic alternative package might include cash and a season ticket to use on local public transport. This can save an organisation money on the cost of the car and on the cost of providing parking, which, as already mentioned, can be substantial.

Provide Office Pool Bikes

Some organisations, such as Cambridgeshire County Council, provide office pool bicycles as an alternative to the car for short journeys.

Car Choice

All cars use energy and cause pollution so there is no such thing as a green car. The green choice is to reduce the company car fleet. However, you can make your car fleet more efficient and achieve significant savings by making sure that you purchase the right cars. More efficient models cause significantly less pollution than gas guzzlers. When choosing a car it is important to look at the whole life cost rather than simply the capital cost. A cheaper model may work out to be more expensive once issues such as fuel consumption and resale value are taken into account.

The Environmental Transport Association provides a guide to choosing the best car. The 1995 Guide ranks small cars such as the Fiat Cinquecento first and large cars such as the BMW 750iL at the bottom.

Choose an Efficient Car

The key points to remember are:

❑ miles per gallon, urban and non-urban;
❑ avoid 'sporty' models;
❑ avoid cars with high acceleration; and
❑ avoid cars with high top speeds.

Monitor Alternative Fuels

The current position of petrol, diesel and alternative fuels was outlined in the section on the Environmental Effects

COMMON PROBLEMS

Cars and Status

❏ Cars are closely related to remuneration and status within many organisations. Measures that seek to encourage senior managers to use smaller cars are potentially highly controversial.

❏ To overcome these problems the key is senior management commitment. The second important principle is to involve staff from the start. Tell your staff what is happening and make them feel part of a positive programme, otherwise they will be suspicious of any changes you introduce.

Sporty Drivers

❏ Good driving technique can reduce fuel consumption by up to 25 per cent, cut accidents and reduce maintenance costs. Driver training and fuel monitoring will curb the budding Damon Hill in your organisation!

Lack of Knowledge of Fuel Cost

❏ Many organisations have only an overall idea of the cost of company cars and business travel. This makes improvement difficult to monitor and report on.

of Transport. This position will change in the future and fleet managers need to monitor the relative merits of all available fuels.

Driving Technique

As well as looking at car choice and maintenance, efficiency of vehicle use can also be improved.

Train all Drivers

Good driving technique can reduce fuel consumption by up to 25 per cent. This means a large reduction in harmful emissions as well as the potential major cost savings. If fuel use is being measured and managed it is possible to monitor improvements and provide incentives to efficient drivers.

The average cost of a claim for accidental damage to a company car is about £1000, to which needs to be added the cost in lost time. Driver training can reduce these costs and the pain and trauma associated with them. Drivers who have attended driver training courses show reduced accident rates and greater fuel efficiency through a smoother driving style. These improvements are being recognised by many insurance companies through reduced premiums.

Provide Route Planning Software

Use of route planning software and real-time traffic information systems can ensure the fastest, least congested route.

Fuel

The Government has pledged to increase rates of duty on road fuels by 5 per cent a year above the rate of inflation. There is pressure to increase this further. Managing fuel consumption is therefore a key to keeping the cost of the car fleet down.

Most companies award senior staff larger cars and higher mileage allowances. These measures encourage the use of less fuel efficient cars and more driving. The perk of free fuel leaves private motoring effectively free and therefore encourages greater distances to be travelled.

End Free Fuel for Personal Use

Organisations should end the perk of free fuel for personal use. Mileage allowances should be the same for all cars. These measures will encourage the selection of smaller cars and reduce the amount of driving.

Monitor Fleet Fuel Use

Monitoring vehicle fuel performance is necessary to control the company car fleet. Although this may seem to entail excessive bureaucracy the systems should be simple to run once in place and will produce a clear picture of a key cost element. The main factors to consider are: the volume of fuel used, the associated cost, and the distance travelled. These will provide a complete record of fuel performance by vehicle. Driver and vehicle performance can then be accurately monitored.

Maintenance and Tyres

A well maintained vehicle can be 10 per cent more efficient than one that is not regularly serviced. One in five roadside breakdowns are the result of bad vehicle maintenance. To minimise the costs and environmental impacts of your car fleet it is essential to keep it well maintained.

Service Your Car Fleet Regularly

Manufacturer's recommendations should be seen as the minimum level for service intervals. These services should check emissions to make sure they are at a minimum level. Your garage should be able to provide a print-out or written record of the emission level. Other important areas are to make sure that tyre pressures are correct and that spark plug leads and connections are in good condition.

Make Drivers Aware of Servicing Intervals

Drivers need to be made aware of their responsibility for helping to ensure regular servicing.

Use a Responsible Garage

Make sure that the garage that carries out the maintenance of your company cars is environmentally

❑ To overcome this use fuel cards to monitor the fuel consumption of individual drivers. There are major savings available from measures such as driver training which will be clearer if you can demonstrate them.

Case Study

Subject –	**COMPANY CAR FLEET**
Organisation –	**NATWEST**
Organisation type –	**BANKING**
Location –	**INTERNATIONAL**
No. of staff –	**APPROXIMATELY 80,000**

BACKGROUND

NatWest Group is committed to achieving environmental best practice throughout its business activities, wherever this is practicable. In line with this commitment a member of the management team at Group Vehicle Services (GVS) was assigned specific responsibility for environmental issues in 1993 and considerable progress has been made in reducing the impact of the company car fleet.

ACTIONS

❏ In 1992 approximately 80 per cent of the 'perk' fleet was downsized to an engine capacity of less than 2000cc, the essential user fleet restricted to a petrol engine capacity of 1600cc and diesel engine of less than 2000cc.

❏ All 'sporty' models (SRi's etc) were removed from the fleet by the end of 1993.

❏ A project looking at alternative fuel vehicles was initiated in 1994. Five cars have now been converted to bi-fuel (natural gas and petrol) operation. These vehicles are being used to promote alternative fuels; three will be based in Bristol, one has been loaned to the WWF and the other is being loaned to bank managers and external organisations ie local councils

❏ In 1995/96, GVS wrote and published a driving booklet giving advice on environmental driving practices and other related issues.

❏ NatWest, through GVS, became a signatory to the London First Clean Air Charter in January 1996. The five year action plan is currently being formulated.

❏ GVS produces annual environmental reports, providing an overview of the department's activities and the current market place.

RESULTS

❏ Introduction of an environmental service level agreement with all suppliers to GVS.

❏ Currently reviewing fuel card and driver training options

❏ Undertaking research into the vehicle supply chain from both an environmental and cost and process angle.

Case Study

Subject –	**REINVENTING COMMUTING**
Organisation –	**HEWLETT PACKARD**
Organisation type –	**COMPUTERS**
Location –	**BRISTOL**
No. of staff –	**1200**

THE PROBLEM

Hewlett Packard's (HP) Bristol site is set in the Bristol 'North Fringe'. It was one of the first major sites established there in 1983; but over the last three years, it has seen very rapid development all around it as other major employers have moved into the area. Such expansion has created a massive, saturating commuting load on the local road system

THE BUSINESS IMPACT

HP's business feels an impact through:

❏ damage to employees' productivity;
❏ damage to employees' well-being; and
❏ direct costs.

Employees do at times arrive late and stressed after being stuck in traffic. As a rule, stressed people can neither enjoy their work nor work effectively.

So far, as the business on site has grown, we have built car parks in direct proportion to headcount. If we can lessen this dependency, we make direct expenditure savings, and increase our return on assets. We also minimise the amount of valuable land we have to devote to a non-productive and ecologically sterile purpose.

THE RESPONSE

HP's response to the gathering transport problem has been to:

TRANSPORT

❏ build on environmentally motivated employee initiatives; and
❏ define a formal transport Hoshin, or breakthrough objective.

In 1990, a series of environmental initiatives were started by employees, among them several on transport. These focused on cycling, lift-sharing, and provision of information about existing public transport services. Out of these initiatives came: experience with building primitive ride sharing systems; an active and well organised cyclists' group; a strong relationship with the County of Avon's Cycling Projects Team; and a new cyclepath running on the periphery of HP's land. In addition, and most important of all, there emerged a wide and general awareness that there are viable alternatives to 'one person, one car' commuting.

A formula Hoshin on transport was defined in mid-1995, when it became clear how severe the problems were going to be. The first task was to characterise and quantify the problem, which we did by:

❏ producing commuting maps, showing (anonymously) home locations of all employees;
❏ conducting a traffic census of all vehicles entering and leaving site; and
❏ issuing and analysing a commuting survey of employees' commuting practices.

From the information these exercises revealed, we then set our priorities and planned how to implement them. These priorities were to:

❏ provide easy access to railway stations;
❏ provide bus access to site; and
❏ increase bicycle commuting from 10 per cent to 20 per cent.

THE IMPLEMENTATION

So how does it actually work on the ground?

Trains

A new station has recently been built which now sees 60 trains a day running to all points of the compass.

Buses

HP has had no handy bus stop, and so no easy access to the network. So in response, we've worked with a local bus service provider to re-route one of their lines through the HP site. Now, at peak commuting times, HP staff can catch the bus from their own stop on-site to either of the local transport hubs or, alternatively, into the middle of Bristol.

Ridesharing

We've tried paper and software rideshare systems, neither of which worked very well; but people on site understood the idea, saw the advantages, and set up their own, informal arrangements – which, in the spirit of a truly distributed system, work much better! Now over 20 per cent of HP commuters rideshare regularly, and over 40 per cent occasionally. We're in the process of publishing lists of lift offerers over the site intranet in order to strengthen this process.

Cycling

Doesn't sound like it can make much difference, does it? But, according to our commuting survey, over 10 per cent of our people cycle to work regularly. The UK government has just launched the Cycle Challenge initiative, and we've worked with our local councils to help them win a government grant and place a cycling information officer in north Bristol (the first, incidentally, in the UK). He and his Project Bike hotline help our people's most serious concern about cycling to work – traffic danger. We're now aiming for 20 per cent commuting. The national average is 3 per cent.

Working from Home

On occasion, this is the ultimate antidote to commuting! It is now technically straightforward to access the workplace computer network from home, or to carry a complete computing environment on a laptop computer.

CONCLUSION

The end result is that HP Bristol is no longer totally dependent on the private car. People have real choices about how they get to work – and, increasingly, whether an electronic presence is sufficient on any given day!

(Contributed by Hewlett Packard, Bristol.)

RESULTS

- ❑ New local train well used by staff.
- ❑ New bus station built on HP's site.
- ❑ Over 20% of staff regularly car share.
- ❑ Over 10% of staff cycle to work.
- ❑ HP Bristol site no longer totally dependent on the car.

SUMMARY GUIDELINES

- ❏ Reduce travel through use of communication technologies such as video conferencing and planning of staff commitments.
- ❏ Make sure that all business travel is by public transport where practicable.
- ❏ Offer staff a realistic alternative package to the company car, perhaps including a season ticket for public transport.
- ❏ Purchase/lease efficient cars and take into account their whole life costs.
- ❏ Train drivers in advanced driving practice.
- ❏ Monitor the fuel performance of each vehicle.
- ❏ Make sure vehicles are well serviced and maintained by a responsible garage.
- ❏ If fleet management is outsourced make sure the company has high environmental standards.

responsible. Ask the garage for details of the environmental precautions it takes. Car maintenance involves washing down oily and greasy surfaces and changing oil at regular intervals. Car washing areas and any area where there may be oil spills should be designed to collect dirty water and prevent its discharge to drains. Waste oil should be disposed of in accordance with the 1996 Special Waste Regulations and never simply emptied down the drain.

Use Retreads for your Tyres

Tyres are a major item of expenditure for a company car fleet. For most fleets they are the third largest item in their operating budget after labour and fuel. They are also a major waste stream that is difficult to dispose of. Retreaded tyres provide both environmental and cost benefits. Fleet managers have found tyre costs can be reduced by 50 per cent by retreading their tyre casings at least twice. This has led to retreads being widely used by transport based organisations such as professional hauliers and taxi companies.

Despite their mixed reputation retreads are already widely in use. All aircraft use retreads, a typical jet aircraft will carry out somewhere in the region of 200 take-offs and landings on a set of tyres that will be remoulded four to five times before being disposed of. In the UK retreads are manufactured to strict legal standards. The retreader you use should work to the British Standard AU 144e, be a member of the Retread Manufacturers Association (RMA) and be certified to the ISO 9002 quality assurance standard. Such a manufacturer will be subject to regular audits to make sure they maintain high quality levels.

The environmental benefits of retreads are also considerable. To manufacture a new passenger car tyre takes on average 7 gallons of oil and 7 kg of rubber compound. To retread the same tyre takes 2.5 gallons of oil and 3 kg of rubber compound. The current savings for the UK from the use of retreads are 33 million gallons of oil and 60,000 tonnes of rubber compound. Retreading also reduces the problems of dealing with scrap tyres. These advantages have led to government support for retreads.

Rochdale Metropolitan Borough Council insists on remoulds on all vehicles except minibuses. This has produced savings of at least 40 per cent on tyre costs.

Contracting Out

Many organisations choose to contract out the management of the company car fleet. Make sure that the standards detailed above are passed on to the management company as part of the contract.

CHAPTER SUMMARY

- ❏ Use the hierarchy: reducing the need to travel, encouraging the use of less polluting modes of transport and improving the use of the car.
- ❏ Gain top level commitment to reducing the cost and environmental impact of your transport.
- ❏ Plan office locations, meetings and business practices to reduce the need for staff to travel.
- ❏ Encourage the use of cycling, public transport and car sharing for commuting and business travel.
- ❏ Provide alternative packages to the company car.
- ❏ Use an efficient and well maintained company car fleet.
- ❏ Train all your staff in advanced driving practice.

Sources of Information

ENERGY EFFICIENCY ENQUIRIES BUREAU

ETSU
Harwell
Didcot
Oxfordshire OX11 0RA
Telephone: 01235 436747
Fax: 01235 433066

ETSU produces guides, case studies and other information to help managers improve fleet efficiency.

GREENER MOTORING FORUM SECRETARIAT

Department of the Environment
RM B247
Rommey House
43 Marsham Street
London SW1P 3PY

The Forum, established between central and local Government aims to promote 'greener' motoring.

THE DEPARTMENT OF TRANSPORT

Transport Policy Unit
Great Minster House
76 Marsham Street
London SW1P 4DR

Advice on transport issues and government policies.

ACFO LTD

The Mint House
Hylton Road
Petersfield GU32 3JY
Telephone: 01730 260162
Fax: 01730 263937

The Association of Car Fleet Operators exists to share information on running fleets of cars and vans.

Lillian Goldberg

ENVIRONMENT DEPARTMENT

Hertfordshire County Council
County Hall
Pegs Lane
Hertford
Herts SG13 8DN
Tel: 01992 556119

Hertfordshire set up the TravelWise scheme outlined in the chapter.

LONDON FIRST

Caxton House
6 Tothill Street
London SW1H 9NA
Telephone: 0171 222 1445
Fax: 0171 222 1448

London First has designed the 'Clean Air Charter for Fleet Best Practice'.

NATIONAL SOCIETY FOR CLEAN AIR

136 North Street
Brighton BN1 1RG

The NSCA produces leaflets on the environmental issues of motor vehicles including 'Choosing and Using a Cleaner Car'.

TRANSPORT 2000

Walkden House
10 Melton St
London MW1 2EJ

Transport 2000 is a national organisation campaigning for environmentally sustainable transport.

8:
Environmental Awareness

INTRODUCTION

With the help of this Manual you will have highlighted a number of areas for environmental improvement in your office practices. The key to the successful implementation of these initiatives is a planned communication programme covering your entire organisation. Individuals need to understand that all their office activities have an environmental impact and have clear guidelines on what they can do to minimise that impact.

The barriers that environmental programmes face are different from organisation to organisation but often revolve around the misconception that the environment is external to most people's working lives. Many people believe that the environment is what you walk the dog around at weekends. The majority of people do care about the environment but do not link this to everyday working activities. The important issue for the creation and development of a successful environmental programme is to make this link.

Most organisations have employees who are interested in environmental issues. Pressure to implement sound environmental practice in an office, particularly recycling, often comes from keen staff rather than management. This enthusiasm should be recognised and reinforced as it represents a valuable source of motivation and awareness.

This chapter describes the planning and launching of a recycling scheme as an example of how to avoid some common

COMMON PROBLEMS

Lack of Senior Management or Officer Commitment

Environmental initiatives can quickly lose momentum without the support of senior staff and management. Highlight the different benefits that environmental initiatives will produce. Senior management can often be persuaded by cost savings.

Poor Perception and Misconceptions

The image of the environment has changed and it is now a central part of the pressures and opportunities all organisations face. Becoming environmentally sound does not have to be a cost; going green saves you money.

Lack of Knowledge and Understanding

Many barriers are based upon a lack of knowledge. Provide clear, factual information to help overcome a lack of understanding.

pitfalls. It also looks at the broader issues of communication, particularly overcoming resistance to change. Creating awareness and understanding of environmental issues is essential to the success of any programme. Effective training programmes play an important role in this, particularly in complex areas such as purchasing. This chapter identifies the key communication issues to consider when planning initiatives and outlines effective ways of integrating environmental considerations into the overall management process.

ENCOURAGING OWNERSHIP

The success or failure of environmental initiatives and programmes are dependent upon the extent to which you can enthuse and involve your staff. Many environmental initiatives are actively dependent upon staff involvement, for example effective recycling schemes can only be developed if all staff are motivated, aware of why they need to take part and know what they need to do to make it work.

Staff involvement can be developed through environmental awareness training, which explains the connections between the actions of people in their working lives and the environment. Provide simple facts such as: every tonne of paper we use contains wood from 17 trees. Information should bridge the gap between the office to the environment.

PRACTICAL ACTION

Obtain Senior Management Commitment

Endorsement from a senior level is an essential part of communicating the importance of the environment to your staff. Establishing an environmental policy signed by senior management will help to give a mandate to the programme (see Chapter 2). You must ensure that senior management have an understanding of the issues so that they are as aware of the reasons for your environmental programme as the rest of your staff. Formal presentations to management outlining the business case can be an effective method of conveying this message.

Promote Individual Action

Individuals need to understand the connection between their day-to-day activities in the office and wider environmental issues. Give staff clear guidelines on what action they can take in their daily work activities and how they can make a difference.

Produce Clear, Relevant Environmental Information

Show the link between your organisation and the environment. Demonstrate the impacts your organisation has upon the environment and the environmental issues associated with those impacts. Use this to explain and support initiatives designed to minimise those impacts and the contribution that each employee can make.

Encourage Participation

Find out which of your staff are already environmental enthusiasts and harness this enthusiasm by encouraging involvement in initiatives within your organisation. Keen individuals can exert considerable peer pressure (see the section on Staff Environment Committees in this chapter).

Promote the Business Case

Explain the reasons why you are introducing an environmental programme. Illustrate the potential cost savings that can be made through the programme, the need to respond to changing environmental legislation and pressures to remain competitive.

Be Professional

You need to show that you are serious about the environment and are approaching the issue in a planned and pragmatic way. A few poorly labelled, tatty boxes for recycling will not inspire cynics! The environment needs to be perceived as an essential, integral part of the way your organisation is run; it is not enough just to shout about it.

SUMMARY GUIDELINES

❑ Explain the connection between work activities and environmental issues.
❑ Make sure you have senior management commitment.
❑ Produce clear and relevant information on the environmental programme.
❑ Highlight any cost savings from environmental measures.
❑ Present initiatives in a professional way.

COMMON PROBLEMS

Lack of Support

Committees become tired and bored if they become a talking shop but are not able to achieve anything because they cannot make funding decisions. Ensure that your committee has representatives from a senior level, endorsement from the board and a formal channel for ideas to be communicated.

Loss of Motivation

Staff can lose interest in the environment if they feel the effort that they have contributed is not recognised and built upon. The environment committee can help to avoid this by encouraging suggestions and providing regular feedback on the success of initiatives.

STAFF ENVIRONMENT COMMITTEES

However energetic and enthusiastic the person leading your programme, they can not green the office on their own. The role of the person driving the programme is to act as a facilitator by encouraging and motivating others within your organisation. If a programme is based on the enthusiasm of one individual, which can often be the case with smaller organisations, there is a danger that the programme will come to a grinding halt if that person leaves. Establishing a staff environment committee can be a very effective way of disseminating information throughout your organisation and of spreading the responsibility for environmental issues. In any organisation, there are usually keen staff who like to be involved and feel that they make a difference. Involving them can improve morale.

An environment committee must have input from different sectors within your organisation and be able to make recommendations at board level. It is essential to recognise that the environment is an interdepartmental issue and is therefore relevant to all activities throughout your organisation.

PRACTICAL ACTION

Establish an Environment Committee

Make sure that you have representation from across departments and different levels of your organisation; this will provide contact points within each department. It is important to have representation from a senior level to ensure the credibility of the group. The success of initiatives that are promoted by your environment committee will often be dependent upon the specific individuals who you choose to be part of it. Environmental champions, people who become identified with the issue and who provide a useful focus, can emerge at this stage. Often champions are those people who are already involved with the environment. If you know of someone in your organisation who is keen on recycling and cutting waste then you may have found your first champion. At Unilever International at Bristol, the green office initiatives are driven by the Green Team, formed by a group of keen and highly motivated staff.

Case Study

Subject –	**STAFF ENVIRONMENT GROUPS**
Organisation –	**DORSET COUNTY COUNCIL**
Organisation type –	**LOCAL AUTHORITY**
Location –	**COUNTY HALL (DORCHESTER) AND DORSET HOUSE (BOURNEMOUTH)**
No. of staff –	**900 AND 180 RESPECTIVELY**

BACKGROUND

Waste Minimisation Audits were conducted at the two main administrative centres of Dorset County Council to identify improvements and implement good housekeeping practices. The County recognised that the key to a successful programme was to involve staff in the implementation of the recommendations. The audit highlighted a high level of enthusiasm and awareness of environmental issues amongst staff and the willingness to participate. Consequently, Staff Environment Groups have been established at County Hall and Dorset House to help implement waste minimisation initiatives and to exchange ideas, particularly ideas for waste reduction. The meetings have shown a high level of awareness amongst staff and a number of new initiatives have been introduced.

ACTION

Cardboard boxes from the delivery of photocopier paper are returned to the Print Room for re-use. The Print Room were previously buying in boxes. This will save an estimated £400–600 pa and reduce the volume of waste.

The typing bureau already use obsolete paper for draft documents. Departments are now encouraged to pass on paper that has only been printed on one side to the typing bureau. Double sided printing has increased particularly for draft contracts and committee reports.

RESULTS

❏ High level of awareness and involvement amongst staff.
❏ Encouraged ownership.
❏ Cost savings achieved estimated at £20,000 pa.
❏ Environmental improvements.
❏ Good publicity.

More use will be made of the scrap pads available from the Print Department.

Several departments were having problems disposing of obsolete equipment or equipment that was no longer needed. Through the Staff Committee, alternative homes for this equipment were found within the authority.

To maintain interest and educate staff, suppliers including Severnside Waste Paper and Greencare (remanufacturer of toner cartridges) have given presentations explaining their products and services and how the recycling process works.

The Agenda 21 Officer explained how the waste minimisation programme within offices linked to Local Agenda 21 and broader issues within the county.

The typing bureau pioneered the collection and successful use of remanufactured toner cartridges within the authority. The extension of this scheme authority wide has resulted in considerable cost savings. The contribution made by the typing bureau was recognised and a prize of a day at a Health Club was given!

The programme was promoted by cartoon graphics personalised to Dorset County Council, created by the resident artist in the office services team!

The achievements at Dorset House were recognised, and a plaque was presented by the Chief Executive to the Staff Environment Group and given to most active greenie!

Local press coverage has been excellent resulting in good publicity for the County and encouragement to the Staff Environment Groups.

The results achieved in a very short time have been excellent. This has been due to the involvement of staff through the Environment Groups.

Select your Chairperson

The chairperson should be senior and be able to report back at board level. The committee should meet regularly, and agendas and minutes should be produced and circulated electronically to maintain a high level of awareness.

Use the Committee as a Forum for Communication

The committee can help internal communication by bringing together people who do not generally work with each other. Excellent ideas, particularly regarding waste reduction measures, can come out of these meetings (see Dorset County Council Case Study in this chapter). Also there may already be informal initiatives in departments that can be extended throughout your organisation. The environment committee is a useful forum to discuss any obstacles that might be faced by the environmental programme and how they can be overcome.

The environment committee can be used to identify and promote good practice, develop new initiatives and to give feedback on existing schemes. The committee must encourage suggestions for improvement and ensure that good ideas are recognised. If the committee includes individuals from different departments it can represent a useful mechanism for sharing ideas.

Introduce Environmental Awareness Training

The committee can be an essential channel for environmental training to improve understanding and awareness of environmental issues amongst all staff. Suppliers such as recycling companies, paper merchants and toner cartridge companies will readily give presentations to staff to explain the processes involved. Visits can also be very useful; a trip to a landfill site can be a memorable experience!

Clarify the Role of the Committee

Make sure that the committee members feel that they have a role in promoting your programme. Where individuals and departments have made significant contributions they should be recognised.

SUMMARY GUIDELINES

- ❑ Choose keen staff who are potential environmental champions.
- ❑ Choose a mix of staff from different departments and levels.
- ❑ Make sure the committee can report to senior management.
- ❑ Give the committee a defined role within your environmental programme.
- ❑ Use the committee to promote environmental awareness amongst all staff.
- ❑ Recognise good practice.

PROMOTIONAL TOOLS

Environmental initiatives need to be creatively promoted; staff do not want to read more memos about the environment and in practice they will not. The aim of your promotional activities is to motivate staff sufficiently to result in a change of behaviour. Any such change to working practice is difficult to initiate and requires a consistent, long term approach to reinforce the message. Therefore promotion of the environment needs to be fun, creative and relevant to daily activities in order to gain interest.

The success of your communication will be reflected in the results of your initiatives. For instance, the amount of paper collected for recycling is dependent upon how many of your staff know about the scheme and understand what they are required to do. This will also determine the likelihood of achieving cost savings and the credibility of the scheme as a whole.

PRACTICAL ACTION

Avoid Paper Based Communication

Use electronic mail wherever possible to update and inform staff about environmental initiatives. Where you have to use paper, be careful – do not send out a single sided two page memo about waste reduction!

Be Creative

Environmental issues, particularly waste, can be seen as very dull. Humour can be very effective in conveying your message. People will remember things that make them laugh.

Use Innovative Communication Techniques

Electronic communication can be a useful tool for communicating and supporting initiatives, a computer based presentation on software such as Power Point and Corel Show can make a scheme come alive and will allow you to move away from using paper.

Many organisations have daily bulletins that are posted on computer networks or log-in screens. Use these to promote initiatives and provide information about your environmental programme. These can also

FIGURE 8.1

Use graphics to communicate environmental issues

be used on a countdown to the launch of a new initiative. For example; publicising your paper consumption and tonnage of waste to landfill will help to promote a forthcoming paper recycling launch. This approach has been used very successfully by the Union Bank of Switzerland (UBS) and significantly raised the profile of the environmental programme.

Create an Identity for Your Environmental Programme

This can be done graphically through a visual image or a cartoon character that can be used to brand any communication that is produced under the environmental programme. Some organisations run competitions for staff to design a character or image, which can be a useful way of promoting involvement and enthusiasm. For example, Her Majesty's Customs and Excise created a cartoon character, the 'Guzzler', for its energy efficiency programme, which is used on all material promoting the programme.

SUMMARY GUIDELINES

❏ Avoid paper based communication.
❏ Utilise electronic communication where available.
❏ Create an identity for the programme.
❏ Reinforce the links between initiatives and environmental benefits.
❏ Provide regular feedback.
❏ Produce guidelines for staff.

Use Display and Notice Boards

Display boards used in your reception or in the canteen can be used to promote initiatives to staff and visitors. Display and notice boards can also provide a valuable focal point where staff will know they can obtain information on the benefits of good environmental practice, successes to date and forthcoming initiatives.

Provide Regular Feedback

Give regular feedback on results. To maintain motivation, staff need to know how they are doing. This feedback should explain clearly the progress made and the environmental benefits. Use electronic communication to produce updated results or highlight areas of weakness. Publish regular updates on the environmental programme that can form a regular feature in your in-house magazine. These are often seen by clients and can help to promote your environmental position externally.

Enclosures in Payslips

If you want something to be read, enclose it with your payslips. This can be an effective way of promoting an environmental programme but you should consider its use very carefully, extra enclosures can be seen as creating waste.

Produce Guidelines for Staff

Many organisations use their head office as a pilot project prior to extending initiatives to other areas. Producing guidelines that highlight lessons learned during the pilot can be a useful promotional tool. Guidelines that provide help and support are invaluable for promoting confidence and continuity. They need to be simple and concise to make sure they are read, and focus on action that can be taken in daily work activities.

LAUNCHING AN INITIATIVE

Staff enthusiasm is a vital resource that should be recognised and harnessed in the design of initiatives. Ideas from staff are often used to help plan the first initiative in environmental programmes. In many cases this will be a recycling scheme. Recycling is something which most staff can relate to and play a part in, so involve your environment committee.

The following section looks at how to plan and implement a recycling scheme. Techniques and ideas are equally applicable to a range of initiatives or a wider environmental programme.

PRACTICAL ACTION

Planning

Logistical problems are often overlooked before a recycling scheme is launched. Some schemes have failed because there were not enough bins close enough to staff, because they were not emptied frequently enough or because the cleaners did not know that recycling bins should be treated differently to general waste. Good planning, involving all parties both internally and externally, can help to avoid such problems. For example, you must identify areas for short-term storage of recyclables prior to launching the scheme.

You must recognise the full implications of embarking on an initiative before starting: nothing damages the long term viability of an environmental programme more than the failure of an initiative. If your staff see a recycling scheme as chaotic, messy and more effort than throwing paper into general waste then they will feel negative about any further initiatives.

Involving Support Services and Contractors

Cleaners

Recycling schemes represent an additional system within the office. Communicate with your cleaning staff to make sure that they know how the new arrangements will work. Recycling schemes do not generally mean more work for cleaners, but they will have to change how they collect waste. Ensure that working with the recycling scheme is built into your cleaning contract.

One company whose staff had thought they had been recycling paper for a number of years found out after a Wastebusters audit that its cleaners had not understood the system and were putting all the paper collected into general waste bins.

Recycling Contractors

Arrangements with recycling companies should always be made to suit the requirements of your organisation. Make sure that the company you choose is aware of how you intend the scheme to work, where the waste can be collected from, and at what intervals. It is important to clarify collection times to coordinate with the cleaning schedule and to establish key contact points between the recycling contractor and your organisation.

Marketing and Publicity

As with any new initiative, a recycling scheme needs to be sold to your staff. A marketing department is ideally placed to help with the production of publicity material. Try to make the maximum use of electronic communication; if you do use paper based communication ensure it is printed double sided on recycled paper, or a size appropriate to the volume of text.

Produce fact sheets on the products being collected for recycling and make them specific to your company. Use any figures you have available to support this information, such as: each tonne of recycled glass used for making new glass saves 30 gallons of fuel oil and reduces our burden on natural resources (for further examples see the Handy Facts section below). Putting results in a graphical form can also help to put your message across as Figure 8.2 below shows.

Recycling schemes can be a good opportunity to raise issues of consumption in general. It is essential to promote waste reduction as well as recycling, eg copying.

Recycling contractors often have publicity and support materials that can be used to communicate schemes to staff and are useful to support your scheme. For example, Save A Cup sells rulers made from vending cups that can be printed with the name of your company.

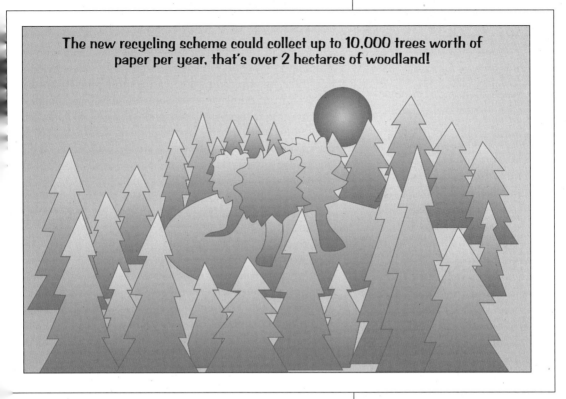

The new recycling scheme could collect up to 10,000 trees worth of paper per year, that's over 2 hectares of woodland!

FIGURE 8.2

Use posters to communicate your results

Promote and Maintain Individual Involvement

Staff need to be educated and motivated in environmental issues so that they are aware of the environmental benefits of their activities. There are many ways in which you can link individual actions to wider environmental issues and it is useful to provide your staff with environmental facts such as: Recycling drinks cans saves 95 per cent of the energy needed to make them from new (for further examples see the Handy Facts section below).

Give the recycling programme a high profile; don't be discreet. Use strong, clear publicity material highlighting environmental benefits. Use posters at recycling points and noticeboards to remind staff.

Give regular feedback on your results. To maintain motivation, staff need to know how they are doing. The feedback you give should include the tonnage of recyclables collected and also the environmental benefits. These need to be identified to ensure that staff are aware of the reasons for the initiatives.

COMMON PROBLEMS

Many recycling programmes fail due to lack of communication, with the following results:

❑ Benefits in waste disposal costs and revenue from quality white paper are never achieved.
❑ The organisation sees recycling as expensive, ineffective and time consuming, and it does nothing for staff morale, resulting in contaminated schemes (for instance, vending cups and cigarette butts end up in the white paper recycling bins).
❑ Recycling contractors are not keen to collect, due to lack of volume and contamination levels.
❑ Problems can be encountered when trying to re-launch the scheme at a later date.

Sponsorship and Incentive Schemes

While it can be relatively easy to achieve staff involvement and motivation in the initial stages of your scheme, this must be maintained on an ongoing basis so that maximum amounts are retrieved for recycling. Incentive schemes are a successful, self-financing way of maintaining motivation. Some organisations achieve this by donating a percentage of cost savings and revenue to an environmental charity or staff social fund. One company has used the revenue generated from a paper recycling scheme to fund their office Christmas party; an idea which was suggested by staff and has proved very successful.

A number of companies link their sponsorship programmes to the volume of paper collected. There are a number of forestry projects and imaginative sponsorship opportunities available (see Useful Contacts section at the end of this chapter).

The environmental groups Friends of the Earth and WWF (World Wide Fund for Nature) have a number of major initiatives operating in conjunction with industry.

There are a number of opportunities to sponsor local community projects. For example, sponsoring the production of an environmental video could assist schools with an environmental education programme.

Use Handy Facts

We have put together a brief list of handy facts (or green soundbites) which you can use on promotional material to reinforce your environmental message.

❑ Each tonne of recycled glass used for making new glass saves 30 gallons of fuel oil.
❑ Seven plastic cups can be recycled to make one ruler.
❑ Switching off your computer overnight can save 200 kg of coal per year.
❑ It takes approximately 10 gallons of water to make a computer chip.
❑ Compact fluorescent lights use up to 25 per cent less energy than standard tubes.
❑ Lighting is usually the second largest user of electricity in the office.
❑ Seventeen trees make one tonne of paper.
❑ Ten trees make one tonne of newsprint.

❑ Decomposing waste in landfill sites is the UK's largest source of the greenhouse gas methane.
❑ Recycling drinks cans saves 95 per cent of the energy needed to make them from new.
❑ The production of retread tyres uses about a third of the oil and rubber needed for new tyres.
❑ An average modern car emits approximately 3 tonnes of CO_2 per year.

DEVELOPING GOOD PRACTICE GUIDELINES

The production of good practice guidelines can be a very useful way to extend successful initiatives throughout your organisation. Guidelines that provide help and support are invaluable for promoting confidence and continuity. A consistent approach to greening your office will also help to maximise the buying power of your organisation. For example, the inclusion of all sites in a national contract for paper recycling will help to ensure that smaller offices are able to have their paper collected. Equally, if you have guidelines which recommend specific brands of recycled paper this will help your purchasing department in their negotiations with suppliers.

Many organisations start their programme with pilot projects prior to extending initiatives to other areas. It is not necessary to audit every location to develop a corporate approach. The issues at sites with similar functions will essentially be the same.

For example, during an Environmental Audit of Abbey National, Wastebusters included four representative branches as well as major head office buildings. This helped us identify: regional differences, restraints of urban and rural locations, and variations in sizes of the branches.

The use of pilot projects allows you to test ideas and produce guidelines specific to your organisation that highlight lessons learnt during the pilot. It also enables you to control the development of the programme by a phased introduction.

SUMMARY GUIDELINES

❑ Plan and communicate to overcome logistical problems.
❑ Use internal communication channels.
❑ Make it easy for staff to recycle.
❑ Run a high-profile launch programme.
❑ Provide regular feedback.
❑ Sponsor a local environmental project.
❑ Make it fun!

PRACTICAL ACTION

Identify Pilot Locations

Choose a cross section of sites and functions. Take into account regional differences, urban and rural locations and the number of staff. Small outlying offices will have different restraints and logistical problems to large city centre locations. Being seen to take these differences into account will add credibility to the programme. Smaller offices often feel rather overlooked. A realistic number of sites is between three and five.

Communicate Your Project Objectives

Make sure that the aims of the project are communicated to the sites and individuals involved. Identify keen staff to help you take it forward and appoint a coordinator at each site. The attitude of the key staff at each site will help or hinder progress. We often find that environmental performance is directly related to the enthusiasm of staff. It is difficult to make progress if the facilities team are not on board.

Conduct Site Audits

Use this *Manual* to conduct site audits and identify areas of improvement and potential cost saving. Highlight areas of existing good practice to give people encouragement. Identify logistical problems to ensure they are overcome. Find out what help people need.

Implement Improvements

Following the audit findings, develop an improvement plan and monitor the results. Provide support and back-up and make sure teething problems are dealt with quickly. Use the results to develop best practice guidelines.

Publicise Results

Make sure the pilot sites benefit from being guinea pigs. Involve them in the development of the guidelines and get their feedback. If the programme is launched formally, ask them to give a first hand account of the project. This will personalise the process and help people identify and relate to the project.

Case Study

Subject –	**WASTEBUSTING FOR SCHOOLS**
Organisation –	**DORSET COUNTY COUNCIL**
Organisation type –	**LOCAL AUTHORITY**
Location –	**DORSET**
No. of staff –	**N/A**

BACKGROUND

Waste is a high profile issue within Dorset, and the District and Borough Councils are working closely with the County to reduce waste and encourage recycling. Schools have an important role in encouraging environmental awareness through environmental education as part of the curriculum and as a focal point for the local community.

Schools are under increasing budgetary constraints and financial pressures and are operating very much as independent business units. Recent increases in the cost of paper and general stationery products give an important incentive for increased control on usage and waste reduction measures.

Environmental education is integrated into the school curriculum and there are educational benefits to be gained from involving the school in environmental initiatives. At primary level this is cross curricular, giving schools flexibility in how they approach this. At middle and senior level it is more structured.

ACTION

The Waste Minimisation Steering Group at County Hall, which is driving waste minimisation initiatives throughout the county, commissioned Wastebusters to audit four schools to see how they could save money and help the environment. The project involved West Moors Middle School, Summerbee School, Gillingham Primary and Prince of Wales First School. These were used as pilot projects from which to extend initia-

RESULTS

The guide:

- ❏ saves money – each school saves approximately £300 pa;
- ❏ promotes environmental awareness and supports curriculum activities;
- ❏ contributes to waste minimisation at a local level;
- ❏ enhances the image of the school within the local community and encourages involvement;
- ❏ generates local publicity for schools;
- ❏ is popular with children/students and parents; and
- ❏ helps waste minimisation become part of the school culture.

tives to other schools in the county. Wastebusters looked at current working practices and identified areas for potential improvement.

Schools currently produce a minimum of one tonne of waste per term and annually spend between £300 and £1000 on waste disposal depending on the size of the school. Therefore measures which reduce the volume of waste and retrieve material for recycling have immediate cost benefits. Better control over usage eg paper will reduce the costs of purchasing and promote the idea of paper as a valuable resource.

Following the results of the school pilots, 'Wastebusting for School' was launched, a practical management guide to produce cost savings and environmental benefits for schools. The guide describes a number of practical environmental initiatives, based on the results found at the four pilot schools, which are cost effective and easy to implement.

The guide also includes a best practice case study featuring West Moors Middle School where a number of initiatives were in place (see Chapter 3). Subjects range from waste reduction measures through to the composting of green waste and how to set up a wormery. For each subject details are provided on the practical action that can be taken. Sources of help and information are also given. The Guide was launched in North Dorset schools in November 1996. Presentations were given by the county and district, Gillingham Primary (one of the pilot schools), and of course Wastebusters!

Launch Best Practice Guidelines

Keep the guidelines concise and communicate electronically where possible. Provide practical guidance on the steps that need to be taken to introduce a range of initiatives, highlighting what can be done, how it can be done, who will do it and the potential cost savings.

Include contact points within your organisation and details of other useful organisations who can provide help and support. Illustrate the implementation of the guidelines with examples from the pilots, highlighting existing good practice and project achievements.

Set up an Environmental Forum

Encourage communication between sites and sharing of good practice through an environmental forum. Develop

Case Study

Subject –	**COMMUNICATION BETWEEN ORGANISATIONS**
Organisation –	**MERCK LTD**
Organisation type –	**CHEMICAL**
Location –	**POOLE, DORSET**
No. of staff –	**N/A**

BACKGROUND

Merck Ltd, a leading UK manufacturer of chemical reagents, disposed of its waste solvents in large drums. These drums were bought externally and disposal was conducted by Merck.

BP Exploration, operating from Wych Farm near Wareham, had to pay for the disposal of their 200l oil drums.

ACTION

Both companies saw an opportunity for exchanging waste and cutting costs. Oil drums are now picked up from BP free of charge by a Merck driver and are used to dispose of Merck refuse, saving money on the purchase of new drums. A win-win situation for both companies.

SUMMARY GUIDELINES

- ❑ Conduct audits of pilot locations.
- ❑ Develop an improvement plan.
- ❑ Implement initiatives at pilots and monitor results.
- ❑ Develop and launch best practice guidelines.
- ❑ Personalise the guidelines to your organisation with case study material.
- ❑ Publicise results and make sure good practice is recognised.

a regular environmental bulletin to keep people up to date with environmental trends, maintain interest and communicate electronically. This approach can help multinational organisations who are aiming for a consistent approach to environmental management. It can also help to bring regional and outlying offices on board. An environmental forum can also provide a good opportunity for organisations to share information and promote good practice within an area.

SPECIALIST TRAINING

Environmental awareness training is appropriate to all staff. However, specific functional areas with significant environmental impacts need more specialist training. In a typical office these will be waste disposal, building management and purchasing

PRACTICAL ACTION

Make Sure Training is Appropriate

Training needs to take into account different levels of commitment and understanding within the organisation and be pitched at the right level. If the environmental programme is new to your organisation, the priority will be to present the business case for the environment rather than providing detailed assessments of environmental effects.

Be Creative

Use innovative training techniques to promote enthusiasm and generate ideas, and facilitate understanding of the issues. For example, role play can be a useful part of environmental awareness training. It is fun and can be a very effective way of getting a message across (see Mercury Case Study).

Supply Relevant Information

Identify the environmental issues relevant to the area of your business and relate them to specific practices within that area. For example, in purchasing training use case studies of products with a high environmental profile to demonstrate the principles of life-cycle analysis. A comparison of differences in suppliers' environmental policies can be very illuminating.

Case Study

Subject –	**ENVIRONMENTAL AWARENESS TRAINING**
Organisation –	**RUSHMOOR BOROUGH COUNCIL**
Organisation type –	**LOCAL AUTHORITY**
Location –	**RUSHMOOR, HAMPSHIRE**
No. of staff –	**N/A**

BACKGROUND

Rushmoor Borough Council is promoting waste minimisation and recycling to the general public, and recognises the importance of being able to demonstrate good housekeeping practices to be consistent with these messages.

The authority has implemented a number of in-house waste minimisation initiatives, however it is recognised that there is considerable scope to improve the effectiveness of these. In a report submitted to the Directors Management Board in March 1996, the following issues were identified:

❑ The policies have not been monitored effectively and have not achieved ownership across the authority.
❑ They have not been communicated effectively and there have been minimal efforts to encourage and educate staff.
❑ Demonstrable commitment from the top from both members and officers is essential to make the policies work.

The result of this is that money is being wasted. The recycling schemes are not fully effective and are therefore not resulting in the potential reduction in waste disposal costs. Purchasing consumption is considerably higher than necessary which results in an increase in purchasing and disposal costs. Schemes can be set up – but nothing happens without individual involvement. The authority is also committed to the Hampshire Waste Minimisation Purchasing Principles, but these have not been introduced very effectively.

ACTION

Environmental and Technical Services who are driving the initiatives recognised that senior management and member support was essential to the success of the programme. Consequently as part of their strategy they decided to run Environmental Awareness Training for Heads of Service and Members on waste minimisation and purchasing. The aim of the workshop was to raise awareness of the issues and provide inspiration and motivation to both audiences to implement sound environmental initiatives in both areas as detailed in the waste strategy.

Summary of Objectives

❏ Develop Action Plans for departments/areas.
❏ Ensure ownership of the programme.
❏ Promote understanding and awareness of the business and environmental issues.
❏ Identify concerns and obstacles.

Short presentations were given to put the training in context and to summarise the environmental and commercial benefits of waste minimisation and green purchasing. This provided the stimulus in the workshop sessions for the generation of ideas which can be applied within their own services. A summary of Wastebusters' presentation was provided on E-mail and was not circulated in paper form.

The 60 participants were divided into workshop groups with a mix of officers, members and political persuasions! Each group was given a specific subject: waste reduction, purchasing, paper consumption, communication and motivation. These followed a brainstorming session in each group to develop action plans which could be implemented by departments.

A number of positive ideas were generated which included re-use of files; increase double sided copying by additional publicity with posters above photocopiers; composting of bedding plants; the inclusion of environmental criteria in the Housing Association tender specifications (and a bike for the Chief Executive!).

A number of groups came up with similar ideas. The most significant was the suggestion from members to reduce the circulation of Committee Papers. This will result in substantial savings to the authority.

RESULTS

The Training:

❏ encouraged active participation;
❏ promoted an exchange of ideas, particularly between members and officers;
❏ achieved a reduction in circulation of Committee Papers and cost savings of £6,000 pa;
❏ increased interest and motivation towards the issues;
❏ gained a positive response from participants – the general consensus was that it was fun; and
❏ achieved an agreement that a range of initiatives would be developed by the corporate group of officers.

Case Study

Subject –	**SPECIALIST TRAINING – ROLE PLAY**
Organisation –	**MERCURY COMMUNICATIONS LTD**
Organisation type –	**TELECOMMUNICATIONS**
Location –	**NATIONWIDE**
No. of staff –	**8200**

BACKGROUND

Mercury Communications Ltd (Mercury) commissioned Wastebusters to assist in the development of a training programme for all waste producers within the company and in particular those responsible for the generation, containment, storage and labelling of special or hazardous waste. The course was designed to ensure that Mercury employees are aware of the legislation covering such waste and the procedures in place within Mercury to cover its production, handling and disposal.

The programme was produced as a series of self-contained modules dealing with general environmental issues, legislation, Mercury internal standards and procedures, identifying wastes, storing, handling and transferring waste and controlling contractors. Approximately 100 employees specifically dealing with waste are expected to attend the full training course over the next 12 months, with up to 1000 further employees receiving some form of environmental awareness training over the same period.

ACTION

The course uses a variety of techniques to communicate:

❏ environmental issues associated with poor waste
  management;
❏ awareness of statutory obligations and duties;
❏ safe waste handling and storage procedures; and
❏ control of contractors conducting waste disposal activities
  on behalf of Mercury.

RESULTS

The exercise allows participants to:

❏ gain an understanding of the complex issues surrounding waste and the environment;

❏ gather information on legislation and company procedures in place to ensure good waste management practice;

❏ understand different perspectives that can be used to improve both their work and their understanding of other people's;

❏ take a role in their own training as active participants; and

❏ have fun.

SUMMARY GUIDELINES

❏ Make sure training is pitched at an appropriate level.

❏ Be creative.

❏ Encourage participation.

❏ Use information that is relevant to your organisation.

❏ Send staff to external seminars to share experience.

One of the modules took the form of a role-play scenario. In the scenario Mercury had commissioned a contractor to conduct some work on its behalf which had resulted in damage to a member of the public's property.

Participants were given background information to the events and were asked, in groups, to take the roles of: Mercury, the contractor, the member of the public and the Environment Agency, whose job was to gather evidence and come to a conclusion. The aim of the exercise was to highlight the complex web of issues that such a situation raises and to understand the motivations of the participants whilst reinforcing the procedures that Mercury have established to cover such a situation.

Encourage Participation

Avoid dry presentations on environmental issues. Assure participation through workshop sessions. Encourage suggestions for improvement – individuals who are actually doing the job and making decisions are in the best position to identify potential improvements to working practices. Include their ideas in the development of policy and action plans (see Case Study on Rushmoor Borough Council).

Participate in External Seminars

Send staff on external seminars. Sharing experiences with other organisations can be very helpful. A recognition that other organisations are working with the same issues can be reassuring, build confidence and increase knowledge and understanding. The seminars run by the Environment Council's Business and Environment Programme are a good example. Organisations that are members are already committed to good practice (see Useful Contacts section at the end of this chapter).

EXTERNAL SUPPORT
Linking to National Initiatives

National environmental initiatives can be useful sources of information, support and ideas for your organisation. Useful national initiatives include: the Energy Efficiency Office Best Practice Programme 'Making a Corporate Commitment' and the CBI Environmental Business Forum.

Agenda 21

Agenda 21, derived from the 1992 Rio Earth Summit, is a global action plan for achieving sustainable development, which has been defined by the Brundtland Commission as 'development that meets the needs of the present without compromising the ability of future generations to meet their own needs'.

All local authorities should be developing a local strategy for achieving sustainability, a Local Agenda 21, and involving the whole community in doing so. Achieving a sustainable community will mean each local authority taking a lead in education and the provision of information, promoting individual lifestyle changes, as well as reviewing its own planning and policy functions.

Agenda 21 recognises the role of business and industry in achieving sustainable development and the need to develop strong partnerships between all sectors within the local community. Local Agenda 21 invites businesses to become part of the community in which they are situated and encourages them to look for opportunities to forge links with the community and their employees and work with them on an environmental strategy that safeguards the future for all.

Business in the Environment (BiE)

Business in the Environment aims to extend business leaders' awareness of environmental issues and to provide practical assistance in improving the environmental performance of business.

Case Study

Subject –	**LOCAL AGENDA 21**
Organisation –	**GPT BUSINESS SYSTEMS**
Organisation type –	**MANUFACTURER AND SUPPLIER OF TELECOMMUNICATION SYSTEMS**
Location –	**BEESTON, NOTTINGHAMSHIRE**
No. of staff –	**1500**

BACKGROUND

GPT's first policy statement on the environment, issued in 1990, placed an objective on the company to promote recycling and environmental awareness throughout the business. In July 1994 the company released an Environmental Policy which committed the company to a process of continuous improvement in minimising its impacts on the environment. In September 1996 the business achieved certification to the environmental management system, BS 7750, which is owned and operated by everyone on site.

ACTION

GPT encourages every employee to become involved in all environmental activities undertaken across the site. To support this, each employee has received at least two hours of environmental awareness training and education. Environmental information is also included in employee induction training.

The implementation of BS 7750 has lead to the development of cross functional teams. These teams are composed of representatives from all areas of the company and aim to generate ideas for environmental improvement and coordinate environmental protection activities.

Such is the enthusiasm of employees that in 1990 they formed an environmental group known as New Leaf. Its aim was and is to draw people together with an interest in the environment and give them the opportunity to exchange ideas research new proposals and promote company wide adoption of worthwhile environmental activities.

Employees have played a significant part in assisting GPT to devise, promote and run viable waste minimisation and recycling schemes. Over 2.5 tonnes of paper and cardboard are now sent for recycling each week. Polystyrene cups are also collected with almost 18,000 cups used each month sent away for recycling. A drinks can recycling project is also run on the site by New Leaf, with proceeds going to support their activities. To facilitate this, can crushers have been bought by GPT using revenue from paper recycling.

Community Involvement and Local Agenda 21

Local Agenda 21 in Nottingham is supported and promoted by Nottingham City Council and Broxtowe Borough Council. GPT is an active partner in Local Agenda 21 through the Nottingham Green Partnership and the company recognises the need for good environmental stewardship and for a company to be involved in the wider community.

Many local businesses and authorities are actual or potential suppliers or customers of GPT, and the company has sought to work in partnership locally to make environmental improvements. GPT is a founder member of the East Midlands Business & Environment Club and a patron of the Business Environment Association for the East Midlands. Through these organisations, small businesses can benefit from the experience and knowledge of larger companies.

As a community of 1500 people, most of whom live in the surrounding area, the company feels that its policy of raising environmental awareness has also provided the stimulus for its employees to become involved in environmental issues in the areas where they live.

GPT has conducted a number of presentations in local schools which have provided an opportunity for children and young people to learn about manufacturing industry and its impact on the environment. Students are encouraged to ask questions and frequently do!

In the spirit of Agenda 21 can crushers have also been donated to local schools by the company and in many cases have initiated environmental projects in the classroom. Feedback from schools is passed on to employees. Pictures and letters from children are photocopied and displayed around the site and on the company's internal Internet system, so that employees can see the positive results of their commitment.

RESULTS

Over £20,000 has been raised from the sale of paper and cardboard for recycling and has been made available to support environmental and other projects in local schools, organisations and charities. This 'paper bank fund' is distributed by employees and acts as an incentive and reward for their help in segregating wastes to enable cost effective recovery.

The company has also achieved the following benefits:

- ❏ An environmentally aware and motivated workforce.
- ❏ Significant reductions in energy and water consumption.
- ❏ Significant reductions in waste stream and material use.
- ❏ On site recycling has meant that the number of waste compactors sent to landfill has dropped from 62 to 8 per month.
- ❏ Certification to BS7750.
- ❏ Reduced environmental risk.
- ❏ A positive contribution to the local community.
- ❏ An improved understanding of stakeholder concerns.

CBI Environment Business Forum

The CBI Environment Business Forum is a cross sectoral voluntary business initiative which aims to support and assist organisations in the development of environmental best practice. The Forum offers advice and services to help plan and implement environmental programmes and the opportunity to learn from businesses which are already successfully taking action. Membership of the Forum is at an organisational level.

Conservers at Work

The Environment Council has developed a membership scheme, called 'Conservers at Work', for people who want to help the environment when they are at work. It provides a guide and produces a newsletter. The scheme has provided help and support to a number of organisations developing environmental programmes (see the Useful Contacts section at the end of this chapter for details).

Green Business Clubs and Local Environmental Fora

The number of green business clubs has increased in recent years as small and medium sized businesses have accepted the importance of the environment and have sought ways of gathering and sharing information. Green business clubs can be an invaluable source of support and information and offer a chance for smaller companies to get together to discuss environmental improvement and share ideas.

There are a number of benefits to joining a green business club, including:

❑ Avoiding re-inventing the wheel; sharing information enables you to use techniques that have been tried and tested.
❑ Talking to other like-minded participants can improve your confidence about developing an environmental programme
❑ Speakers and events can provide you with information on wider environmental issues and trends as well as initiatives suppliers and contractors in your area.

Case Study

Subject –	**GREEN BUSINESS CLUBS**
Organisation –	**SURREY AND HAMPSHIRE ENVIRONMENTAL BUSINESS ASSOCIATION (SHEBA)**
Organisation type –	**GREEN BUSINESS CLUB**
Location –	**FARNHAM, SURREY**
No. of staff –	**120 MEMBERS**

BACKGROUND

Sheba is an initiative created by the Surrey Institute of Art and Design in association with SC Johnson Ltd to develop practical environmental support for business.

Sheba exists to:

❑ provide a forum for information exchange on environmental issues which affect profitability; and
❑ promulgate the highest achievable standards of environmental responsibility in the creation and conduct of business and industrial activities.

ACTION

Sheba has established two programmes to support the needs of organisations in Surrey and Hampshire, the Sheba Environmental Management Programme and the Sheba Environmental Technology Programme.

Within these programmes four key services are offered:

❑ events;
❑ training;
❑ information; and
❑ contract event management.

RESULTS

In its first two years Sheba has reached 120 members. There have been over 1000 attendees to 27 seminars, conferences and training courses, including six events organised for the Government Office of the South East. All Sheba events have achieved a 70–90% excellence rating from delegates.

Sheba also offers a wide range of training and information resources on subjects which include environmental management systems, exporting environmental technology and managing eco-design. Existing Sheba members include small and large businesses, consultancies, local authorities and universities.

International Chamber of Commerce

ICC UK is the British affiliate of the world organisation concerned with international business issues and practice. Through its Business Charter for Sustainable Development, the ICC seeks to spread good environmental practice throughout business.

The Institute of Environmental Management (IEM)

The Institute of Environmental Management (IEM) provides professional and practical support for individuals involved in environmental management in industry, commerce and local government. The Institute aims to:

❏ establish and uphold the profession of environmental management; and
❏ promote and continually improve the competence of environmental managers.

Membership of the Institute is on an individual basis.
    There are also a number of national organisations who can provide support to local authorities in meeting the aims of Agenda 21 through the introduction of specific initiatives. The main organisations are described below.

Eco-Schools

Eco-Schools is a programme run by the Tidy Britain Group that encourages teachers and pupils to integrate concepts and ideas from environmental education into the everyday life of their school. Schools register for an award scheme and receive the Eco-Schools Pack consisting of a Handbook, an Environmental Review and the current curriculum unit on waste. Eco-Schools can provide useful additional support to existing environmental education initiatives.

Wildlife Watch (Watch)

Watch is the junior branch of the Wildlife Trusts and is a national environmental club for children and young people. The Watch Education Service (WES) provides an information service to schools and informal groups.

World Wide Fund for Nature (WWF)

The WWF produces a wide range of education publications and services for schools; both print and IT based. The material is designed to support the curriculum, stimulate learning and be fun to use.

Global Action Plan

Global Action Plan (GAP) is a non-profit organisation, sponsored by the Department of the Environment, whose aim is to encourage individuals to take practical environmental action in their daily lives. GAP works with local authorities to develop specific programmes promoting environmental initiatives to households.

It can provide Action Packs to households covering waste, energy, transport, water use, shopping and how to become involved in the local community.

Going for Green

Going for Green is a government and private sector financed public awareness campaign which aims to improve public understanding of sustainable development and develop the part that individuals can play. Its aims are to encourage, support and enhance green campaigns and initiatives involving the public across the country and provide evidence of the environmental benefits achieved.

The campaign seeks to use all channels of information to give simple, clear advice to individuals in the many roles they play in their daily lives.

CHAPTER SUMMARY

❑ Enlist senior management support.
❑ Involve staff from all areas of your organisation.
❑ Give your environmental programme a high profile.
❑ Monitor the programme and give regular feedback.
❑ Make sound environmental practice part of the company culture.

The Henry Doubleday Research Association

The Henry Doubleday Research Association is committed to researching and promoting organic gardening as a productive and sustainable means of food production. In April 1996 the Association launched the 'Go Organic in the School Grounds' project. This three year campaign is funded by the Department of the Environment and aims to encourage and enable schools to manage their grounds in an environmentally sound way.

National Recycling Forum and Local Authority Recycling Advisory Committee

Additional support for local authorities is provided by the National Recycling Forum (NRF) and the Local Authority Recycling Advisory Committee (LARAC). The NRF is a non profit organisation that brings together industry, individuals local authorities and the voluntary sector to promote the principles of waste reduction, re-use and recycling. It is committed to raising awareness across a range of waste and recycling issues. LARAC is a national local authority organisation promoting waste reduction and recycling.

Sources of Information

Environmental Organisations

CONSERVATION FOUNDATION
1 Kensington Gore
London SW7 2AR
Tel: 0171 823 8842
Fax: 0171 823 8791

FRIENDS OF THE EARTH (FOE)
26–28 Underwood Street
London N1 7JQ
Tel: 0171 490 1555
Fax: 0171 490 0881

GREENPEACE
Canonbury Villas
London N1 2PN
Tel: 0171 865 8100
Fax: 0171 862 8200

PROGRAMME FOR BELIZE
PO Box 99
Saxmundham
Suffolk IP17 2LB

ROYAL SOCIETY FOR THE PROTECTION OF BIRDS (RSPB)
The Lodge
Sandy
Bedfordshire SG19 2DI
Tel: 01767 680551
Fax: 01767 692365

TREE COUNCIL
51 Catherine Place
London SW1E 6DY
Tel: 0171 828 9928
Fax: 0171 828 9060

WILDLIFE WATCH
The Green
Witham Park
Waterside South
Lincoln LN5 7JR
Tel: 01522 544 400
Fax: 01522 511 616

WOODLAND TRUST
Autumn Park
Dysart Road
Grantham
Lincolnshire NG31 6LL
Tel: 01476 74297
Fax: 01476 590 808

WORLD WIDE FUND FOR NATURE (WWF)
Panda House
Weyside Park
Godalming
Surrey GU7 1XR
Tel: 01483 426 444
Fax: 01483 426 409

Industry Organisations

BUSINESS IN THE ENVIRONMENT (BIE)
8 Stratton Street
London W1X 5FD
Tel: 0171 629 1600

CONSERVERS AT WORK/ENVIRONMENT COUNCIL.
21 Elizabeth Street
London SW1W 9RP
Tel: 0171 824 8411
Fax: 0171 730 9941

HENRY DOUBLEDAY RESEARCH ASSOCIATION
Ryton Organic Gardens
Coventry CV8 3LG
Tel: 01203 303 517
Fax: 01203 639 229

ECO-SCHOOLS
Tidy Britain Group
The Pier
Wigan WN3 4EX
Tel: 01942 824 620
Fax: 01942 824 778

GLOBAL ACTION PLAN
3rd Floor
42 Kingsway
London WC2B 6EX
Tel: 0171 405 5633
Fax: 0171 831 6244

GOING FOR GREEN
1st Floor
Churchgate House
56 Oxford Street
Manchester M60 7HJ
Tel: 0161 2374158
Fax: 0161 237 4155

INTERNATIONAL CHAMBER OF COMMERCE
14–15 Belgrave Square
London SW1X 8PS
Tel: 0171 823 2811

9: Environmental Management

INTRODUCTION

This Manual has guided you through the areas where your office has an impact on the environment and the practical actions you can take to reduce this burden. A common experience of organisations who have reached this stage is that as time gets tight and initial enthusiasm runs out, environmental initiatives can fade. To avoid this pitfall many organisations have formal procedures to implement their commitment to responsible practice.

The formal approach has a number of advantages. By integrating responsibility for environmental issues into day to day work it makes sure that initiatives last beyond initial enthusiasm. It also helps organisations to identify all their environmental effects in a structured way rather than responding to outside pressures on an *ad hoc* basis. These effects, or impacts, can be wide ranging but can be defined as 'Any change to the environment, whether adverse or beneficial, wholly or partially resulting from activities, products and services of the organisation' (BSI, 1996).

Environmental management has received a great deal of support from policy makers. Agenda 21, the programme for action agreed at the Earth Summit at Rio, states that 'Business and industry should recognise environmental management as among the highest corporate priorities and as a key determinant to sustainable development.' In the UK the Government is committed to promoting a proactive approach to environmental management. As part of this commitment it has set a challenge to industry: '50% of companies with more than 200 employees to have management systems in place to give effect to their environmental policies by the end of 1999' (DoE, 1995).

This chapter guides you through the principles of formal environmental management for an office. It explains how to systematically review where you are at, develop an environmental policy and set out a programme to implement your policy. The chapter does not aim to guide you through certification to a specific management standard but to be applicable to any formal environmental management system. The chapter includes a section on benchmarking your environmental effects, a step by step approach to developing a simple environmental 'fingerprint' of your organisation. The chapter also summarises the independent standards, other guidance and the sources of help that are available.

Standards

October 1996 saw the launch of an international environmental management system standard (ISO 14001). This was developed from the first such standard: British Standard (BS7750) which has now been withdrawn. In addition there is a European Regulation, the Eco-Management and Audit Scheme (EMAS), which establishes a standard for environmental management for industry and a local authority version of this (LA-EMAS). These management standards have created an international blueprint for integrating environmental issues into the management structure of an organisation. They provide an opportunity for independent certification of an organisation's commitment to responsible environmental practice.

Who Can Implement a Management System?

Environmental management systems provide a structure for managing all the significant environmental effects of any organisation. The steps to a management system in this chapter focus on the office. However, the principles in it are applicable to all organisations. If you are implementing a management system for an office and factory together on one site the guidance will remain valid.

Environmental management systems are flexible enough be applied to: a whole organisation, an operational unit such as a head office, or even a particular activity. However this flexibility is limited by the need for the unit implementing the system to have management responsibility for all significant environmental effects. For instance if you share a building with other parts of your organisation you are unlikely to have control over areas such as waste, energy and air conditioning. This will make it difficult to implement a system independently.

To date management systems have been implemented almost exclusively by larger companies. However, they are equally beneficial for smaller organisations. The Government is encouraging small and medium sized organisations through a grant scheme called SCEEMAS that contributes up to half of the consultancy costs of obtaining the European standard EMAS.

Advantages of a Systematic Approach

No successful organisation leaves the management of areas like sales and performance to chance. Successful management involves setting clear goals and a strategy to meet them. A management system provides a structure in which to set these goals, implement a programme to achieve them and monitor the progress achieved.

Environmental performance is no different to other corporate goals in benefiting from this systematic approach. Indeed the fast changing nature of the issues and the range of interested stakeholders from the public to insurance companies make a systematic approach even more important. The benefit to be gained are set out below.

LEGISLATIVE COMPLIANCE

Legislation remains the key driver behind responsible environmental practice for business. There is already a comprehensive programme of environmental legislation, much of which has been outlined in this *Manual*. A management system will ensure that you are aware of forthcoming environmental legislation and the impact it will have on your organisation rather than finding out about it when it is already in place.

A management system also sends a clear message to regulators such as the Environment Agency that you are taking environmental issues seriously.

COMPETITIVE ADVANTAGE

It is extremely difficult to win contracts within industry without a quality system following ISO 9001. Environmental issues are beginning to follow a similar path. Indeed a formal policy and management system is already necessary to win contracts from organisations such as British Telecom.

Until recently environmental procurement policies did not affect the service sector. This is changing as requirements move down the supply chain from major purchasers in business and local authority sectors. B&Q, for instance, delists suppliers who do not show a commitment to environmental improvement.

MAXIMISING ACHIEVEMENT

Everything we do has an effect on the environment. It is clearly not possible to manage all of these effects. A central feature of an environmental management system is the systematic evaluation of the effects you are having on the environment to identify key areas that are worth managing. This evaluation ensures that the effort you put into your environmental programme is spent on your main effects rather than wasted on minor issues.

IDENTIFYING POTENTIAL LIABILITIES

By systematically identifying all your environmental effects, actual or potential, you will ensure that you are aware of any areas that might lead to liability for environmental damage. Contaminated land, for instance, is potentially very expensive to clear up. Insurance companies and banks are already including environmental risk in their assessments of companies that they insure or lend to. The Co-operative Bank, for instance refuses to lend to any company it does not consider to be ethically or environmentally sound.

Systematic assessment of your environmental effects can also alert you to any potential public relations issues. Public environmental campaigns can develop very quickly and have a major impact. The 1995 Greenpeace campaign against the dumping of the Brent Spar at sea cost Shell many millions of pounds.

MAINTAINING PROGRESS

Once environmental responsibilities are integrated into procedures and job descriptions it is much harder for initiatives to fade away after the initial start up. If targets are not met this will be flagged up by auditing procedures.

COMMON PROBLEMS

Bureaucracy

The key problem of a formal system is that a lot of time, and paper, can be spent on bureaucracy that could have been spent on actual improvements. Vague policy statements and action plans can be drawn up without any real improvements taking place.

There are three key steps to preventing your environmental programme turning into a paper chase. The first is to integrate new procedures into the existing management culture of your organisation rather than creating a large pile of new documents. The second is to encourage ownership of procedures by the staff who are going to be carrying them out. The third is to use a system to improve your management rather than seeing the end result as a badge, such as ISO 14001.

Small Businesses

Very few small companies have environmental policies let alone environmental management systems. Environmental issues are often recognised as important but they are outweighed by other pressures. The everyday pressures of running a business in a competitive world tend to leave little time to respond to anything not seen as an immediate priority.

Small companies can however gain considerable benefits from environmental awareness. Energy efficiency and waste minimisation measures can be implemented with no capital investment and can produce surprising savings. A simple environmental policy and action programme can have marketing benefits and may well become essential for selling to some companies and local authorities.

A management system also gives all staff environmental responsibilities as part of their day to day work. This avoids the problem common to those following a less structured approach where environmental initiatives are loaded on to one keen individual.

MEETING AGENDA 21

One of the first steps for a local authority encouraging a community response to LA 21 is to put its own house in order. A management system will help with a systematic approach to improving environmental performance in council buildings and to integrating sustainable development into the services the council provides. The Government and Local Government Management Board have identified environmental management for local authorities as a major part of the LA21 initiative

Summary of Benefits

Formal environmental management systems will help your organisation to:

❑ ensure compliance with environmental legislation;
❑ develop a systematic approach;
❑ identify potential liabilities;
❑ develop competitive advantage; and
❑ develop effective, targeted objectives to manage environmental effects.

INDUSTRY STANDARDS/INITIATIVES

There are now two independent standards that organisation can gain to recognise their environmental management systems. The standards set out an approach to environmental management that has been widely taken up even where formal certification is not being sought. The advantage of independent certification of your environmental programme is that will give your customers and the public confidence that you are taking real steps to improve your environmental performance. The disadvantage is that these standards can require high levels of bureaucracy to comply with their requirement An organisation that does not already have an ISO 9000 quali system in place needs to consider very carefully whether it is ready to work in this way.

Environmental management standards grew out of the recognition that, as the environment moved from a fringe concern to a mainstream business issue, a systematic approach to help companies deal with complex environmental challenges was needed. They are part of a general European move to encourage companies to improve voluntarily. The first environmental management system standard was the British Standard BS7750 which was based on the approach of the widely used quality standard BS5750. In Europe EMAS was developed specifically for manufacturing companies. The International Standards Organisation has now developed a standard, ISO 14001 that has replaced BS7750 and is recognised world-wide.

ISO/CD 14001

ISO 14001 describes an environmental management system for ensuring and demonstrating compliance with stated environmental policies and objectives.

ISO 14001 is designed to enable any organisation to establish an effective standardised management system, as a foundation for sound environmental performance and to ensure compliance with environmental legislation and regulations. It does not specify absolute levels of environmental performance, with the exception of compliance with legislation and a commitment to continual improvement. Thus two organisations carrying out similar activities but having different environmental performance may both comply with its requirements.

Although it is not required by the standard, the first step for almost all organisations who wish to have a management system certified to ISO 14001 is to conduct a review of their current environmental position. The information from this will help with the first requirement of the standard: the environmental policy statement. The policy must set out the aims and commitments of the organisation and be publicly available.

At the heart of the standard is a requirement to identify the environmental aspects of the organisation's activities which define its base level of performance. The environmental policy must include a commitment to continuous improvement from this base level. This improvement is achieved through a set of objectives and targets and a programme for implementing them.

What turns the standard into a management system is that the responsibilities of staff in implementing the policy and

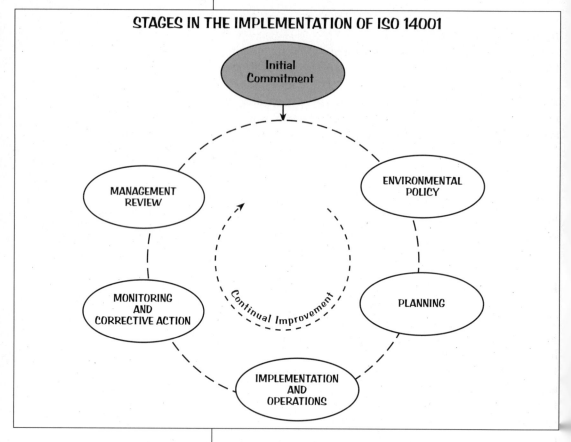

STAGES IN THE IMPLEMENTATION OF ISO 14001

FIGURE 9.1

Stages in the Implementation of ISO 14001

objectives must be documented in a set of procedures. These procedures should set out who is responsible for achieving what, when.

The standard requires that your system is regularly audited to ensure the procedures are being followed. Periodic management reviews of the success of the system in achieving the aims of the environmental policy must also be carried out.

Certification for compliance with the standard is carried out by external certifiers who are formally accredited under a scheme run by UK Accreditation Services (UKAS).

EMAS

EMAS is a voluntary European Community scheme for companies performing industrial activities which aims to encourage evaluation and improvement of environmental performance and the provision of relevant information to the public. Unlike ISO 14001 it is only available to industrial companies and local authorities.

EMAS is compatible with ISO 14001. To gain EMAS the main additional requirement is the publication of a concise and comprehensible statement for each participating site to ensure that the public and interested parties understand the environmental impacts of the site and how they are being managed. Publication is usually yearly and should contain up to date information on progress against the objectives and time scales agreed by the site's management team.

This environmental statement must be verified by an independent, accredited environmental verifier at the end of each cycle. The policy, programme, management system and audit procedure also have to be validated. Verifiers are accredited under a scheme run by UKAS on behalf of the Department of the Environment.

Local Authority (LA) EMAS

The Department of the Environment in association with the Local Government Management Board (LGMB) has established a version of EMAS for local authorities called LA-EMAS. The system is voluntary and is aimed to help local authorities improve their management of environmental issues. Hereford City Council and Sutton Council have already been validated to LA-EMAS. The scheme is closely modelled on the industrial version but has three key differences:

1) The industrial scheme is specific to a particular site. For local authorities a more appropriate management unit is a department or division.
2) The industrial scheme can be achieved by one site in a company. A local authority can also register one department, however a corporate overview and coordination scheme is also required and the whole authority must commit itself eventually to seek corporate registration.
3) The industrial scheme focuses on the environmental effects of production activities such as energy use and air pollution. These direct effects are also applicable to local authorities but the main impact of, for instance, a planning department, is likely to be in the way the service is delivered. LA-EMAS would be ridiculed if it concentrated on the energy use of the planning department and ignored the effect of a planning decision on an application to open a large quarry. The local authority scheme therefore also aims to manage these service effects.

Which Standard?

If you want to gain certification to a standard, which one do you choose? For office and service sector companies ISO 14001 is the only choice as it is applicable to any company and is internationally recognised.

For local authorities LA-EMAS is the best option. It has been specifically adapted and there is a dedicated help desk run by the LGMB to assist authorities with the process.

For manufacturing companies the choice between ISO and EMAS is more difficult. A company should take into account that EMAS is a more demanding scheme which requires a detailed public statement and should, therefore, have greater credibility. The choice however, will probably rest on which is most recognised in the particular market sector in question.

You should remember that you are not tied to the standard you first choose. EMAS and ISO 14001 have many similarities and once you have achieved one standard it will be a much simpler process to fulfil the criteria of the other.

CBI Environment Forum

The Environment Business Forum is a service for all businesses which want to aim for environmental excellence. The Forum provides an opportunity to further promote your environmental position. It is a two way commitment:

❑ by the CBI, to help businesses improve their environmental performance; and
❑ by business, to demonstrate the action which they are taking.

At the heart of the Forum is the Agenda for Voluntary Action which outlines eight key steps which every business can and should take.

❑ Designating a board level director with responsibility for the environment, if there is not a board then the most senior representative should be nominated.
❑ Publishing a corporate environmental policy statement.
❑ Setting clear targets and publishing objectives for achieving the policy.
❑ Measuring current performance against targets.

Case Study

Subject –	**ENVIRONMENTAL MANAGEMENT SYSTEMS**
Organisation –	**BICC CABLES LTD**
Organisation type –	**TELECOMMUNICATION CABLES**
Location –	**HQ HELSBY, CHESHIRE**
No. of staff –	**400**

BACKGROUND

The Communications Installation Unit (CIU) business of BICC Cables specialises in the installation and maintenance of cable networks for the telecommunications sector. Operations are organised from regional offices, with all central functions located at Helsby (35 staff). The Unit's services are undertaken nationally by field engineers in a fleet of approximately 300 vehicles.

BICC Cables made a corporate commitment to environmental improvement in its environmental policy issued in 1995. Following this commitment CIU began looking at its environmental effects in early 1995. The decision was taken to go for certification to the environmental management system (EMS) BS7750 which was achieved in May 1996.

As a transport-based operation, the CIU is unusual in implementing BS7750. The majority of companies with formal EMSs are in the manufacturing sector and have a different set of environmental effects.

ACTION

The Unit began reviewing its environmental impacts with an independent report by Lancaster University which looked at: relevant legislation, identification of environmental effects, existing management systems and structures.

A key decision was taken to integrate the requirements of BS7750 into the existing quality management system to create

RESULTS

CIU was the first multi-site business operating services from a transport fleet to achieve BS7750.

Among the first year's environmental objectives the Unit is committed to:

- ❑ reducing fuel consumption;
- ❑ reducing waste to landfill;
- ❑ reducing electricity consumption; and
- ❑ evaluating environmental performance of its suppliers.

Implementation of BS 7750 has been the kick start to many innovative business improvements, and is now part of the way we do business. It has been cost effective as well as benefiting the environment, and given a base line for future development. Commercially our environmental initiatives are a key inclusion in contract tenders in a highly competitive sector.

One surprising but pleasing aspect of the exercise was the enthusiastic commitment demonstrated by our workforce. The majority of employees can relate to and are passionate in protecting the environment.

The discipline of an independently certified EMS will enable CIU to continue to improve efficiency, and be responsive to the expectations of customers, employees, government agencies and the public.

one business management system which fulfilled BS7750 and ISO 9002. To this end the Unit employed an environmental officer to work within the Quality Department.

A significance evaluation of the Unit's environmental effects revealed initial objectives should be focused on diesel consumption, vehicles, waste disposal and energy consumption. Project teams and reporting methods were developed. All staff received environmental training or awareness sessions, and will receive this at least annually on refresher programmes.

(Contributed by Communications Installation Unit, BICC Cables Ltd.)

❑ Implementing improvement plans.
❑ Communicating company environmental policy and objectives to employees, seeking their contribution to improvement and providing appropriate training.
❑ Reporting publicly on progress in achieving the objectives.

The Business Charter for Sustainable Development

The International Chamber of Commerce launched the Business Charter for Sustainable Development in 1991. The charter consists of 16 principles for environmental management.

1) Corporate priority. To recognise environmental management as among the highest corporate priorities and as a key determinant to sustainable development; to establish policies, programmes and practices for conducting operations in an environmentally sound manner.
2) Integrated management. To integrate these policies, programmes and practices fully into each business as an essential element of management in all its functions.
3) Process of improvement. To continue to improve corporate policies, programmes and environmental performance,

taking into account technical developments, scientific developments, scientific understanding, consumer needs and community expectations, with legal regulations as a starting point; and to apply the same environmental criteria internationally.

4) Employee education. To educate, train and motivate employees to conduct their activities in an environmentally responsible manner.

5) Prior assessment. To assess environmental impacts before starting a new activity or project and before decommissioning a facility or leaving a site.

6) Products and services. To develop and provide products or services that have no undue environmental impact and are safe in their intended use, that are efficient in their consumption of energy and natural resources, and that can be recycled reused, or disposed of safely.

7) Customer advice. To advise, and where relevant educate, customers, distributors and the public in the safe use, transportation, storage and disposal of products provided; and to apply similar considerations to the provisions of services.

8) Facilities and operations. To develop, design and operate facilities and conduct activities taking into consideration the efficient use of energy and materials, the sustainable use of renewable resources, the minimisation of adverse environmental impact and waste generation, and the safe and responsible disposal of residual wastes.

9) Research. To conduct or support research on the environmental impacts of raw materials, products, processes, emissions and waste associated with the enterprise and on the means of minimising such adverse impacts.

10) Precautionary approach. To modify the manufacture, marketing or use of products or services or the conduct of activities, consistent with scientific and technical understanding, to prevent serious or irreversible environmental degradation.

11) Contractors and suppliers. To promote the adoption of these principles by contractors acting on behalf of the enterprise, encouraging and, where appropriate, requiring improvements in their practices to make them consistent with those of the enterprise; and to encourage the wider adoption of these principles by suppliers.

12) Emergency preparedness. To develop and maintain, where significant hazards exist, emergency preparedness plans in conjunction with emergency services, relevant authorities and the local community, recognising potential transboundary impacts.

13) Transfer of technology. To contribute to the transfer of environmentally sound technology and management methods throughout the industrial and public sectors.

14) Contributing to the common effort. To contribute to the development of public policy and to business, governmental and intergovernmental programmes and educational initiatives that will enhance environmental awareness and protection.

15) Openness to concerns. To foster openness and dialogue with employees and the public, anticipating and responding to their concerns about the potential hazards and impacts of operations, products, wastes or services, including those of transboundary or global significance.

16) Compliance and reporting. To measure environmental performance; to conduct regular environmental audits and assessments of compliance with company requirements, legal requirements and these principles; and periodically to provide appropriate information to the board of directors, shareholders, employees, the authorities and the public.

STEPS TO A MANAGEMENT SYSTEM

An environmental management system is a tool. It does not set levels of performance but a structure in which to achieve the performance targets you set yourself. The approach follows the simple cycle of planning what you will do, doing it, checking that it is working and reviewing your approach.

FIGURE 9.2
The Improvement Loop

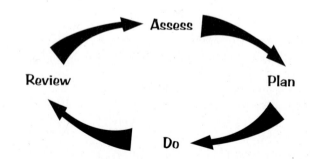

THE IMPROVEMENT LOOP

Assess

Review

Plan

Do

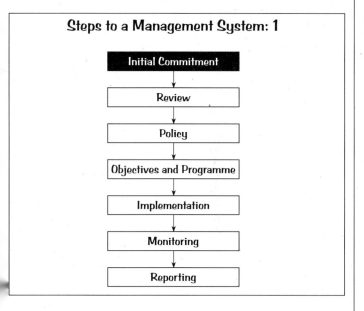

FIGURE 9.3
The Steps to a Management System: 1

The details of the system you implement must fit in with the way your organisation works but the basic steps are more or less the same for all systems.

Step 1: Initial Commitment

The successful development of a system is dependent on commitment from the highest level to carry it through. An environmental management system is a programme of change. It will take significant resources to develop and will have an impact on all areas of your organisation and the way all managers and staff carry out their jobs.

Before committing themselves to this change top management will need an understanding of the implications as well as the benefits. If there are members of your senior management who are sceptical about environmental issues, a presentation covering the key business drivers outlined in Chapter 1 can help bring them on board.

It is equally important to keep staff informed and involved from the start. When you ask staff to take on new roles and responsibilities, the benefits must be very clear if it is not to be dismissed as another management gimmick (a guide to successful communication is given in Chapter 8).

FIGURE 9.4

The Steps to a Management System: 2

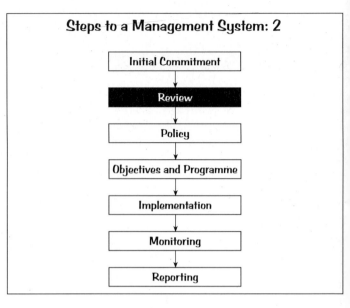

Step 2: Review

Step 2: Review

Your office has a range of effects on the environment, some of which you may not have been aware of until picking up this Manual. For many of these effects you will already have management procedures due to legislation and cost. To develop a system to manage and reduce these effects you need to know what they are and how you currently deal with them. Thus the second stage for an organisation developing a formal environmental management system is a structured assessment of its current position

Most offices who have decided to consider a management system will already have taken some action on environmental issues. Having worked through this Manual you will have identified a range of practical actions you can use to improve on your performance. This work can be used as part of the more structured approach of a formal review.

HOW TO PLAN A REVIEW

Establish a Co-ordinating Group

The first step of a review is to establish who is going to carry i out. One successful approach is to set up a project team of staf who cover the key areas of your organisation. You may alread have a group looking at environmental issues on a less forma basis on which you can draw. Using a team based approach wi draw in a wide range of knowledge and spread the load. It wi also involve a range of staff in the environmental programme at an early stage and improve communication between areas.

Decide on Training Needs

Consider whether the group has the necessary range of skills and expertise to conduct the review. If you have no staff who have experience in environmental management and auditing then training in these areas will add value to the review. Knowledge gained at this stage will also be helpful in developing the rest of the management system. If training is required then you need to identify what the needs are, how staff will be trained and who will conduct the training.

Plan Scope of Review

The project team should define carefully the scope and aims of the review before starting. Different areas of the review can be allocated among the members of the work group.

Guidance on what topics to cover within the review is dealt with in more detail below.

Consider a Two Stage Review Process

If you are dealing with a large complex office it can be helpful to divide the process into a scoping and detailed review. The aim of a scoping review is to do a first stage assessment of all of your environmental effects and to identify those that merit further investigation. Once you have identified key areas you can undertake a detailed review focusing purely on those areas.

The two stage review is recommended for local authorities in the LGMB guidance. Local authorities have a wide range of environmental effects and a scoping review can make the process seem less daunting.

Decide on Methods

It is best to use a range of methods to gather information. For instance if you are examining your existing recycling scheme a simple check of waste bins will tell you a great deal. The most common methods are questionnaires/ worksheets which require staff to fill in information, interviews with key staff and direct observation.

When deciding on your methods you should consider how similar projects work in your organisation, the area you are examining and what information you already have. To minimise your work make sure you do not duplicate this information.

WHAT TO COVER

Your review should cover the following key areas:

Main Environmental Effects

Identify your key environmental effects. This is a key part of the review and is looked at in more detail below.

Legislative And Regulatory Requirements

Record all the environmental legislation relevant to your operations. Each chapter in the *Manual* contains a section on legislation which will help you identify these regulations. This information should not be taken as a comprehensive listing of environmental legislation. Where legislation applies to your organisation seek further details from the appropriate regulatory body.

The Environment Agency is responsible for enforcing a large amount of environmental legislation and can provide further information on specific areas.

Record any policy commitments by any wider corporate body or industry sector of which you are a part.

Existing Management Procedures

You will already have procedures or practices to manage important cost areas such as energy use, or health and safety measures for items such as hazardous chemicals.

Recording these will help with designing your environmental management system to make the best use of existing procedures rather than imposing a completely new system.

Previous Incidents or Problems

Previous incidents can provide valuable information as to current weaknesses in your control of environmental issues. For instance your recycling company may have complained about contamination of paper for recycling with other wastes such as plastic cups and food wrappers.

ASSESSING ENVIRONMENTAL EFFECTS

The assessment of the effects you are having on the environment is the most time consuming and challenging part of a review. Your approach needs to be comprehensive but concentrate on the key areas rather than getting bogged down identifying the environmental effects of every last biro

Wherever possible you should seek to measure and quantify the effect, this will enable you to set targets and measure the progress you are making.

Direct and Service Effects

This *Manual* covers the direct effects of the office, however many offices will also have effects arising from the services they provide. The difference between these two types are illustrated by the example of a solicitor's office:

1) 'Direct effects' are those which result not from the nature of the service provided, such as legal advice, but from the general activities required to provide that service eg energy use, transport use, paper purchasing etc. These areas are covered in detail in the *Manual*.
2) 'Service effects' are those which arise from the actual service, such as legal advice provided in areas like takeover bids, contaminated land and environmental law. These are specific to the organisation and are outside the scope of the *Manual*.

For some office based organisations, such as an office attached to a factory, service effects will not be relevant.

Identifying Effects

Step 1

Divide your operations into activities, products and services as appropriate to your organisation. For direct effects you can divide your offices by the chapters of this *Manual*: office waste, purchasing products, purchasing services, office equipment, building and energy management, and transport. To assess service effects you can use the different departments in your office. For instance, a solicitor's office could be divided by the different legal areas it deals with.

Step 2

Identify the inputs and outputs from each of the areas you have divided your activities into. For example, inputs for transport would include cars and fuel and the outputs would include, carbon dioxide emissions and waste tyres. You should make sure you have covered inputs and outputs in the following areas:

- ❑ emissions to air;
- ❑ discharges to water;
- ❑ waste;
- ❑ contamination of land;
- ❑ use of raw material and natural resources; and
- ❑ other local environmental issues.

Some inputs and outputs such as office waste, will arise as part of your normal daily operations. Others may only occur during abnormal conditions or in an emergency such as a fire causing release of hazardous cleaning and building maintenance chemicals. It is important that you consider these potential issues as well as the normal ones.

You should also take into account past incidents and future plans. For example if you are planning an office relocation the effects of your energy and transport may change dramatically.

Step 3

Identify the environmental effects of the inputs and outputs, both positive and negative. For instance, the key environmental impact of carbon dioxide release is contribution to the greenhouse effect.

Concentrating on the Important Areas

Following this assessment process, focus on the effects that are important enough to require more detailed consideration and management. Keep in mind the following criteria when assessing your inputs and outputs to determine whether they give rise to effects that are significant.

- ❑ Whether there is any relevant legislation.
- ❑ The scale of the effect.
- ❑ The importance of the environmental issue.
- ❑ The chance of the effect occurring.

RECOMMENDATIONS

The review should include recommendations for improvements. Whilst reviewing your environmental position the project team is likely to have plenty of ideas which will help to set objectives and targets. At this stage the review does not need to contain polished and costed initiatives but a wide range of ideas to take forward.

The review is also a good time to encourage ideas from other members of staff. It is usually those carrying out a particular activity that have the best ideas as to how it can be done better.

REPORTING THE REVIEW

The Review Report

The review report will be used in all the stages of your management system. It should contain a clear presentation of the review. In particular it should detail environmental effects in a systematic way to allow objectives and targets to be developed to set your organisation on the path to continuous environmental improvement.

The Effects Register

You can take your review of significant environmental effects a step further by compiling a formal register of all your effects based on your earlier assessment. This is a major component of EMAS.

The advantage of this approach is that you can clearly justify the objectives you set and evaluate and report progress objectively against the register of effects. For organisations with a high environmental profile, such as manufacturing companies or local authorities, this is a major advantage. For other organisations it is important to carefully weigh the advantages against the resource demand.

SWOT ANALYSIS

A useful way of summarising the finding of your review is by analysing the strengths and weakness of your organisation and the opportunities and threats environmental issues present. Table 9.1 illustrates how you might present your analysis.

Step 3: Environmental Policy

An environmental policy is a mission statement for your whole organisation. Its aim is to set out and communicate key environmental commitments to all stakeholders. The policy should therefore be a clear statement of the organisation's overall aims and approach.

It should be possible to implement the overall aims in the policy through practical action. It is important to realise that your aims may be subject to close scrutiny and you should make sure that you are ready to fulfil them. For instance, a

COMMON PROBLEMS

Getting a Positive Response

Staff may well see someone giving them questionnaires or interviews about how they do their job as a threat. If this is the case you are unlikely to get the information you are looking for. It is important to involve all staff from the beginning so they see it as a positive exercise which they want to contribute to rather than a threat.

Identifying the Information You Need

Since all aspects of your organisation have some effect on the environment there is a danger of being swamped in information when undertaking your review.

The key is to follow a structured approach such as that outlined above so that you know what information you are looking for and can ignore anything that is not relevant.

STRENGTHS	WEAKNESS
A. Model Ltd has committed itself at top level to an environmental management system A. Model has in place procedures to ensure environmental liabilities are considered in investment decisions	There is a lack of knowledge and measurement of the organisation's environmental effects Environmental management is currently on an *ad hoc* basis There is a lack of knowledge of relevant environmental legislation Environmental issues not taken seriously by middle management
OPPORTUNITIES	THREATS
Environmental improvements would show A. Model as a responsible company Environmental management will assist in competing for contracts. Environmental measures could provide cost savings by cutting waste	There is increasing pressure from customers for A. Model to demonstrate that it is an environmentally responsible company An environmental management system could create bureaucracy

TABLE 9.1
SWOT analysis of A. Model Investment Bank

SUMMARY GUIDELINES

❏ Establish a review coordinating group and plan scope of review.
❏ Decide on any training needs.
❏ Decide on methods you will use.
❏ Assess your environmental effects using a structured approach.
❏ Review relevant legislation, existing management procedures and previous incidents.
❏ Make recommendations based on your findings.

broad policy commitment to minimise air pollution from your activities will need to be implemented with specific actions and measurable improvements. It is not necessary for the specific actions or targets to be detailed in your policy, these should come in the environmental management system you put in place to implement it.

HOW TO COMPILE YOUR POLICY

Involve Senior Management

Senior management should be involved in initiating, designing and supporting the environmental policy. They should fully understand the business reasons behind the policy and the resource commitment that is required to implement it.

Review your Environmental Impacts

The review, outlined in the previous section, will give you a good idea of your main areas of environmental impact. These should serve as the basis for the specific areas to be covered in the policy.

Review Existing Policies and Guidelines

Most large organisations have publicly available environmental

Steps to a Management System: 3

```
Initial Commitment
        ↓
     Review
        ↓
     Policy
        ↓
Objectives and Programme
        ↓
  Implementation
        ↓
    Monitoring
        ↓
    Reporting
```

FIGURE 9.5
The Steps to a Management System: 3

policies. Obtaining a selection of these can help you with ideas of layout, style and content for your own policy. Those in your own sector of business will be particularly relevant.

The CBI publishes a booklet *Corporate environmental policy statements* (1992) which provides guidance on drawing up a policy and case studies of existing corporate policy statements. The booklet identifies four themes running through these statements:

'1. A recognition of responsibilities.
2. A commitment from top level.
3. A commitment towards training for employees and dissemi-nation of information concerning the detail of the corporate environmental policy statement.
4. A technical understanding and the willingness to imple-ment targets.'

A useful guide to the principles you should include in your policy is the International Chamber of Commerce (ICC) Business Charter for Sustainable Development which was adopted in April 1991 and relaunched in 1996. The Charter is an influential statement of the principles of good business practice to which many companies worldwide have signed. This is reproduced in full earlier in this chapter.

The Local Government Management Board EMAS Help-Desk produces guidance notes for LA-EMAS. These provide some of the most useful guidance to all the stages of a manage-ment system. They are aimed at local authorities, however the principles will be valuable for any organisation.

KEY FEATURES OF A POLICY

Complies With Corporate Policy

If the organisation is part of a broader corporate body your environmental policy should comply with any corporate policy. However you should not just copy the corporate approach but ensure you take account of specific issues which affect your organisation or division. The environmental policy should also be consistent with health and safety policies.

Has Senior Management Commitment

A policy that is not clearly endorsed by the senior management of the organisation will have no credibility for staff members or for stakeholders such as customers and the public. Your policy should therefore be signed by a senior manager.

Covers the Main Environmental Issues

To have credibility your policy must cover the key environmental issues affecting the organisation. The policy of a nuclear power station, for instance, will not be taken seriously if it does not mention potential radioactive emissions. Equally a policy for a bank which did not mention investment would have little credibility.

Includes a Commitment to Continuous Improvement

Environmental management should not be seen as a one off process but an ongoing move towards an environmentally sustainable organisation. The policy should therefore include a commitment to continuous improvement of environmental performance. This should be taken to mean an improvement each year in overall environmental performance rather than an improvement in all areas at all times.

Includes A Commitment To Comply With Legislation

A commitment to meet all relevant legislative and regulatory commitments is required by environmental management standards. More ambitious companies often set a policy commitment to aim to exceed the requirements of legislation.

Makes Clear Commitments

To be credible your policy should include clear environmental commitments that can be implemented through practical action.

Is Publicly Available

Openness to the concerns of the public is a key principle of an environmentally aware business. You should publicise your policy within the local community, perhaps through local media or by providing local authorities with a copy. The policy should also be available to anybody that requests a copy (see GPT case study, Chapter 8).

Is Clearly Written and Concise

The policy should be written clearly and concisely with the minimum of jargon. This will encourage people to read it and help to ensure that it gives a clear message of your aims and values.

Model Policy

We have outlined below a model policy to provide an example of how these key features and the CBI and ICC guidance can be put together in a policy. The policy is nominally for a banking organisation. It therefore focuses on the environmental impacts of the banking service provided as well as of the operation of the business.

There is of course no ideal policy, your policy needs to reflect the main issues for your business, to be realistic as to what you can achieve and to fit with the style of your organisation.

OFFICE ENVIRONMENTAL POLICY

If your office is part of a wider organisational environmental management system it can help to have a specific office policy to make sure that specific issues relating to the office are not ignored. An office policy does not need to cover areas that do not come under its remit. The model office policy below provides an idea of what this might look like.

A. MODEL OFFICE ENVIRONMENTAL POLICY

The A. Model Corporate Environmental Policy states that 'We regard ecological protection and sustainable development as key priorities for all organisations and as essential for the future success of our business.'

This Policy sets out how we aim to fulfil this commitment in the office by continuously improving our environmental performance. We will:

COMMON PROBLEMS

Waffle

Some organisations use their environmental policy to reassure everybody about how wonderful they are and fail to make any meaningful commitments. Such a policy will have no credibility within or outside the organisation.

All organisations have scope to improve their environmental performance. A recognition of the impacts your organisation is having and credible commitments to improve must be at the heart of your policy.

Lack of Understanding of the Consequences

Organisations and individuals can sometimes fail to realise that a policy statement means what it says. Meaningful environmental commitments will mean change in all areas of the organisation. Once you have made a public commitment then failure to fulfil the policy will lose credibility and you will be open to negative publicity.

You must make sure that all your staff are aware that policy statements will have to be carried through and are not just meaningless standard statements to appease the green lobby.

❑ assign responsibility for implementing the office environmental policy to a senior manager;
❑ minimise our use of resources by applying the hierarchy of 'Reduce, Re-use and Recycle';
❑ dispose of any remaining waste safely, and in accordance with all relevant legislation;
❑ minimise our energy use in all areas of our office through staff awareness and the use of energy efficient heating, air conditioning, lighting and office equipment;
❑ consider the environmental impact of products and services in our purchasing decisions and purchase environmentally preferable products where practicable;
❑ phase out the use of CFCs and HCFCs;
❑ reduce the environmental effect of commuting to work and business travel by efficient use of travel and by encouraging cycling and public transport; and
❑ encourage staff ideas and keep staff informed on new environmental initiatives.

To implement the environmental policy we will put in place an environmental action plan each year setting out our environmental objectives and target dates for that year.

Signed Ms Big Cheese

Step 4: Objectives and Programme

The basic aim of any environmental programme is to reduce your impact on the environment. Your environmental policy will have committed you to this aim. The objectives and action programme are where you turn these fine words into real change.

The environmental effects identified in your environmental review will provide you with the basis for setting your objectives. Not all significant effects need to be addressed at once but they will need to be managed in due course. Each objective should have an implementation programme with management responsibility and resources identified together with targets and performance indicators to monitor progress.

OBJECTIVES

It is important to set demanding objectives that are seen to be

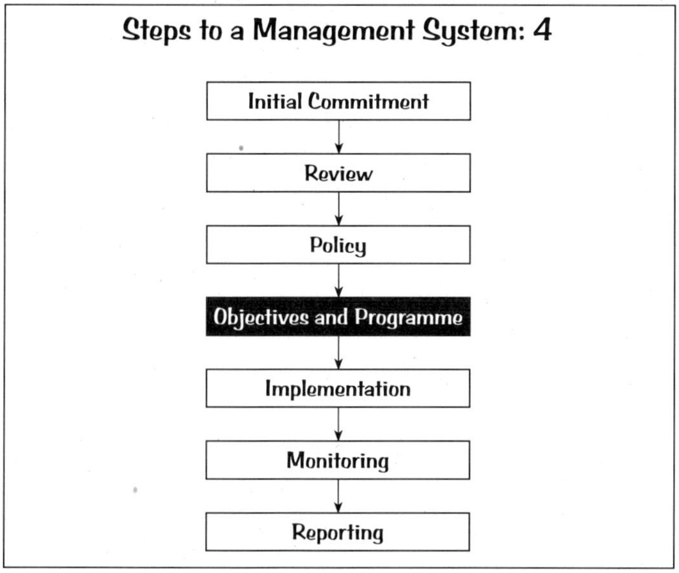

Steps to a Management System: 4

Initial Commitment

↓

Review

↓

Policy

↓

Objectives and Programme

↓

Implementation

↓

Monitoring

↓

Reporting

FIGURE 9.6
The Steps to a Management System: 4

making a real change rather than just reinforcing the status quo. They must also be achievable. Failure to achieve your objectives will be demoralising, so consider carefully whether you are being realistic or whether you need to concentrate on a smaller number of key issues.

Criteria

Objectives should closely reflect the policy commitments they are designed to implement. In setting objectives you should take into account the following criteria:

- ❏ policy commitments;
- ❏ the review of environmental effects;
- ❏ legislation and compliance issues;
- ❏ ease of implementation;
- ❏ views of interested parties; and
- ❏ cost, time and potential savings.

ENVIRONMENTAL PROGRAMME

Each objective should be supported with a specific action plan, detailing who is going to do what and when they are going to do it. This will link the objectives into the management system you use to implement your policy by establishing management control and monitoring procedures.

Types of Actions

It is important to be clear exactly what each of your actions is

A. Model Ltd Corporate Environmental Policy

CBI

ICC

Recognition of responsibilities

A. Model Ltd UK recognises that banking has an impact on the environment through the direct impact of our operations and the indirect impacts of our customers. We regard ecological protection and sustainable development as key priorities for all organisations and as essential for the future success of our business.

Principle 1

Our environmental programme aims to achieve continuous improvement in reducing our environmental impacts. To achieve this goal we will develop and implement an environmental management system as an integral component of the management of our business. We will set targets for improvement in the following areas:

Principle 3

Principle 2

We will meet and, where appropriate, strive to exceed the requirements of all relevant legislation

Principle 3

We will include environmental criteria in our standard risk assessment and management procedures and apply environmental criteria to loan policies and company evaluations.

Principle 10

Technical understanding & target setting

We will encourage our clients to assess the environmental effects of their business and provide them with information on best practice for environmental management.

Principle 7

We will minimise our waste, our consumption of natural resources and our energy use in all areas of our business.

Principle 8

We will minimise the release of any pollutant that may cause environmental damage to the air, water, earth, or its inhabitants.

Principle 8

Commitment towards training & dissemination of information

Through our purchasing policy we will support those companies which demonstrate best practice in environmental management and purchase environmentally preferable goods and services.

Principle 11

All employees are encouraged to play a full part in the implementation of our policy and will be given appropriate training and education to enable them to do so. We will work with our suppliers, customers and the community in improving our environmental performance.

Principle 4

Principle 15

We will regularly review our environmental programme and report on our progress to the Board of Directors, shareholders, employees and the public.

Principle 16

Commitment from top level

Signed, Ms Big Cheese

trying to achieve. Confusion can arise between those which aim to achieve an actual improvement, such as reducing energy use and those which aim to gather further information or achieve better control. The LGMB EMAS guidance notes (EMAS Help-Desk, 1996) divide actions into three categories:

❑ Improvement actions that directly fulfil your commitment to continuous improvement, such as installing energy efficient lighting.
❑ Further analysis actions that improve the information you have in order to judge the importance of an environmental effect, such as surveying how staff commute to work.
❑ Control actions that ensure an actual or potential environmental effect is properly controlled to minimise risk, such as a procedure to ensure hazardous waste is properly stored and disposed of.

If you are clear as to what type of action you are setting it will make it much simpler to define and monitor it. An extension of this approach is to have three separate programmes: improvement, control and further analysis.

Criteria

Actions you set should fulfil the following criteria.

❑ Be clearly designed to achieve the objective you have set.
❑ Have a specific person responsible for achievement.
❑ Have an identified timescale.
❑ Be measurable so that progress and achievement can be assessed.
❑ Have adequate resources allocated.

In Table 9.2 we have set out a model programme structure with some example actions. The actual structure you choose should be tailored to fit in with your existing management practices.

Step 5: Implementation

PROCEDURES AND DOCUMENTATION

An environmental management system requires that you document the key procedures needed to implement your policy. In most people's minds documentation means bureaucracy and bureaucracy is to be avoided at all costs. Yet all

COMMON PROBLEMS

Under Ambition

Your policy should include a commitment to the overall objective of continuous improvement as well as specific aims. You do not need to tackle all areas at all times but your objectives need to be sufficiently ambitious to show you are making a real commitment to improvement. Objectives that just reinforce the status quo will undermine the credibility of your programme and the morale of those implementing it.

Over Ambition

Setting hundreds of objectives that you do not have the time or money to fulfil will undermine confidence in your environmental programme. You should concentrate on a relatively small number of demanding targets.

POLICY COMMITMENT:	We will minimise our waste, our consumption of natural resources and our energy use in all areas of our business
OBJECTIVE 1:	To reduce office waste arisings by 5% by Jan 1998
PROJECT LEADER:	A Manager
MONITORING PROCEDURE:	Total figures of different waste streams and progress against previous figures, to be recorded on a monthly basis
BASELINE:	kg per person

ACTION PROGRAMME	TARGET DATE	RESPONS-IBILITY INDICATOR	PERFORM-ANCE	RESOURCE COST	NON COMPLIANCE AND CORRECTIVE ACTION TAKEN
Develop general good housekeeping guidelines for staff	1 June 1997	Office Manager	Production of guidelines	2 days	Completed on time
Place poster above all photocopiers to remind staff to double side	1 March 1997	Clerk	Production of poster	1 day	Completed on time
Train all staff in use of electronic mail for internal communication	1 January 1998	IT Manager	Number of staff trained	One hour training for 300 staff	Training of 50 staff delayed – lack of resources. Completed 1 March
Assess all computer report print-outs to examine whether information could be accessed on line	1 June 1997	IT Manager	Number of reports assessed	1 day	Completed on time

TABLE 9.2

A. Model UK Ltd – Environmental Programme 1997

organisations use letters, filing systems and records as part of their day to day work. The key is to not shy away from developing procedures but to ensure they form a streamlined system with only essential documents.

What to Cover

Your documented procedures need to translate the environmental policy and objectives into specific responsibilities for staff. In other words who does what when to make sure that the policy is met. Procedures also need to cover what happens when things go wrong and the corrective action that will be taken. This documentation will help ensure staff are aware of their responsibilities, provide continuity when staff take up new jobs and give you a set of procedures against which the system can be audited. The documents could include organisational charts, emergency plans and procedures describing specific tasks.

Your environmental programme links into this system by documenting who is responsible for implementing environmental objectives, how they are going to do it and when they are going to do it.

TRAINING

There will inevitably be some nervousness amongst your staff about the change of culture that environmental management will bring. The aim of a training programme is to overcome this concern by giving staff a clear idea about their roles under the new system and to equip staff with the skills they need to make that system work. The previous chapter outlined a number of methods for raising staff awareness which will help you to implement the training which you need.

To implement training for all your staff you will need a structured programme which ensures all staff are trained, including

SUMMARY GUIDELINES

Your Objectives Should:

- ❏ implement your policy commitments;
- ❏ be demanding but achievable;
- ❏ cover your main environmental effects; and
- ❏ cover any issues of legislative compliance you have identified.

Your Action Programme Should:

- ❏ have responsibilities and resources defined;
- ❏ be monitored against a given timescale; and
- ❏ achieve the objective you have set.

Steps to a Management System: 5

Initial Commitment
↓
Review
↓
Policy
↓
Objectives and Programme
↓
Implementation
↓
Monitoring
↓
Reporting

FIGURE 9.7
The Steps to a Management System: 5

COMMON PROBLEMS

Procedures That Nobody Follows

The danger is that you will create procedures that sit on a shelf and which everybody ignores until there is an audit. To avoid this each document should be owned by a specific job holder who is responsible for keeping it up to date and making any changes. That person should be involved in writing the procedure so that it reflects what they actually do. Any documentation should be clearly written with a minimum of jargon and have a clear purpose.

induction training for new recruits. You will need to identify what training staff are going to receive and who is going to deliver it. Training programmes for staff should cover the following areas:

❏ The system and what it means to staff. All staff in your organisation should feel involved in the development of your system from day one and understand the business reasons for environmental management. As you put the system in place train your staff in how your environmental policy and procedures will function and the importance of conforming with these. This training must emphasise the potential environmental consequences of not following the procedures. Staff also need to understand their individual role and responsibility in the system.

❏ The environmental effects of their work. In your review you will have identified your key environmental effects. The staff who are carrying out the activities that give rise to these effects should be aware of them and why they are important. They need to understand how improved performance of their activities will reduce these environmental effects.

❏ Specific skills. In some areas specific skills training will be required to enable staff to put in place an objective. For instance an office with a product design team will need to train designers in considering environmental issues in the design process.

Ease of Use

You should aim to complement existing management procedures rather than set up an entirely new management system. Very often it will be a case of signposting existing documents concerned with areas like health and safety or emergency procedures. This should avoid the development of a weighty tome stuffed with procedures. For organisations that have a quality system in place this will provide a base on which to add environmental procedures. It can be of help to create a central manual as an overview of the system.

Step 6: Monitoring

A management system needs to be self-repairing to be successful. Monitoring and corrective action when problems arise are key features of a successful system. There is little point in

Steps to a Management System: 6

```
┌─────────────────────────┐
│   Initial Commitment    │
└─────────────────────────┘
            ↓
┌─────────────────────────┐
│         Review          │
└─────────────────────────┘
            ↓
┌─────────────────────────┐
│         Policy          │
└─────────────────────────┘
            ↓
┌─────────────────────────┐
│ Objectives and Programme│
└─────────────────────────┘
            ↓
┌─────────────────────────┐
│     Implementation      │
└─────────────────────────┘
            ↓
┌─────────────────────────┐
│       Monitoring        │
└─────────────────────────┘
            ↓
┌─────────────────────────┐
│        Reporting        │
└─────────────────────────┘
```

FIGURE 9.8
The Steps to a Management System: 6

setting objectives if you never check to see they have been achieved. Checking should occur at three levels:

1) Day to day monitoring. On a day to day basis the management system should include checks on compliance. For instance your environmental objectives and programme are to a set timescale. Where targets are not met this should trigger corrective action.

2) Management system audits. The purpose of a regular audit is to have a more comprehensive and independent assessment of how the system is working. Auditing will highlight areas of weakness in your system and the strengths that you can build upon. The audit programme should cover:
   – Whether environmental management activities are happening as planned; and
   – the effectiveness of the system in fulfilling your environmental policy.
   Audits should be carried out by a trained person who is independent of the area they are auditing. If you do not have a specific audit team you should train a range of staff to carry out auditing. This has the additional benefit of being an effective method of increasing understanding of environmental management.

3) Management review. The management review is a periodic strategic review of the effectiveness of your system by the top level management. It provides an opportunity to examine the success of the policy and management system in responding to the business drivers that led to its adoption.

Step 7 – Reporting

FIGURE 9.9
The Steps to a Management System: 7

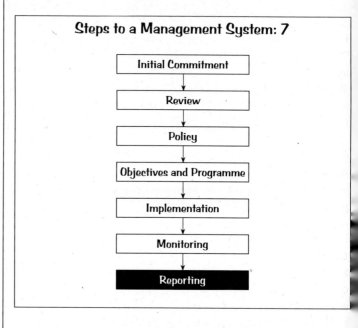

Steps to a Management System: 7

- Initial Commitment
- Review
- Policy
- Objectives and Programme
- Implementation
- Monitoring
- Reporting

Openness to the concerns of interested parties is an important principle of an environmentally aware organisation. We have looked at the importance of internal training and communication for the success of the system in the previous chapter. Equally important is external communication with stakeholders. There are three common ways in which organisations report on their environmental performance:

OPENNESS TO CONCERNS

The first principle of environmental reporting is to be open to complaints and communications from interested parties, such as the public and customers, regarding your environmental effects and to respond promptly. When setting your environmental policy and prioritising your objectives take these communications into account to ensure you are tackling the issues of concern to stakeholders.

PUBLICLY AVAILABLE POLICY

A publicly available policy provides a basic tool for taking a more proactive approach to demonstrating your environmental awareness and commitment to responsible practice. It sets out your aims and values in a short and clear format which will be accessible to a wide range of people.

PUBLIC REPORTING

An increasing number of major organisations are taking a proactive approach to communicating with stakeholders a stage further by producing an annual regular environmental report. The Chartered Association of Certified Accountants has an annual environmental reporting award which has been won by Thorn EMI for the last two years. The Body Shop has also been a pioneer of open reporting including auditing of its social impact as well as its environmental impact.

A public report should set out clearly the results of your environmental review and the objectives and targets you have set to improve. Many businesses have found this a valuable way of focusing their management programme. It can also provide a basis for dialogue with any interested parties and enhance the reputation of your organisation. Most companies have sought some degree of independent endorsement of their review along the lines of the independent audit of a business's financial accounts. An in depth public report is a requirement of EMAS and validation of the report is an important part of achieving EMAS.

Local authorities have also seen benefits in a public environmental statement which enables them to report back to residents on their environmental position in a rigorous way. Sutton Borough Council and Hereford City Council have both published statements as part of their EMAS programmes. These have the added advantage of being independently validated.

ENVIRONMENTAL MANAGEMENT SOFTWARE

Environmental management entails keeping and controlling large amounts of information. This may be in addition to related issues such as quality systems and health and safety. Software packages can provide a useful way of structuring this information and preventing your organisation being buried in piles of paperwork.

There are a number of competitively priced software packages on the market which are dedicated to environmental management. This is a fast developing field and new systems may become available. The two packages we see as the most useful at present are outlined below.

BSI Electronic Manager for ISO 14001

SCOPE

The Electronic Manager is produced by BSI and Intelex Technologies Inc. It is a fully integrated software system designed specifically for the development of a complete environmental management system.

The software provides a framework to guide the user through the stages of ISO 14001 using best practice information to help the organisation set up records, track actions and report on appropriate elements. A system of green ticks and red crosses provides an overview of the organisation's state of compliance with the system. Document control is automated within the system.

There is also an Electronic Manager for ISO9001 and QS–9000 which enables organisations to take the same approach to quality and environment.

PERFORMANCE

The system is comprehensive, well presented and the involvement of BSI ensures it is authoritative. It contains a great deal of useful information on developing a standard. It is probably the simplest method of achieving ISO 14001 available in that it provides a step by step guide to the system.

The approach of guiding you through the standard does have one potential drawback which is a lack of flexibility in the overall design of your system. A well designed management system should primarily document how you manage your organisation and then fulfil an independent standard almost as a side issue. Following the Electronic Manager approach may leave you with a system that meets the standard but does not fit with the way your organisation works.

For this reason the system is less likely be suitable for organisations that already have ISO 14001 than those who are developing it for the first time.

Granherne EQS

SCOPE

The Granherne system has four modules, Environment

Case Study

Subject –	**ENVIRONMENTAL MANAGEMENT SOFTWARE**
Organisation –	**BRENT EUROPE**
Organisation type –	**CHEMICAL**
Location –	**MILTON KEYNES**
No. of staff –	**45 AT MILTON KEYNES SITE**

BACKGROUND

Brent Europe specialises in manufacture of chemical products used by the aerospace industry, and metal treatment chemicals. It uses more than 500 chemical raw materials to create over 600 finished products.

When Brent Europe took the decision to develop an environmental management system and to apply for BS 7750 and then ISO 14001 accreditation, the company decided to look at computer-based management systems.

ACTION

The company wanted a user friendly tool that would help them to build an EMS, and provide ongoing support afterwards. Environmental safety manager Anthony Oswald looked at five or six packages, before selecting AIMS, from Intelex Press.

AIMS – Advanced Intelex Management System – consists of three elements: an assessment and development system, a management system, and a reference library. The questionnaire-based assessment system was particularly attractive to Oswald, along with the clear interface running under Microsoft Windows. AIMS has now been upgraded to BSI Electronic Manager developed jointly by Intelex and the British Standards Institute (BSI).

The assessment engine helps an organisation to prepare for accreditation, by prompting it to record existing good practice and pointing out any shortcomings.

RESULTS

❏ Brent Europe was certified to BS7750, and then to the new international standard ISO 14001, by BSI in 1996.

Although BS 7750 and ISO 14001 do not require a review, both BSI and AIMS recommend it. This was one of the most useful parts of the package, Oswald feels, and the time spent on the review has paid dividends. The structured format of a computer package is a great aid to the review process.

Oswald points out that even though Brent Europe had embarked on environmental management projects, such as waste reduction, they had not been documented properly. 'It was a case of formalising what we were doing already,' he says. AIMS facilitated this.

Having the guidance for accreditation on-line in the package was also a 'tremendous help', Oswald believes, and much easier to use than a book.

Once an EMS has been built, AIMS' management module ensures it is used. On boot-up, for example, the software shows graphically any tasks that need to be carried out, with a series of ticks and crosses. The software will list areas that need attention, and provides advice on how problems might be addressed.

'With other software, you have to delve quite deep to find out what needs to be done,' says Oswald. 'If you have to rely on going in and hunting for information, you may not do that regularly. That small detail is of great value.'

Oswald would like to be able to customise the package more, for example in the reports. But he says that this, and other criticisms, are minor.

(Contributed by Environment Business Magazine.)

Quality, Safety and a central Management core module. The system reflects the fact that the three disciplines share many common elements, however the user has the freedom to choose to implement an individual module such as Environment and then bring in the others as time and resources permit.

The system provides a framework in which to document and control your environmental management. It does not guide the user through the system or assess whether the organisation is compliant.

PERFORMANCE

The system is well presented and comprehensive. It provides a flexible structure within which to move to an electronic system

This is particularly appropriate if you already have a accredited system in place or wish to design your environmental management system to extend your quality system.

Both the EQS and Electronic Manager are useful products. The choice of which to use will primarily depend on whether you are looking for a detailed guide to achieve ISO 14001, with the advantages of an electronic system, or a simple and flexible electronic system for organising your existing system.

BENCHMARKING YOUR EFFECTS

This section is designed to help you develop a picture of the environmental 'fingerprint' of your office. The key typical environmental effects of an office fall into three areas:

❑ emissions to atmosphere;
❑ resource use; and
❑ waste.

In each of these areas the typical office will have significant effects on the environment. The tables below will allow you to calculate these effects. Taken together these provide a summary of your environmental performance. This summary can then be used to monitor and report on the success of your environmental performance.

Industry benchmarks are given where relevant, against which you can assess your current performance. However whether your current performance is good or poor, the key is to reduce your environmental 'fingerprint'.

Emissions to Atmosphere

ACTIVITY: USE OF ENERGY

A key indicator of the environmental effects of energy use is the amount of carbon dioxide released. Carbon dioxide is generated by the burning of fossil fuels and is the main gas contributing to the greenhouse effect. Figure 9.10 and Table 9.3 show how you can calculate your releases and compare them to performance norms. (Treated floor area is your gross floor area multiplied by 0.9.)

FIGURE 9.10

Calculating your emissions.

Source: BRESCU, 1995

	Annual kWh		Treated floor area(m²)		Annual kWh/m²		CO_2 Conversion factors		Annual CO_2 emissions kg/m²
Gas	[ ]	X	[ ]	=	[ ]	X	0.20	=	[ ]
Oil	[ ]	X	[ ]	=	[ ]	X	0.29	=	[ ]
Coal	[ ]	X	[ ]	=	[ ]	X	0.32	=	[ ]
Electricity	[ ]	X	[ ]	=	[ ]	X	0.70	=	[ ]

Total CO_2 emissions kg/m² [ ]

TABLE 9.3

Benchmarking your emissions.

Source: BRESCU, 1995

	LOW EMISSIONS KG/M²	MEDIUM EMISSIONS KG/M²	HIGH EMISSIONS KG/M²
	Less than ⟶	Between ⟵ ⟶	Greater than ⟵
Smaller office	44		74
Naturally ventilated open plan	62		100
Air conditioned open plan	112		186
Headquarters (computer room and catering)	209		307

ACTIVITY: TRANSPORT

The amount of carbon dioxide released is also a key indicator for the environmental effects of transport. Figure 9.11 shows how you can calculate your releases from business and/or commuter travel. Levels vary too much by type of organisation to provide a performance benchmark but the total will enable you to monitor your progress.

ACTIVITY: AIR CONDITIONING, REFRIGERATION AND FIRE FIGHTING

The key impact of these activities is the release of CFC, HCFC and Halon gases which deplete the ozone layer. Table 9.4 allows you to calculate this potential. Ozone depleting potential

	Annual usage (litres)		Conversion factor		CO_2 emissions (kg pa)
Petrol	☐	X	2.3	=	☐
Diesel	☐	X	2.7	=	☐
Total					☐

FIGURE 9.11
Calculating your transport emissions

GAS	ODP	GAS	ODP
R11 & R12	1.00	R502	0.33
R123	0.02	Halon 1301	10.00
R22	0.05	Halon 1211	3.00

TABLE 9.4
Ozone depleting potential of gases

(ODP) of each gas is measured in relation to that of CFC 11. Production of CFCs and halons have been banned in the EU and HCFC production is being phased out, therefore the relevant benchmark for performance is zero ozone depleting potential (Figure 9.12).

To work out your loss rates of these chemicals ask your maintenance contractors how much is replaced when they are serviced.

Chemical	Ozone depleting potential		Quantity used (kg pa)		Loss rate		Ozone depletion (kg CFC R11 pa)
☐	☐	X	☐	X	☐	=	☐
☐	☐	X	☐	X	☐	=	☐
☐	☐	X	☐	X	☐	=	☐
Total							☐
Benchmark							0

FIGURE 9.12
Calculating your emissions

Resource Use

ACTIVITY: WATER USE

Water takes energy to treat and deliver to your office. Abstraction of water from rivers can damage habitats during periods of drought. The benchmark for water use will highlight if you have any major areas of wastage (Figure 9.13).

FIGURE 9.13
Calculating your water use

Annual water use (cubic metres)	No of staff	Water use per person (cubic metres/per person per year)
☐	/ ☐	= ☐
Benchmark		12

ACTIVITY: PAPER PURCHASING

Paper manufacture creates a range of effects throughout its lifecycle of forestry, manufacture and disposal. The key to reducing this impact is to use less paper. Figure 9.14 gives a benchmark from our audits for a standard office. Some offices, such as local authorities and solicitors tend to use a much higher level and will find this benchmark figure difficult to reach, however it is a feasible target.

FIGURE 9.14
Calculating your resource use

Annual copier and laser paper use (reams)	No of staff	Paper use per person (reams/per person per year)
☐	/ ☐	= ☐
Benchmark: Standard Office		6

Waste

ACTIVITY: ALL AREAS

Fifteen million tonnes of waste are thrown away by the commercial sector each year in the UK, most of this is landfilled or incinerated. This is a waste of natural resources

Volume of your bins		Conversion factor		No of collections pa		Total waste (kg pa)
☐	x	☐	x	☐	=	☐

FIGURE 9.15
Calculating the weight of your waste per person

and causes air and water pollution. Using Figures 9.15 and 9.16 you can calculate the weight of waste you dispose of per person every year. If your bins are not full when collected you will need to take this into account. If your bins are cubic yard containers use 0.15 instead of 0.2 as the conversion factor.

Total waste (kg pa)		No of staff		Waste per person (kg pa)
☐	/	☐	=	☐
Benchmark				200

FIGURE 9.16
Calculating your waste

ACTIVITY: IT USE

Offices are heavy users of IT equipment. With the pace of change of technology this has a short life, resulting in huge quantities of waste. The majority of this waste is plastic material but it also contains toxic materials such as heavy metals.

Record the average lifetime of IT equipment in your office using Figure 9.17.

Average lifetime of photocopies, printers, PCs and faxes	=	☐

FIGURE 9.17
Average lifetime of IT equipment

Environmental Fingerprint

Table 9.5 will provide a summary of your environmental position. By updating this yearly you can develop an objective measure of the success of your programme in reducing the environmental fingerprint of your organisation.

ACTIVITY		IMPACT
Energy use		CO_2 emissions in kg/m2 pa
Refrigeration, fire fighting, air conditioning		ozone depletion potential in kg CFC RI I pa
Transport		tonnes CO_2 pa
Water use		m^3 water per person pa
Paper purchasing		reams paper per person pa
Waste from all areas		kg waste per person pa
IT waste		average lifetime in years

WHO CAN HELP?

Business and Environment Programme

The Business and Environment Programme is designed to inform managers about the commercial implications of environment issues. It promotes the message: environmental sense is commercial sense.

Its seminars, briefings, workshops and publications are all designed to explore and disseminate views, information and techniques within the emerging field of environmental management.

Its major publication is the Business and Environment Programme Handbook. This performs a dual role of documenting information on business and environment written by leading experts. The seminars provide a mechanism for addressing new issues and helping form opinions and appropriate responses.'

SCEEMAS

The Small Company Environmental And Energy Management Assistance Scheme (SCEEMAS) is a grant scheme offered by the Department of the Environment, which is designed to help smaller companies establish a recognised environmental management system and register their site(s) under the EC

Eco-Management and Audit Scheme (EMAS). This in turn should help achieve increased profits, improved image and better environmental performance.

The conditions necessary for a company to apply for a grant are:

❏ it has fewer than 250 employees worldwide;
❏ it has an annual turnover of less than £32 million; and
❏ it is involved in manufacturing, power generation, waste disposal or recycling.

SCEEMAS provides up to 50 per cent towards the cost of hiring experts to guide you to EMAS registration.

ETBPP

The Environmental Technology Best Practice Programme (ETBPP) is a government initiative which aims to promote better environmental performance while increasing the competitiveness of UK industry and commerce. The Programme runs the Environmental Helpline which gives free up-to-date information on a wide range of environmental issues, legislation and technology.

The Helpline will either answer your query on the spot or arrange for a specialist to contact you. The specialist can work on your enquiry for up to two hours free of charge.

Local Authority EMAS Help-Desk

The LA-EMAS Help-Desk, jointly funded by the Department of the Environment, Transport and the Regions and the Local Government Management Board, was established in January 1995. Its aims are to promote the scheme and provide the practical tools necessary for implementation. A range of publications and services have been developed to support local authorities.

Consultants

It should be clear from this chapter that an environmental management system is not something you can purchase off the

CHAPTER SUMMARY

❏ Decide whether a formal management system will work for your organisation.

❏ Decide which independent standard is most appropriate for your business.

❏ Get senior management support for the programme.

❏ Make sure that everybody in your organisation is aware that implementing a management system will involve significant changes in the way they work.

❏ Integrate your system within your existing management structure.

❏ Keep all staff informed of the programme, and get their ideas and feedback.

❏ Aim for real, continuous, improvement in your environmental performance.

shelf from consultants. A successful system will involve all staff in the development of your management system and its integration within your existing management practice. Simply paying consultants to implement your system will leave you with a pile of documents rather than a management system.

The right consultant can however be a major help to guide you through the steps to a formal system. In particular you may find a methodology for the review of your environmental effects difficult to develop without outside expertise. You will get much more value from your consultant's work and be in a better position to evaluate competitive tenders if you:

❏ have a clear understanding of the structure and aims of the management system you are implementing; and

❏ are able to provide a consultant with a clear brief of the work you want them to carry out.

The consultant you choose should, as a minimum, have:

❏ experience of implementing environmental management systems; and

❏ understanding of your business area.

Case Study

Subject –	**ENVIRONMENTAL MANAGEMENT**
Organisation –	**BEACON PRESS**
Organisation type –	**PRINTING**
Location –	**UCKFIELD, EAST SUSSEX**
No. of staff –	**75**

BACKGROUND

Beacon has formally committed itself to an ambitious long-term environmental management programme designed to minimise the negative impacts of its activities on the environment and, eventually, to eliminate them entirely. The company has set out to establish itself as a centre of environmental excellence within its industry. It has introduced a comprehensive programme of on-site working practices which actively discriminate in favour of the environment; carries out a programme of environmental education activities aimed at staff, customers and the community; and takes a leading role in the printing industry's internal debate on its environmental impact and the way in which it can be improved. Beacon has been awarded both BS 7750 and EMAS accreditation and has won many awards for its environmental management system.

ACTION

Beacon explores every avenue open to it to ensure that care of the environment is a key consideration in all the company's work practices, processes and methods of operation. Specific action has been taken to ensure that environmentally compatible and recyclable material is used whenever possible in product manufacture. Another priority is the elimination or minimisation of waste at source and the re-use or recycling of a wide range of materials ranging from photographic fix to fluorescent light tubes.

Major efforts have been made to reduce the emission of

RESULTS

❏ A 67 per cent drop in alcohol use.

❏ A 48 per cent reduction in water consumption.

❏ A 10 per cent reduction in paper waste.

❏ Recycling some 85 per cent of our 1.8 million litres of dry waste.

❏ A 25 per cent reduction in VOC cleaning solvents.

damaging volatile organic compounds (VOCs) which arise mainly from the use of isopropanol alcohol in the printing process. Beacon has invested heavily in waterless printing technology which does away with alcohol use as well as eliminating the use of water and creating less paper waste.

Other measures taken include the use of chemicals and inks more friendly to the environment (eg based on vegetable derivatives) and the introduction of a programme designed to reduce energy consumption.

Sources of Information

Case Studies

BEACON PRESS
Brambleside, Bellbrook Park
Uckfield
East Sussex TN22 1PL
Tel: 01825 768611
Fax: 01825 768042

COMMUNICATIONS INSTALLATIONS UNIT
BICC Cables Ltd
18 Kingsland Grange
Woolston
Warrington
Cheshire WA1 4RW
Tel: 01928 722727

ENVIRONMENT BUSINESS MAGAZINE
18–29 Ridgeway
London SW19 4QN
Tel: 0181 944 2930
Fax: 0181 944 1982

Standards and Awards Bodies

BRITISH STANDARDS INSTITUTION
389 Chiswick High Road
London W4 4AL
Tel 0181 996 9000
Fax 0181 996 7400

CHARTERED ASSOCIATION OF CERTIFIED ACCOUNTANTS
29 Lincoln Inn Fields
London WC2
Tel: 0171 396 5700
Fax: 0171 396 5757

ENVIRONMENTAL AUDITORS REGISTRATION ASSOCIATION
Welton House
Limekiln Way
Lincoln
Tel: 01522 540 069
Fax: 01522 540 090

INTERNATIONAL CHAMBER OF COMMERCE UK
14–15 Belgrave Square
London SW1X 8PS
Tel: 0171 823 2811
Fax: 0171 235 5447

SCEEMAS
NIFES Consulting Group
NIFES House, Sinderland Road
Broadheath, Altrincham
Cheshire WA14 5QH
Tel: 0345 023423
Fax: 0161 926 8718

THE UNITED KINGDOM ACCREDITATION SERVICE
Audley House
13 Palace Street
London SW1E 5HS
Tel: 0171 233 7111
Fax: 0171 233 5115

UK COMPETENT BODY FOR THE ECO-MANAGEMENT AND AUDIT SCHEME
Department of the Environment
Room C11/21
2 Marsham Street
London SW1P 3EP
Tel: 0171 276 0595
Fax: 0171 276 3731

Organizations Which May Help

CONFEDERATION OF BRITISH INDUSTRY
Centre Point
103 New Oxford Street
London WC1A 1DU
Tel: 0171 379 7400
Fax: 0171 240 1578

LOCAL GOVERNMENT MANAGEMENT BOARD
Woyden House
76–86 Turnmill Street
London EC1M 5QU
Tel: 0171 296 6600
Fax 0171 296 6666

ENVIRONMENT COUNCIL
212 High Holborn
London WC1V 7VW
Tel: 0171 836 2626
Fax: 0171 242 1180
Email: environment.council@ukonline.co.uk

ENVIRONMENTAL INDUSTRIES COMMISSION
45 Weymouth Street
London W1N 3LD
Tel: 0171 935 1675
Fax: 0171 486 3455

ENVIRONMENTAL TECHNOLOGY BEST PRACTICE PROGRAMME ENVIRONMENTAL HELPLINE
0800 585 794

BIFM
67 High Street
Saffron Walden
Essex CB10 1AA
Tel: 01799 508608
Fax: 01799 513237

PREMISES & FACILITIES MANAGEMENT
IML Group
Blair House
High Street
Tonbridge
Kent TN9 1BQ
Tel: 01732 359990
Fax: 01732 770049

INSTITUTE OF ENVIRONMENTAL MANAGEMENT
58/59 Timber Bush
Edinburgh EH6 6QH
Tel: 0131 555 5334
Fax: 0131 555 5217

WASTEBUSTERS LTD
3rd Floor
Brighton House
9 Brighton Terrace
London SW9 8DJ
Tel: 0171 207 3434
Fax: 0171 207 2051

Environmental Software Companies

GRANHERNE INFORMATION SYSTEMS LTD
Chester House
76–86 Chertsey Road
Woking
Surrey GU21 5BJ
Tel: 01483 729661
Fax: 01483 750418

INTELEX TECHNOLOGIES LTD
62 King Street
Maidenhead
Berks SL6 1EQ
Tel: 01628 770037
Fax: 01628 770031

References

NOTES TO CHAPTER I

Department of the Environment (1995) *Making Waste Work – A Strategy for Sustainable Waste Management in England and Wales*, HMSO, London

World Commission on Environment and Development (1987) *Our Common Future* Oxford University Press, Oxford

NOTES TO CHAPTER 3

DoE (1995) *Waste Management Licensing Regulations*, HMSO

DoE (1996) *Waste Management: the Duty of Care – a Code of Practice*, HMSO

NOTES TO CHAPTER 4

BRECSU (1996) *Managing Energy Use: Minimising office equipment consumption*, Presentation to the International Seminar on Optimizing Energy Efficiency in Office Equipment and Consumer Electronics. Stockholm, September 1996

WBCSD (1996) *A Changing Future for Paper*, World Business Council for Sustainable Development, Geneva

WWF (1995) *Pulp Fact*, World Wide Fund for Nature, Gland

NOTES TO CHAPTER 5

DoE (1995) *Making Waste Work: A Strategy for Sustainable Waste Management*, HMSO, London

NSCA (1996) *1996 Pollution Handbook*, National Society for Clean Air, Brighton

WBCSD (1996) *A Changing Future for Paper*, World Business Council for Sustainable Development, Geneva

ENDS (1996a) 'Printworks show reluctance to move to low-solvent products', *The Ends Report* No 259 August 1996, pp 12–13

ENDS (1996b) 'Metropolitan councils show support for EC Eco-labelling scheme', *The Ends Report* No 259 August 1996, pp 27–28

Groundwork (1996) *Purchasing and Sustainability*, The Groundwork Foundation, Birmingham

NOTES TO CHAPTER 6

BRECSU (1995) Introduction to Energy Efficiency in Offices, Department of the Environment Energy Efficiency Best

REFERENCES

Practice Programme, Watford

The British Fire Protection Systems Association (1995) Code of Practice for Gaseous Fire Fighting Systems, BFPSA, Kingston Upon Thames

BSRIA (1994) *The Environmental Code of Practice for Buildings and their Services*, Building Services Research and Information Association

Department of the Environment (1996) Circular 6/96 – Environmental Protection Act 1990: Part II, HMSO, London

Department of the Environment (1995) *Making Waste Work – A Strategy for Sustainable Waste Management in England and Wales*, HMSO, London

ETSU (1995a) *Good Practice Guide 84 – Managing and Motivating Staff to Save Energy*, Department of the Environment Energy Efficiency Best Practice Programme, ETSU, Oxfordshire

ETSU (1995b) *Good Practice Guide 133 – Energy Efficiency in the Work Place – A Guide For Managers and Staff*, Department of the Environment Energy Efficiency Best Practice Programme, ETSU, Oxfordshire

Department of Trade and Industry ETSU (1995a) *Refrigeration and Air Conditioning – CFC Phase Out: Advice on Alternatives and Guidelines for Users*, DTI, London

Department of Trade and Industry (1995) *Fire Fighting – Halon Phase Out: Advice on Alternatives and Guidelines for Users*, DTI, London

HAG Report *A review of the toxic and asphyxiating hazards of clean agent replacements for Halon 1301* and The British Fire Protection Systems Association Code of Practice for Gaseous Fire Fighting Systems

Intergovernmental Panel on Climate Change (1995) *Second Assessment Report* Cambridge University Press, Cambridge

NSCA (1995) *1996 Pollution Handbook*, NSCA, Brighton

NOTES TO CHAPTER 7

Department of Transport (1993) *Road Traffic Statistics of Great Britain*, HMSO, London

Department of Transport (1996) *Transport – The Way Forward*,

HMSO, London

Department of Transport (1996) *The National Cycling Strategy*, DoT, London

ETSU (1995) *The Company, The Fleet And The Environment*, Energy Efficiency Best Practice Programme, ETSU, Harwell

Environmental Technology Support Unit (1996), private communication

London First (1996) Clean Air Charter For Fleet Best Practice, London First, London

Royal Commission on Environmental Pollution (1994) Eighteenth Report – *Transport And The Environment*, HMSO, London

Transport 2000 (1996) *Company Cars*, Transport 2000, London

NOTES TO CHAPTER 9

British Standards Institute (1996) *ISO 14001*, BSI, London

Confederation of British Industry (1992) *Corporate Environmental Policy Statements*, CBI, London

EMAS Help Desk (1996) *Writing an Environmental Programme*, LGMB, London

Index

Page numbers in *italics* refer to tables and those in **bold** to figures